THE STRANGE STORY OF STANLEY SUSPECT

JC COMPTON

Spectrum Books

CONTENTS

Gender can be different from the sex assigned at birth. Transgender, intersex, nonbinary and genderfluid people are the gender they self-identify as. The author will therefore refer to each character using the pronouns matching their gender identity.

PROLOGUE

STANLEY OPENED HIS EYES to a bright electric light flashing in his face. He was tied to a chair and in a straitjacket. They knew how dangerous he was.

"So... 'Stanley'," a man in a brown suit said, leaning over him, "do you know where you are?"

Standing around him were four other men, all dressed in white. Muscle. They stood with their hands behind their backs, ready to intervene if the prisoner made any move. What did they think he could do, anyway?

"An insane asylum, I suppose?" Stanley replied with a grin.

"And do you know why you are here?" the man in the suit asked, flashing the light in his eyes again.

"What are you trying to do, grandpa? Check the color of my eyes?" Stanley retorted.

"Maybe," the man said.

"I think you'll find they're black. Just boring black," Stanley said.

The man backed away somewhat.

"Do you know why you are here?" he repeated.

"Refresh my memory," Stanley said.

Now he could actually see him. He was an average-sized man, with gray hair and a beard. An absolutely ordinary human.

"Do you believe in demons?" the man then asked.

"Lie," Cornelius said, appearing in a corner of the room.

They couldn't see or hear him. Stanley raised an eyebrow.

"Demons? They live in Hell and poke your ass if you've been naughty," he said.

"They also leave a mark on the people they make a pact with..." the man said. "Should we undress you, what would we find?"

Probably not what they expected, but certainly no demon mark on his skin. Stanley laughed.

"I thought the witch trials were over," he said. "But feel free to examine my awesome body. You will have to remove the straitjacket for that..."

His answer seemed to anger the man.

"And what do you know about vampires?" he asked, pursuing his interrogation.

Stanley chuckled again.

"You mean the ones who live in coffins and turn into bats at night?"

"They don't do just that," the man answered.

He gestured to one of the men in white to come forth, and the man placed himself before Stanley, holding a silver cross.

"Vampires cannot touch silver, it will burn their skin," the man in the suit said.

"Interesting," Stanley said.

"Kiss the cross," the man ordered.

Stanley frowned.

"Are you serious?"

"Is there any reason why you cannot?"

"Have you ever heard of germs, you nincompoop?"

In his corner, Cornelius laughed softly. The man was definitely trying to get somewhere, but he was not going to, not with Stanley.

"Open the shutters!" the man in the suit then ordered, and Stanley froze.

He drew in his breath as one of the men in white walked over to the window behind him.

"Are you sure you have nothing to tell us, 'Stanley Suspect'?" the man in the suit asked again.

Stanley could feel the sweat dripping down his temples. So this was how the Order eliminated undesirable elements: they left it up to priests and vampire hunters. With them, you were not even allowed a glorious ending.

"Let them do it," Cornelius told him.

Stanley closed his eyes as the man threw the shutters open and he felt the hot sunlight hitting the back of his head. Seconds passed, and nothing happened. He opened his eyes again and saw the man in the suit's eyes moving from the window to him, then back to the window.

"So this is what this was all about? You think I'm a vampire?" Stanley laughed.

"What? This can't be!" the man said, furious.

He grabbed the silver cross from the other man's hands and pressed it against Stanley's forehead. The young man looked him straight in the eyes and grinned.

"Guess what?" he said in a victorious voice. "You were wrong. I'm much more than that!"

And then he suddenly vanished from his chair, leaving only the scent of woodfire smoke in the air behind him. The men in the room gazed at each other with stupor.

He materialized again on the road beyond the gates of the insane asylum where he had been only minutes before. He had rid himself from the straitjacket and walked casually in his black morning suit minus his top hat – he didn't know what they had done with it. Cornelius quietly followed him.

"That was close," he remarked.

"Not one bit," Stanley said. He turned around and stretched out his arms in the sunshine. "What a beautiful day... I think I might even get a tan!"

He stopped as he heard someone clapping their hands and turned around. A man stood behind him on the dirt road. No carriage or horse anywhere, he had to have come on foot. Like him, he was wearing a nice gray suit, nothing unusual. He was of average height, in his late twenties to early thirties, with a handsome face. Tall forehead, mysterious green eyes under rounded eyebrows, square jaw, neatly cut blond hair, and a light blond mustache and goatee. If his almost too perfect features were not suspicious enough, his perfect build and his confident, straight stance seemed designed to appeal to most women and certain men too, as though he was in the business of seduction. Stanley, who had absolutely no interest in men, walked on, ignoring him, but the man followed him.

"Stanley Suspect, that was a marvelous trick you played on them," he said in a friendly voice.

"Am I a celebrity now or what?" Stanley grunted.

"No, not in their world."

"And who the hell are you? Their boss?"

"Not quite," the mysterious man said, and he suddenly disappeared and reappeared before him, holding a business card. He, too, smelled like woodfire smoke. Stanley took the business card, read it, then smirked.

"You don't sound French, Mister Baille."

"I travel a lot... for business," the man said. "Were you also traveling?"

"I am, in fact. To France," Stanley said.

"Well, that is perfect. I'm on my way back to Rouen now," the man said.

"Ru- what?" Stanley said, who did not speak much French.

"Small town on the banks of the Seine River. Lovely place, and their croissants and frog legs are amazing," the man said, his smile widening, especially as he said the word 'frog'.

"Listen up stranger, I don't know who you are, but I have to be on my way," Stanley said, who was getting annoyed.

"Because it's difficult being out here, right?" the man said. "Might I take you to a more comfortable place to talk? I rent a closed room nearby - no windows. And I have brandy."

"And why would I want to talk to you?" Stanley asked.

"Because I need you, and you need me."

"Who says?"

The man gazed up at the bright sunlight above them, then back to him.

"It's five miles on foot to the next village. Think you can make it there?" he asked.

Stanley grunted again. He knew what the man was, but not who he worked for. His kind usually conducted business at night, so he probably wanted this daytime meeting to remain secret.

"Alright, I'll follow you, but I'd better get cigars, too."

"But of course," the man said, stretching out his hand to him. "So, shall we go?"

Stanley took it, and they disappeared together. They reappeared moments later in the dark room of a hotel, like the man had said, and it had no windows. He clapped his hands and all the oil lamps lit at once. Stanley gazed around the room: it was richly furnished and decorated, all in crimson and gold tones. Two comfortable red velvet sofas awaited them, and on a table brandy and cigars. Stanley did not hesitate and helped himself to the cigars before having a seat. The blond man followed him and poured them both drinks. He sat across from him and smiled.

"So who are you?" Stanley asked after lighting a cigar and taking a sip from his drink.

"I gave you my business card," the man replied.

"You gave me your human name. I want your demon name," Stanley said.

The man seemed pleased by his response.

"It's on the card. It's only a matter of how you read it..."

"Mister 'Luc Baille'," Stanley said, leaning forward. "You're the one who wants something from me, but you won't get it unless you prove yourself to me first."

"Quite the negotiator..." the man said.

"I have experience with your kind."

"Shouldn't you say 'our' kind?"

"What makes you think I'm like you?" Stanley said, leaning back on the sofa.

The man finished his glass and set it down on the table.

"Fine," he said. "Rather than telling you my name, I will tell you my place in the hierarchy. There is no demon above me – not in this part of the world."

Stanley appraised him with his eyes. His mind, which had the bad habit of mixing up the letters in words, was already playing around with his last name and he had it all figured out. He was sitting in a hotel room and having drinks with none other than Lucifer himself.

"Lucifer Belial... Why do you have two names?"

The demon seemed both impressed and intensely satisfied.

"Lucifer is my former name; I prefer to be called Belial. To most demons, I am just a major demon who oversees them, like many others."

"Why? Don't you want people to worship you or something?" Stanley asked, somewhat confused, and Belial laughed.

"I like to be worshipped – in bed," he said. "But in everyday life, I am an attorney, and also the overseer of European demons."

After all Stanley had seen and done, nothing really surprised him anymore.

"I really hope you didn't bring me here to proposition me. I have absolutely no interest in men," Stanley said, crossing his arms.

"I didn't. I was just answering your question," the demon said. "I brought you here because you are one of the most feared people in the underworld."

"How did you find out who I was? Who's your informant?" Stanley asked.

"No one," Belial said. "I was actually tracking down your father, Henry Suspect. But he mysteriously disappeared a few years ago. So then I moved on to the next candidate on my list: you. And when I saw your powers at work, I immediately knew what you were."

"And what do you want from me?" Stanley asked him.

"I want to offer you a deal."

"Ah," Stanley said as though he didn't care.

"I know you bear a demon's mark," Belial then said, serious.

"Prove it," Stanley said.

"I cannot," Belial said. "Of course I have the means to *make you speak*, but I'd much rather have a friendly conversation with you."

"You won't seduce or coerce me. I've been down that road before," Stanley said flatly. "So what are you offering me? Money? Power? You think I would fall for that?"

"Stanley, you are a brilliant young man and I would not insult you by offering you some trivial thing," Belial replied. "I have in mind something much better, which you seem to be lacking: happiness."

Stanley smirked.

"I'm perfectly happy."

"Then please tell me what makes you happy in your life right now," the man said, and Stanley could not answer him. In his short life, he had done more than any other human and perhaps even creatures of the underworld, and yet he could not say that he had ever been truly happy. Rather the opposite.

"No one can ever give me happiness," he said.

"I love a good challenge," Belial said.

"And what do you want me to do for you?" Stanley asked with a frown.

Demons never did anything for free. There was always a pact involved that primarily benefited them.

"I want you to be my joker card - loyal only to me," Belial said, taking another sip from his glass.

"You mean your hitman?"

"No, my joker card."

"And what does the job entail?"

"Just spying and reporting to me, and obeying occasional orders," the demon said. "I will however need you to tell me who you currently work for, just to make sure you have no conflict of interest."

"And you think I will?" Stanley said.

"It depends on how much you want happiness," Belial said. "But I think my proposal is a lot better than anything you have been offered so far. And I will even add this to it: I bet I can make you happy without using any sort of trick or magic."

"And what if I refuse?"

"I can also make sure you never work for anyone else."

They gazed at each other quietly for a moment, then Stanley said: "So that's it? You think you just threw a royal flush on the table and won this little game?"

Belial laughed.

"You remain the joker card," he said. "And my intent is to make *you* win."

"Alright then," Stanley said. "So where do we start?"

"How about you start by telling me your story?" the demon said. "How did you come to be so many things in one man?"

"It's a long story. I hope you have more brandy."

Stanley gazed at the now empty bottle on the table between them, then back to Belial, who seemed very satisfied.

"I certainly do..." he said.

CHAPTER 1

"SO, WHAT DID YOU find, Mister...?" the client said.

Stanley jumped in his seat, suddenly pulled away from his thoughts.

"Suspect... Stanley Suspect," he said calmly.

The man was, like many of Stanley's clients, in his forties, middle-class, a boring black suit and a thick brown mustache men his age thought gave them an air of authority. This one was a banker wanting to sell one of his family's homes, except there was a little problem with it.

"Suspect, huh... Any relation to Barnabus Suspect?" he asked.

"Never heard of him, Sir," Stanley said. "Besides, my name is only a mistranslation of the French name 'Souchet'. My ancestors were French."

"Oh... *Buongiorno!*" the man said in his best Italian.

You nincompoop, Stanley thought.

"Well then... did you get rid of the 'problem'?" the man asked.

Stanley placed a thin brown folder on his desk.

"Here is my report," he said. "I found a few orbs in the attic, that's very common but not a threat to anyone, an ecto-mist in the basement, also extremely common, and a poltergeist. She said her name was Claudia."

The man's face suddenly turned pale. He took the folder and read through the notes.

"Anyone you know?" Stanley asked with a grin.

Of course he knew the answer, because Claudia had spent three hours telling him all about her life, from her childhood in a boarding school to being invited to a royal tea party, before she finally revealed to him how she had died and why she could not move on to the other side.

"Claudia was my sister-in-law," the man said, putting the folder down. "Did you get rid of all the ghosts?"

"I smudged all the rooms with sage, which will take care of the orbs and ecto-mist," Stanley said.

"What about Claudia?"

"Claudia remained in the house because she had unfinished business with you. I'm sure you don't need me to tell you what that business is. I asked her to leave, but..." Stanley said, shaking his head.

"What... what can I do?" the man asked, frightened. Pearls of sweat dripped down his brow. He pulled out a handkerchief and wiped them off.

"But she wouldn't, so I had to perform an exorcism," Stanley said. "That will be an extra five pounds," he added in a persuasive whisper.

"Oh... t-thank you!" the man said in a trembling voice. "I tried everything. You were my last hope!"

"And you hired the right person. Make sure to send me any of your friends with similar issues. I charge fair rates and take your secrets to the grave," Stanley said, placing his business card on top of the folder.

"Of course I will! Thank you so very much!" the man said.

He pulled out a thick leather wallet, rummaged through it, and handed him the money. Stanley counted it then put it away and shook his hand.

"It was a pleasure working with you, Mister Oswald," he said, before taking his leave.

London, December tenth, 1886. Almost a decade had passed since Stanley left his family home in Kensington and moved to the East End. He had worked many jobs until he finally saved up enough to rent a building – a shitty one on the outskirts of Whitechapel – and opened his own business as a paranormal investigator. A largely unsuccessful one. He was late on rent and already facing eviction after two grim years. But that day, business had brought him back to his home neighborhood and its busy streets, and even in his best suit, he knew he looked like the pauper he now was. The sun was dimming in the gray sky, but that was a good thing: he hated the sun. He lowered his hat over his face as to avoid the dozens of pairs of eyes he thought were staring at him. He hated being looked at, and in this neighborhood, there was always the risk that someone would recognize him. He did not know a Barnabus Suspect, but he was sure they were related if he lived in Kensington, and this Barnabus did not need to know about him. But since he was here, he thought he ought to stop by his old home and pick up the mail at least, so he headed there.

The old, abandoned three-story mansion still stood in the same spot, in-between newer mansions. They were all middle or upper middle-class homes, and, if they did not all have much staff, everyone had at least one maid of all work – because posh people could not possibly wash their own laundry or take their children to the park, it would make them look poor. He stopped and pretended to light himself a cigarette as the maids, some only thirteen years old, came back from the market carrying heavy baskets of vegetables, and returned to their kitchens in the basements of the houses around him. When the street was clear, he snuck up to the front door of his house and stuck his hand in the mailbox. Along with cobwebs, he pulled out a handful of letters that had apparently been sitting there for a long time and slipped them in his coat pocket. There was no point in trying the door since the locks had been changed, and he was not ready to burglarize his own home for some mail. He walked away, smoking his cigarette, and when he was done, he called a cab. Though he was used to walking everywhere, he would much rather spend some of the money he just earned on a comfortable ride back to the East End rather than walk in this cold weather.

In the cab, he pulled out the letters and sorted them. Many were from Mister Scarborough, his father's former lawyer and administrator of his estate, still searching for a 'Miss Sophie' he would never find. The other letters were about property taxes which would never get paid. Stanley put away the letters with an exasperated sigh and gazed out the foggy cab window at the streets. Sometimes he missed having enough food and a warm house, but he did not miss the people in West Kensington or his relatives. It was a shallow world, full of shallow people, in which he had always felt completely out of place. At least in the East End, people minded their own business, which was the same as his: survival. He did not like the rough, cussing workers who sometimes bumped into him because they thought they owned the sidewalk, or the loud, rude matrons arguing with their neighbors over their extended use of the shared privies, but at least they were entertaining. Traveling to Kensington made him uncomfortable, and the more distance between him and that neighborhood, and the closer he got to the East End, the more he felt at home. He relaxed somewhat and closed his eyes as he listened to the rain now battering the quiet cab. It was cold and uncomfortable, but it was peaceful.

The cab came to a sudden halt. Stanley opened his eyes and looked out the window. They had not arrived yet, but the coachman opened the door.

"I'm not going down Whitechapel Road at night," he said.

The sun had already set during the short ride and the sky was getting dark.

"But I live there," Stanley said.

"Sorry Sir. Please get off here," the man said.

Stanley grunted but got out and paid him, and then he left. Well, that was what you got for calling a cab in a posh neighborhood. Whitechapel Road could be dangerous after most people went to bed, but it was barely six o'clock, and the streets would still be crowded. It was safe enough, if one avoided the dark alleyways and the pickpockets. Furthermore, at this time of year, the greatest danger would probably be carolers annoying everyone with their stupid Christmas songs. Stanley shrugged and began to walk.

He crossed the street quickly with his hands in his coat pockets and walked back to his small office in the old building he rented, and the first thing he did when he arrived was light a fire in the chimney, then he let himself fall heavily onto the old chair, lifting a cloud of dust. He coughed. Dammit. He really needed someone to take care of the cleaning and the paperwork. Of course, he could do it himself, but that would leave him little time to meet with his clients. Meeting people in person was as unpleasant to him as receiving an enema, but he could not work by correspondence only, and a fake smile and a handshake were often the first step to getting the job. He had put an ad for some help in the local newspaper, but so far, the applicants were not rushing in. Few maids were literate enough to write business letters or do the accounting, and few secretaries were willing to take care of the cleaning. Not like he had much of anything to pay the unfortunate applicants, if there were any.

"Did you get the silverware?" Cornelius asked, suddenly appearing in a corner.

William also appeared, slouching on the sofa. He and the child ghost were always there whenever Stanley returned home.

"No... nothing valuable in that old house," Stanley said. "The old man is completely broke. He's selling everything he owns. He didn't lie about that, only about how he lost all his money."

He pulled out his wallet and took out a coin and began tossing it in his hand.

"Heads or tails?"

William and Cornelius both stared at him.

"Come on..." Stanley grunted. "Heads we pay rent, tails we go out and have the biggest meal ever!"

Neither of them answered.

"Party poopers..." Stanley muttered, tossing the coin.

"We don't eat," Cornelius finally said, and William chuckled softly.

Stanley rolled his eyes at them. He checked the coin that had fallen onto his hand: it was heads.

"Well, I guess it's just bread again tonight," he sighed.

And now the stupid carolers were singing outside again... Couldn't Christmas just be over yet? It was not the 'happiest time of the year', it was the slowest time of the year for Stanley's type of business. People mainly found out their houses were haunted when they went into rooms they usually didn't use, for example, when doing some spring cleaning. Nobody wanted to investigate or deal with a ghost in the attic in the middle of winter, and most preferred to ignore it until it became too loud or obnoxious.

Chains rattled in the hallway. Stanley's father's ghost was there too, taunting him. He had never believed in Stanley, and he thought he would never get anywhere in life, between his shyness, his speech impediment, and the fact he identified as a boy. Well, Stanley got somewhere: to the East End. It was a lot better than the life his father envisioned for him as some stupid man's mealy-mouthed housewife and baby-birthing machine.

"Watch me, Father!" Stanley said aloud, lighting himself a cigarette. His father also did not want him to smoke.

A knock on the front door startled him as he was slowly getting out of his chair to get started on the cleaning, the cigarette still hanging from his lips. He checked the clock: six thirty. He was still open for business. So he walked out into the dark hallway and opened the door cautiously, more worried this was about some charity than about business. But before him stood a beautiful youth in her early twenties – long, black curly hair, olive skin, and big black eyes with long lashes in which the innocent sparkle of teenage mischief was not quite dead yet. She wore a black, tight-fitting silk dress with a lace collar covering her gorgeous bosom, and, in a daring fashion, a gentleman's silk top hat. They stared at each other for some time, both curious about the other.

"I was looking for Mister Suspect..." she then said in a voice that was both clear and sensuous.

Though Stanley praised himself for always being professional with his clients, this one sure had his attention elsewhere and his eyes were naturally drawn to the perfect mounds of her chest and the beautiful curvature of her hips under her tiny, corseted waist. He didn't hate all people; he liked women – brunettes especially – but he generally lacked the motivation to approach them. Not like they would have wanted him, anyway.

"That would be me," he said, removing the cigarette from his lips.

"Stanley... Suspect?" she asked, seeming confused.

He was not very much taller than her, so he straightened his back to appear a little more so. She was definitely his type. Now was not the time to be caught off-guard and start stuttering – his biggest fear when interacting with people. He smirked.

"My grandfather was an Indian soldier by the name of 'Sachdev', and when my father moved back to England it became 'Suspect'," he said.

"Oh..." she said. "But you don't look Indian..."

"My mother was a Russian princess. Anyway, it's a long story, but that's my name," he said.

"Uh..." she said.

She looked at the flyer she had been holding once more and he thought it was the one advertising for a secretary.

"Did you come for the ad?" he asked her.

"I think... I may have made a mistake," she said. "Because of your name, I thought..."

"You thought...?"

"I didn't expect you to be..."

"To be... what?"

"Human," she said. "I do apologize, I will look for another investigator."

"Wait, I am a paranormal investigator," he said as she was about to leave. "I refuse no customers. Why don't you give me a try?"

She gazed at him and hesitated.

"I promise you, whatever your story, I will believe it. Trust me, I've seen it all," he said.

"No, I don't think you would believe me, but thanks," she politely said before walking away.

"Well, excuse me for being too *human...*" he muttered as she left.

What was she even looking for? A ghost to hunt down another ghost? How bizarre.

"Business is not looking good," Cornelius said when Stanley returned to his office.

"You should have asked your client for more," William said, as he looked at the money Stanley had placed on the table.

"What? Twenty pounds for a little exorcism and cleansing? He would never have given me that much, and he might have reported me to the police as a fraud," Stanley said.

"He's got a point," Cornelius said.

"See, the kid is on my side," Stanley said, lighting himself another cigarette. He started coughing and both Cornelius and William giggled.

"Oh, shut up! It's the dust," he said.

"Sure it is..." Cornelius said.

"Well, I guess it's just going to be bread for the next few days. I have to pay rent," Stanley sighed.

He didn't mind being poor, but he hated being hungry. The weekly rents in the area ranged from three to six shillings, and his landlord charged him twelve for the building he rented. It looked terrible on the outside, but the interior was acceptable. It had a small office on the first floor, a bedroom and a spare room upstairs, and a small basement with a kitchen, which he only used to boil water for tea. He had lived in worse places before. But with work being so scarce, he already owed his landlord several months of rent, and he was quite sure if he hadn't told him that his father was a wealthy merchant in America and he was sending him funds later this month, he would have been evicted.

That night again he faced a meager dinner of bread and tea. He set them down on his desk and sat down. The kitchen was too cold to eat in, and he only had enough money to heat one room, so it had to be the office. He wore an old brown smoking jacket to keep himself warm at home, and sometimes wrapped a blanket around himself too.

He rummaged through the papers on his desk as he slowly ate a piece of coarse bread. He had grown up eating much finer foods, but this was not bad. White bread was widely available, even in the slums, but bakers added all sorts of whitening ingredients to it that had nothing to do with flour and made his stomach churn. Luckily, he never liked sugar or sweets, and he preferred his tea with nothing added. He had very basic tastes in everything, from clothing to food.

On his desk were the latest newspapers, a few thank-you letters from clients, bills, and threats from his landlord. He read through the newspapers, looking for a story that might become a business opportunity for him, and though there were a few bizarre and gruesome murder cases, none involved ghosts. All the East End revenants were behaving right now. He let out a loud sigh and went to extinguish the fire; there was no need to waste the rest of that log tonight, he had blankets upstairs. As usual, he read another boring book about demonology before going to bed, and, that night again, he had that dream.

Stanley had become so used to nightmares now he simply thought of them as dreams, and in this dream he found himself again in his old house, standing in the staircase that led up to the attic. It had always frightened him as a child. His home was full of spirits and he had been able to sense them since he was born, and later see them and talk to them. But whatever was up in the attic was so dark, its presence so heavy and hateful, that even he never dared to go up there. Unlike the rest of his house, the walls of the staircase had not been repainted in decades and looked grayer than white. Vague brown spots formed in some places from water infiltration, and clusters of black mold could be seen at the top of the walls. The wooden stairs were warped and creaked with every footstep, as to warn the *thing* in the attic of potential intruders, and they had an odd smell. And he could hear that clock again. He knew there was no clock in the attic; it was just a storage room, and yet he could clearly hear a loud *tick-tock*. He observed the attic's door for a long time, and then the black mold on the walls around it. There was a door to his right, the door to warmth, light, and safety. He tried it, but it was locked from the other side. His dream would not let him go anywhere but up to the attic. As he hesitated, he saw something black and thick pouring down the stairs. He watched it pour down the stairs slowly and wrap around his bare feet. And then he noticed that the black mold clusters on the walls beside him had turned into eyeballs, all simultaneously observing him.

"Don't look at me..." he whispered, breathing heavily.

Something hit his foot. He looked down and saw four tarot cards floating in the black liquid: the Hanged man, the Tower, the Devil, and Death. He bent over and picked up a random card: the Hanged Man.

Having no choice but to go up, he took one step forward, then another, until he finally reached the attic's door and gazed at it. The air around him was so heavy and dark it was almost electrifying, and his heart was racing furiously. The tick-tock of the clock behind the door was louder than ever, and the walls around him were now covered with eyeballs watching him. But before he could think, the clock's chime rang, and a loud shriek resounded right behind the door. It was a cry of absolute terror, like someone's time had come and they were dying in a horrible way. Startled, he fell backward and rolled down the slick stairs, and at their bottom was a pond of this thick black liquid in which he began to drown. The last thing he remembered was that it smelled and tasted like blood and woodfire smoke at the same time, and then he opened his eyes outside, in the small yard behind the house. He was laying in the dirt, under the rain, and he was freezing. But before he could get up, a tiny, blueish child's hand emerged from the dirt, its crooked fingers seemingly trying to grab onto something, and he screamed in terror.

He suddenly awakened in his room and sat up in his bed, sweating profusely. The bedroom was empty, and yet he could hear heavy footsteps in a corner. Their sound had probably created that of the clock in his dream. He rolled over and covered his face with the pillow, muttering: "No... leave me alone William!"

"Stanley... time to wake up..." the ghost teased him.

"Shut up!" Stanley said.

William laughed and disappeared just as Stanley was throwing the pillow in his direction. He sat up in the bed again, grumpy and disheveled. He didn't really want to get up, but he probably would have a hard time going back to sleep now. This life... His name was Stanley Suspect, but it might as well have been Ebenezer Scrooge with the three ghosts haunting him, and he wanted to yell "Bah, humbug!" at those annoying happy-faced carolers who seemed to rejoice in singing right underneath his window during the holidays.

He sat alone in his bed for some time, contemplating the darkness around him. The dark ceiling, the dirty green wallpaper falling off the wall in large chunks here and there, the wood floor that had probably seen better days, the gray wool blanket on the bed... He lived in the darkness. Since his childhood, he had been visited by various ghosts and spirits and some had even remained with him, like Cornelius. William was attached to this house. But at least his life was probably more interesting than that of his parents, who didn't believe in anything, be it God or ghosts, and were only interested in money and how society perceived them.

He finally rolled out of bed in his nightshirt and staggered over to an old and stained tall mirror in a corner of the room. He looked dreadful. And if the bags under his hazel eyes were not enough to scare away his customers, his overgrown brown hair probably would. He needed a haircut, but for that he needed another client, because he had little money to spare. Food or haircut: a tough choice when one wanted to look decent for business, but his stomach was growling now and demanded to be fed... or else. So food it would be. He removed his nightshirt and quickly washed in the washbasin because the room was not heated. He then strapped a binder made of tight fabric around his chest, put on his trousers, his shirt, a matching vest, and a tie.

Living as a man was essential to him, because it was who he truly was, but he'd had to work hard, especially on his voice and intonation, to be able to pass as a man in everyday life. Female children were taught to use different words and intonation when they spoke, and because a high-pitched voice was preferred in women, many subconsciously adopted a higher pitch. Stanley's voice, too, had a high pitch at first, but he had trained himself to lower it, like he had trained himself not to stutter as a child. As for the rest of him, he had a skinny, androgynous shape and a square face, and he even naturally grew a few facial hairs. He had persistent pimples around his jaw and on his neck, as though adolescence never quite wanted to leave his body, and no medicated soap or ointment ever got rid of them – probably because he couldn't be bothered to take care of his skin every single day and quickly gave up on any kind of treatment. Combing his hair was enough of a chore, he didn't have the time to be a dandy.

He wouldn't go as far as saying he looked good in his old brown suit that day, but he looked decent, and that was enough. He then returned to the dresser, on top of which was a small oval mirror. In front of it was a box of Rimmel's mascara – the only cosmetic product he owned. He opened it, dipped the brush on the charcoal bar, and used it to darken his light mustache and the hair around his chin. He didn't do this every single day because using something feminine like makeup made him deeply uncomfortable, but once he saw the result, he felt more confident, which was why he kept it. He then combed his hair with some pomade and smiled, satisfied.

His first stop that morning was his landlord's house, where he dropped off part of the rent money he owed, and then he headed to the bakery to get a loaf of fresh bread. He was too hungry to wait until he got home, so he ate half of it while walking down the street. Another reason why he liked living in the East End: nobody cared what you looked like or what you did, and if people were looking at him, it was probably because they were hungrier than him. But this was all he had to eat for the day and he did not know what he would be eating the rest of the week unless he found more work quickly. He was running out of options, so he decided to return to the last place where he had worked, a bookstore called 'The Lantern', in a better part of this sordid neighborhood.

After leaving home at seventeen, he ended up on the streets and had to fend for himself. With no place to go and no one to turn to, he found shelter in the basement of an abandoned building. There were a lot of dangers on the streets for someone like him who had barely ever set foot outside of his comfortable middle-class home, and he had to learn to hide from rapists and cutthroats. He often found himself in dangerous situations, but Cornelius was always there to protect him by scaring his attackers almost to death. He tried looking for work but he had no idea how to approach employers and his dirty clothes did not make a very good impression, so he first became a pickpocket, and found that he was very good at it. With the money he gathered stealing, he bought himself better clothes, got a neat haircut, and found work selling matches on the streets at first. It didn't provide much of an income, but he was soon approached by shopkeepers for his attractiveness - all the ladies' shops wanted handsome young men as their salespeople to attract women - as well as lecherous old men who promised him money in exchange for sex. Had he been approached by women, he might have said yes, but men were repulsive to him, so he chose to work in department stores instead, and when he finally had a decent income, he was able to move into a small room with Cornelius and look for a more interesting job than selling corsets and petticoats, and he was eventually hired at The Lantern. It was before his father died, and he did not have the burden of his inheritance problems then, nor did he have so many nightmares. Life was a little better, but now it was getting tough again. So perhaps he could help old Marvin stock shelves or something. He stopped in front of the door and drew in a deep breath. He hid the paper bag containing the rest of his loaf of bread in the pocket of his coat and stepped inside.

The old bookstore was just like he remembered it: dark, warm, cozy, and filled with the smell of books. There were few things he enjoyed in life more than reading a book in a cozy place like this, and he liked working for Marvin, but he had to quit eventually. As he got older, his voice and his appearance would raise questions.

"Hey, Marvin!" he hollered, and the owner soon came out from behind a shelf.

Marvin was a short and rounded man with thinning gray hair and jolly red cheeks. He always wore a brown suit, whatever the season, whatever the occasion, and some of his regular clients nicknamed him 'Mister Brown'.

"Hey! Stanley boy! How is it going?" he asked, while giving his former employee a firm handshake.

"I'm doing well," Stanley said.

"You still got that chirpy little voice! How old are you now?" Marvin asked.

"Twenty-five," Stanley said, frowning.

"Gotta eat more meat boy, it'll make you grow a beard!" Marvin said, and he gave him one of his powerful taps in the back.

"Thanks, I'll try," Stanley said.

"So, what can I help you with?" Marvin asked.

"Well, I was just wondering if... there was any work I could help with today?" Stanley said, lowering his eyes and shifting from one foot to the other. He hated begging, but he had come to that point again.

"Business not going well?" Marvin asked in a compassionate voice.

"Oh, it's going great. I just miss working in a bookstore, that's all," Stanley lied, but Marvin understood.

"You don't have to lie to me boy, I understand," he said. "Well, I can't really afford to hire anyone right now, but I'll give you two shillings if you help me put away the new arrivals. My old back sure could use some rest!"

"Thanks," Stanley said softly.

He appreciated Marvin's kindness, but he knew it had its limits. He did not know how he would react if he ever came to know his birth name. At best, he would still offer him work, but only pay him what he was legally obligated to pay a woman or a female bodied person – half the wages of a man – and at worse he could report him to the police, and Stanley could be arrested for crossdressing. Most people were only good to others as long as they fit within the narrow frame of their world, and the moment one crossed the established lines, even friends and family who claimed to love them could turn against them in a second. Stanley had learned it the hard way.

"Sorry I can't offer you more," Marvin said, mistaking Stanley's solemn face for disappointment.

"No, it's great, really," Stanley said, putting on a smile. "What should I start with?"

Marvin showed him the boxes of books he had received in the back of the store. Stanley didn't need any instructions to put them away: he knew every shelf by heart, so Marvin returned to the counter and his bookkeeping while he worked.

It was another cold, rainy day, and customers were few and far apart. Everyone was either busy shopping for Christmas or working longer hours so they could get their family something, at least. One of the benefits of living alone – or with ghosts – was that Stanley did not have to worry about those things. All the money he earned was for himself.

"So, any plans for Christmas? Family dinner?" Marvin said after a while.

"I have no family," Stanley reminded him.

"I thought you might be married now," Marvin said. "No sweetheart, huh?"

Stanley slowly placed the book he was holding on the shelf before him. He did not like it when Marvin got nosy about his private life.

"You mean 'too many sweethearts'," he replied. "I've got so many girls beating down my door every night I have to use exorcisms to keep them away!"

Marvin burst into laughter.

"Oh Stanley, I've missed your sense of humor!"

Stanley put away the last book from the box he was working on, then went to the next one. One of the books in it seemed out of place. He picked it up.

"Eve Chauvin's 'Kitchen Witch's Guide to the Supernatural World'..." he said. "Shouldn't this one go with the girly romances rather than the demonology and witchcraft books?"

"Oh no, that's definitely a book about the occult," Marvin said, joining him.

"But it's written by a woman..." Stanley said, and Marvin laughed again.

"You should read books written by women now and then. It would broaden your perspective," he said. "Here, I'll give you a free copy, and if you don't like it, just bring it back."

Stanley frowned, not convinced. He was an avid reader, mainly of thrillers and forensics books, and everything that had to do with the occult, not women's pillow books. But he could not refuse a free book so he said: "Alright then."

He tucked the book into the inner pocket of his coat and finished his work. And as he put away the last box in the storage, he noticed an old, heavy wooden table in a corner - the one Marvin brought out for signing events. He remembered the last time he had brought it out, a few years ago.

That night, they were preparing for an upcoming book signing event with an author of romance novels. Most of those novels were written under men's pen names by women, so he had expected the author to be a woman, but he turned out to be a real man. He was accompanied by his publisher,

Mister Chapman, whom Stanley and Marvin knew well. They knocked on the door late after the business had closed, and Stanley unlocked the door for them, then returned to his work while Marvin went to greet them.

"Billy! Long time no see!" he told Mister Chapman, and they shook hands.

"Marvin!" Mister Chapman said with a smile. "So finally, and after much negotiation, the great vampire romance author John Silverstake has agreed to show his face," he then said, turning to the man accompanying him.

He was a young and rather short man with a pale white complexion, black eyes, curly black hair, and a somewhat feminine aura. He wore an all-black suit with a silk top hat, and his hands were gloved. Rather than shake hands with the owner of the bookstore, he tipped his hat and offered him a polite smile. *Silverstake*, what a ridiculous pen name, Stanley thought. He shrugged and ignored them. To his surprise though, rather than partake in the conversation between Marvin and his publisher, Silverstake came over to the table Stanley was setting up to help him.

"You don't have to help me, Sir," Stanley told him.

"Those tables are heavy. Let me take care of it," the man told him with a smile.

And, with the same ease as if he had been lifting a twig, he picked up the heavy table and placed it where they wanted it. He then took the box filled with books his publisher had brought in and began to place them on the table. Cornelius suddenly appeared and leaned against the table, gazing at the stranger with curious eyes. Stanley gazed at him sadly. The poor child ghost sometimes wanted humans to notice him, people who looked kind or sweet, but apart from Stanley, no one could see him. He was stuck, forever hidden from people's eyes when he so wanted to be seen and heard, and if he moved objects or made noise, he only scared them. But the man by Stanley's side once again surprised him. He stopped and looked at Cornelius, then smiled.

"Well, hello there. Are you attached to this young man?" he asked him directly.

"You... you can see him?" Stanley whispered, astounded.

Silverstake turned back to him.

"He's lucky to have found a clairvoyant friend," he said, before returning to the box of books.

"A-Are you..." Stanley began to say, but his stuttering was coming back. "A-Are..." he tried again, then he closed his eyes and breathed in deeply.

"Take your time," Silverstake said in a warm and peaceful voice.

"T-Thank you Sir," Stanley finally said. "Sorry, it happens to me sometimes."

"You have nothing to apologize for," Silverstake said.

He placed all the books on the table neatly.

"Sir, I know you must be busy, but could we meet up for lunch tomorrow or another day, perhaps? I have never met someone like me before," Stanley said, but Silverstake seemed troubled by his proposal.

"Lunch... I'm afraid that will not be possible," he said.

"We could meet up in the evening if you prefer," Stanley insisted.

Silverstake seemed troubled again and avoided his gaze.

"I'm afraid I am always busy these days," he finally said, and then his publisher called him over to discuss the book signing.

He did not speak to Stanley again that night, and they never met again. Stanley could, of course, have gone to one of his evening book signings, but hadn't the man clearly let him know he was not interested? Even when he met people like him, Stanley could not make friends.

"Everything alright in there?" Marvin hollered.

"Oh, yes. Just thinking," Stanley said, coming back out into the bookstore. "That romance author, did he ever come back?"

"Which one?"

"Silverstake."

"Silverstake? Yes, I think he came back last year for another signing. Always nighttime, he doesn't seem to like the sunlight very much – like his vampires."

"And did he say anything special?" Stanley asked.

He did not expect the man would remember him, let alone inquire about him.

"Nothing special. He's very shy, you know. He rarely appears in public," Marvin said. "Were you hoping to see him? I can probably arrange something with Billy."

"Not really. I'm not a big reader of romance," Stanley shrugged.

"Well, I might as well start closing. It's getting dark outside, no one is going to come at this hour," Marvin said with a sigh. "Here's your two shillings. Go get yourself a good meal, you look like you need it."

He placed the money on the counter and Stanley took it. It was only five thirty, but it was already getting dark outside, and the rain would indeed discourage potential customers.

"Are you sure you don't want me to help with the closing?" he asked.

Marvin shook his head opinionatedly.

"You're as thin as a twig. You need some food, boy," he said.

"Alright then," Stanley said.

He put on his coat and hat and headed out.

"Let me know how you liked the book!" Marvin said.

"Sure will!" Stanley said, tipping his hat.

The sky was dark outside and the cold rain immediately hit his face when he stepped out onto the street. He lowered his hat on his head and began walking, but stopped when he heard some commotion: a carriage had just run over someone. It happened often, and he needed to get home, so he began to cross the street. Unsurprisingly, a ghost stood in the middle of the street – that of a little girl. She was dressed in rags and looked around her as though she wondered what had just happened. Mechanically, Stanley grabbed her cold hand as he walked past her and took her to the other side of the street. People were converging to the accident scene now and paid no attention to them. Stanley gazed sadly at the carriage in the distance. Dealing with death and spirits rarely stirred any emotion in him, except when it came to children. Even he who thought himself so detached from the rest of the world felt something when he witnessed or heard of the death of a child.

"What's going on, Sir?" the little girl asked. "Why are people screaming?"

He turned to her and kneeled beside her.

"I'm afraid you were hit by that carriage..." he said in a soft voice.

She seemed confused at first, then turned her eyes to the accident scene and they filled with tears.

"I was on my way home... My mum is waiting for me," she said.

"You won't be going there. You must go to another home now," he said.

"Which one?"

His eyes also filled with tears and a vague pain gripped his chest. He could already sense the light coming for the little girl, and he needed to convince her to step into it, or she would face an eternity of loneliness and roaming like Cornelius. And yet he knew that she did not want to leave her home and everything she knew in this world. She still had unfulfilled dreams, and the desire to live burned in her pale pupils, but this cold and cruel world had decided that her journey ended there. She would never grow up or grow old; everything ended right here for her. If only he had a way to reverse time, Stanley thought, he would prevent such tragedies from happening, but no one had such powers.

"Soon, a warm blue light will come searching for you. You must let it take you," he explained, still holding her hand.

"What will happen to me if I do?" she asked.

"You will go to a better place."

"What if I stayed here instead?" she asked, clinging to his hand. She was scared.

"I will stay with you until you get to the other side if you want," he said. "And I will tell your mother that I sent you off safely."

"You will?" she sobbed.

"Where do you live?"

She pointed to the slums beyond the carriage, but before he could ask for her mother's name, the light came for her. No one but him and the spirits could see it. He watched her being pulled into the light and he held her hand until the very last moment so she would not be scared. And when she was gone, a great sense of emptiness crept over him. It was what he did, what he felt compelled to do: spirits came to him and he helped them on to the other side, hoping they would find something better there. It had to be better than this world; he could not think of a worse place to be.

"Goodbye, sweet one," he whispered.

CHAPTER 2

STANLEY SAT ALONE IN the chair in his office, holding his head in his hands. His eyes were red and swollen from crying. Sending the little girl on to the other side was difficult enough but having to tell her mother and watch her break down before him was even harder, even if she did find comfort in knowing that someone was there to hold her little girl's hand as she moved on to the light. William stood silently in a corner, and Cornelius sat on the desk near him.

"Stanley, it was her destiny," the child ghost finally said in a soft voice.

"I know..." Stanley said, wiping away one last tear.

"No one is ever ready to see children go," William told Cornelius.

"And children are never ready to go," Cornelius reminded him.

Stanley got up and removed his coat. The book Marvin had given him slipped out of his pocket and fell onto the floor. He had forgotten about it.

"You should go to bed now," Cornelius said.

Stanley nodded. He picked up the book and went upstairs to his room. There, he undressed and changed into his nightshirt, not overly worried about William and Cornelius, who had followed him. Living with ghosts meant that one had no privacy.

He sat in his bed and decided to read a little before going to sleep. Cornelius slipped into the bed and sat beside him, and William did the same. Stanley smiled at them.

"Thank you. I really need company right now," he said in a small voice.

"We care about you, even if you are quite rude sometimes," William said.

"Yes, I guess I am. Sorry about that," Stanley said.

"But we understand," Cornelius added.

They both wrapped their cold arms around him and hugged him. At least he was not completely alone.

He then opened the book and browsed through it, mostly to clear his thoughts. Despite loving books, reading was not his forte, and he had the hardest time learning how to read and write as a child. His mind somehow mixed up the letters of words and the words on a page, and he really had to focus to be able to understand anything. But Cornelius was always there to help him, and eventually he was able to master reading to what he thought was the same level as other people, only he had to do it slower. He liked reading because it was something he could do alone, and books did not judge him like people did.

The book contained chapters about different dream topics, tarot cards, undead creatures and revenants, a few recipes for bedtime herbal teas, and healthy living advice. The author was a French herbalist who also owned a cosmetics shop in Paris, and at the end of the book was an address where fans could write her. If they provided their date and place of birth, she offered astrology guidance and tarot readings. Boring. He skipped the first chapters of the book to read the one about ghosts and found it quite intriguing, though. The author made a few mistakes, and he did not think she had ever seen a ghost, but she believed in them, not as frightening entities wanting to give humans nightmares, but as natural inhabitants of this world whose existence humans had simply chosen to forget. The chapters about werewolves and vampires were also very detailed, and one could almost think she advocated for the acceptance of supernatural creatures in society. She also believed in 'links' between people and places, and how they explained why sometimes people experienced strong feelings of *déjà vu*.

"Do you think she's a real witch?" Cornelius asked.

"I don't know, I've never met one – nor a vampire," Stanley said, who did not believe in either. Witches were simply women who knew of the herb lore and had been persecuted by the men who feared them. As for vampires and werewolves, he only believed in what he could see, and so far, ghosts were the only supernatural creatures he had ever come across.

"Why don't you read the chapters about dreams and tarot cards? Perhaps they could explain your dream," William said.

"I always have that dream. I just never saw tarot cards in it before," Stanley said, but still he went to that chapter and read it. According to the book, the Hanged Man card represented stagnation, sacrifice, or surrendering. The Devil represented temptation, money, or being seduced by the obscure, the Tower represented imminent danger, destruction, or a sudden change, and Death represented illness or transformation rather than death itself.

"Perhaps you are facing an imminent danger and choosing sacrifice instead?" William suggested.

"Or this imminent danger could come from sacrifice," Cornelius said.

"So what should I do? Choose the Devil's card instead and dive into the obscure? Don't I already live there?" Stanley said, cynical.

"You could ask her," Cornelius said.

"Oh, please... I'm sure she receives dozens of letters from women every day asking her the same things," Stanley said.

"But you're different, since you actually interact with the supernatural world," William said.

"Perhaps if she could explain your dreams, you would stop having them," Cornelius then said.

Stanley looked at both of them and sighed. Indeed, despite his attraction to the obscure, it was not by choice he had stepped into that world, and at first it terrified him. It made sense that, in his dream, he would choose the card representing stagnation rather than go up to the attic and face his fears. He could, of course, return to his old home and investigate it, and probably encounter some vengeful poltergeist up there, but something inside him told him not to.

"Cornelius, you're a ghost. What sort of ghost lived up in the attic in my old home?" he asked his friend, who shook his head.

"I never sensed any ghost up there," he said. "There were a few soldiers living in the walls on each floor, elderly people, a woman who died in childbirth, and me. I died from the pox in 1732."

"1732? You are so young!" William joked, who had died in 1610.

"Old man," Cornelius retorted, and Stanley finally laughed.

"Alright, friends, let's go to bed. And hopefully this time I won't have nightmares," he said, closing the book.

He placed it on the nightstand and turned off the oil lamp. Cornelius and William then tucked him underneath the blankets like a child and sat beside him as he closed his eyes. Sometimes, Stanley needed his friends. No, he always needed them...

The dream he had that night still took place in his old house, but it was a little different. He was laying in the garden, on a patch of cold, wet dirt, and again the rain was falling on him.

He sat up and looked around him. The small garden, with its little stone path and a few flower beds, was surrounded by brick walls, just like he remembered it. He could hear the distant *tick, tock* of a clock, and he looked up to the house and the attic. Through its only window, he could distinguish a flickering red light. Something was going on up there, but it was not a fire. He heard that same loud shriek, then silence fell upon the house and the light disappeared. Whatever happened in the attic, he was now witnessing it from a different part of the house, and he thought perhaps if he went up there now, he could safely investigate it. He was about to get up when he felt the dirt shifting underneath him. Frightened, he scrambled to his feet and turned around. He had been laying on a grave, and at its head was a blank stone.

"What the hell?" he said.

There had never been a grave in his garden, he was sure of it. Besides, the city did not allow families to bury their dead wherever they wanted, they had to be buried in cemeteries.

He then noticed someone standing behind the grave. A woman. The lavender color of her dress blended so well with the gray walls surrounding them that he had not noticed her until then. She wore a thick black veil over her head, covering her face, and she held her gloved hands together. Stanley observed her for a moment, wondering what she was doing in his dream, and she also seemed to be observing him. The dirt shifted and stirred again, and a blueish child's hand reached out of it. Stanley wanted to run away, but the woman's presence reassured him enough to want to stay and see who or what would come out of the grave. Another hand came out of the dirt, and then a face and a torso, and a disheveled child in a white dress emerged from the grave and pointed an accusing finger at him. Sophie.

Stanley's eyes opened wide with terror as he saw the child: it was him.

He awakened terrified in his room again, and it no longer surprised his ghost friends, who sat quietly on either side of his bed.

"Did you have that dream again?" Cornelius asked him.

"Yes, but this time I was in the garden..." Stanley said. "And there was a woman and a grave... my grave!"

"But you're not dead," William remarked.

"I know, but... It was like I somehow died as a child. Am I a ghost?" Stanley asked, turning to each of them.

"Can you put your hand through the wall?" William asked him.

Stanley turned around and punched the wall behind his bed so hard he hurt himself.

"Ouch!"

"Definitely not a ghost," Cornelius said.

"Then what am I and why am I having these dreams?" Stanley said, resting his head in his hands.

He didn't mind being a clairvoyant and clairaudient and living with ghosts, but he was tired of all these inexplicable dreams.

He got out of bed and quickly washed before getting dressed in the cold. He then headed downstairs to the kitchen and started boiling a kettle of water on the iron cookstove to make some tea. The problem with having grown up with house staff was that he never learned how to cook, otherwise he might have been able to enjoy real meals without having to spend so much money on restaurants. He warmed his hands by the cookstove as he waited for the water to boil. And then he remembered the words 'kitchen witch' from that book. It was, in fact, a book mostly aimed at women, but the author seemed to know a thing or two about dreams and the sort of world he lived in. And if others had dreams similar to his, perhaps this old witch had already worked with them to interpret them. It couldn't hurt to ask her. So when the tea was ready, he brought it upstairs to his office and set it on the desk. As usual, Cornelius and William joined him because they were ghosts and ghost life was apparently quite boring. Stanley ignored them and lit a fire in the chimney, then he opened the window and the shutters to let in the sunlight. Across the already busy street were again those pests singing carols.

"Oh, can't you just shut up! It's only eight o'clock!" he snapped at them.

They looked appalled and some children laughed and started chanting: "Scrooge! Scrooge!"

"You also shut up or I'll box your ears!" Stanley said before shutting the window.

Cornelius and William also giggled in a corner.

"Want me to perform an exorcism?" he warned them, before going back to his desk, and they came to him.

"What are you doing?" Cornelius asked as he saw him pull out a clean sheet of paper and an old dip pen.

"You're the ones who told me I should ask this old lady about my dreams..." he remarked.

"Is she old?" William asked.

Stanley rolled his eyes at him.

"She's got years and years of experience making potions, interpreting dreams, and doing tarot readings. I doubt she's fifteen."

He dipped the pen in an ink bottle and began to write. Even on his best days, his cursive was atrocious and he hoped she would be able to decipher what he wrote:

Dear Madame Chauvin,

I had the pleasure of reading your Kitchen Witch's Guide to the Supernatural World and found it most interesting. I know you must be very busy, so please excuse me in advance for taking up your precious time with this letter, but I have a few questions I hoped you might be able to answer. I was born with the ability to see and hear the spirits of the dead, and I grew up in a very crowded home (crowded with spirits, that is). Since I moved out, I have been having recurring dreams about the attic, a place that terrified me as a child, as well as the backyard.'

He then went on to describe his latest dreams in detail, from the moment he found himself in the staircase leading up to the attic to his drowning in that thick black liquid and the grave in the garden and the woman in the lavender dress.

"Stanley is not nearly as rude when he writes as when he talks..." William commented, who had been reading over his shoulder.

"I think he's trying to impress her," Cornelius said.

Stanley turned back to them with a dark look.

He hesitated before signing the letter, but finally wrote: 'Ernest S.'. And, in case it was of any use to her, he wrote his birth date: December eighteenth, 1860. He had not realized it was coming up so soon. He was turning twenty-six this month. Where had all those years gone without his noticing?

"Why didn't you sign it 'Stanley'?" Cornelius wondered.

"Because if this is actually just a pillow book for women and she doesn't believe in any of it, she will think I'm deranged and I don't really want to end up in an insane asylum."

"You shouldn't sign it 'Ernest' if you're not being earnest. 'Billy' would be better," William remarked.

"Ha. Ha," Stanley replied, frowning.

"But why don't you want to tell her your name?" Cornelius insisted, who did not always understand grown-ups.

"Who is truthful nowadays, anyway? Eve is probably only her pen name," Stanley said.

He read the letter again, but as he did, he realized how silly it sounded. He, a grown-up man, was writing a letter to someone who claimed to be a kitchen witch to ask her to interpret his dreams.

"I shouldn't have done this, it's stupid," he said.

He crumpled the letter and tossed it across the room.

"Stanley, no!" Cornelius said.

"Your cursive was not that bad," William said.

"It's not about my cursive," Stanley said as he walked across the room.

"Then why not send it?" William wondered.

"Because it's a waste of time. No one can understand me," Stanley said, somber.

"And what are we? No one?" William said, offended, and Stanley regretted his words. He turned to his friends, who now both looked deeply hurt.

"Sorry. I meant no living human can understand me," he said, and with this he put on his hat and coat and left the building.

Cornelius immediately flew across the room and picked up the crumpled letter.

"What are you doing?" William asked him.

"Being naughty," Cornelius said.

He uncrumpled the letter and flattened it on the desk as best he could, then grabbed an envelope. Not all ghosts could touch and move objects, but he had been around for so long that he had developed that ability. William could sit on chairs, but he could not move objects very well, despite being older. Cornelius took the pen and turned to him.

"What?" William asked, puzzled.

"I need help to write the address. I'm just a child," Cornelius said.

Stanley walked briskly down the street, trying to clear his thoughts. The air was cold that morning, but the sky was clear. He liked winter days like this one, and he always believed he had chosen to be born in winter, the season when all things were dead. It suited someone like him. He slowed down his pace as he reached a street lined with shops and even stopped to look at a few men's suits in the window of a tailor. They were too expensive for him right now, but not out of reach. Perhaps when he had a little more money he would get himself a new suit. He could definitely picture himself in that brown cutaway morning suit with black trousers and a black tie. He did not like most colors, only earth tones and black. He was not a dandy, rather an old man in a young body. Well, if he could not afford a suit, at least with his two shillings he could afford a trip to the barber, so he made that his next stop.

His usual barber, Sam, was quick and precise, and he never asked any personal questions. He served not only men but also bold young women who wore their hair in a bob and went out without a hat. Some called them prostitutes, but they called themselves 'feminists' and 'suffragettes' instead, and they claimed they did not owe men beauty or long hair. Stanley rather liked them, but not enough to join their meetings. Too much feminine energy around him made him uncomfortable.

He was the only customer in Sam's shop that morning, and Sam cut his hair very short, just the way he liked it.

"It's a lovely day out there, isn't it?" Sam said as he worked on his mane.

"Indeed," Stanley said.

"Any holiday plans?" Sam asked. Now he was becoming annoying.

"Not really. Have you any plans?" Stanley asked, not because he cared, but because it was the polite thing to do.

"Oh, I'll just be spending Christmas with my other half, as usual," Sam said.

"I didn't know you were married," Stanley said, surprised.

Sam looked like he had unwillingly said too much, but since they were alone, he relaxed somewhat.

"The law does not allow me to marry the person I've been living with for years," he said, and Stanley realized he was probably living with another man. He had never imagined he was one of those men.

"You won't tell anyone, right?" Sam then said.

Stanley smirked.

"Who would I tell? The law doesn't allow me to be who I am either," he said, and Sam smiled. He understood.

"There you go, all done and looking like a prince!" he said when he was finished.

Stanley disagreed with him. Though others seemed to find him handsome, he thought he looked more like a frog than a prince, but the haircut was nice.

"Thanks," he said, getting out of his chair.

A man he had never seen before walked into the shop and embraced Sam before realizing there was a customer.

"Don't worry Daniel, this is Stanley, and he is as quiet as a mouse," Sam told his partner.

Stanley tipped his hat. He paid Sam and left and resumed his morning stroll.

He knew the city of London was probably full of people like him and Sam, whose very existence was illegal, and he sometimes wondered if they could gather, like the suffragettes, and make things change. After all, who was he harming? Who was Sam harming? But, so far, he had not heard of any such groups.

He walked down the street aimlessly until he noticed a set of three china dolls in a toy store. He hated dolls; they terrified him as a child. He remembered laying in his bed at night in the dark, staring at the three dolls on the dresser. As always, he could hear footsteps and things moving in the attic when everyone was supposed to be asleep. His was a comfortable, middle-class home, but it was haunted, and he never knew what he might hear or see in a dark corner, in the staircase, or even under his bed. He had tried telling his governess Mary and the little maid Annie, but both of them laughed at him. Only he could hear or see anything. Then, one night, he noticed that the three dolls were gone. He sat up in his bed and looked around the room, but he did not see them anywhere, which meant they could either be under his bed or in the old wardrobe. His heart began to race and his palms were sweating. He was stuck on his bed. If he got up, wouldn't the dolls come crawling after him, possessed by whatever lived inside the walls and the attic? What would they do to him? He then heard a noise in the wardrobe. They were in there. He could not risk angering the adults in the house by waking them up over something they couldn't even see. He would have to fight alone. So he quietly slipped out of his bed, went to the small bookcase, and picked up a heavy encyclopedia. Could a six-year-old like him kill possessed dolls with an encyclopedia? But that was all he had. So he tiptoed over to the wardrobe, waited, and listened. More rattling. He drew in a deep breath, swung the door open, and raised the encyclopedia above his head, then froze. Instead of the dolls, he saw a pale little face looking up at him. It was that of a child about his age, only he looked too pale to be alive, and his clothing seemed to be from the last century. He sat in the wardrobe and gazed at him with imploring eyes. Beside him were the three dolls, sitting quietly. All fear left Stanley at once.

"Who are you?" he asked.

"My name is Cornelius," the little boy said.

Stanley put down the encyclopedia and sat on the floor facing him, more curious than frightened now.

"How did you get inside my wardrobe?"

"I live here," the little boy said.

"That's not true, I live here," Stanley said. "Why are my dolls in the wardrobe?"

"I noticed that they frightened you at night, so I thought I would put them away," Cornelius said.

"Oh... thank you," Stanley said, who never dared touch the cursed things.

"I think we should leave them here," Cornelius said.

"Yes, let's do that."

Stanley smiled, but Cornelius seemed hesitant.

"What's your name?" he asked.

"I don't have a name," Stanley answered.

"What do your parents call you?"

"Sophie..." Stanley said, lowering his eyes.

"But it makes you sad. So why do they do it?" Cornelius asked.

Stanley raised his shoulders. He did not know why his parents desperately wanted him to be a girl. He was a boy.

"We can choose another name for you," Cornelius suggested. "Pick a name you like."

"Stanley," he immediately said.

Cornelius now smiled.

"Can we be friends, Stanley, even if I am a ghost?"

"Oh, I would love to have a kind ghost as my friend!" Stanley said, smiling brightly.

"You're not scared?"

"A little, but you protected me from those dolls and you don't call me 'Sophie'. You're already a good friend."

He offered the little ghost his hand and the boy took it. His touch was like cold air touching Stanley's fingers. It was his first visual encounter with a ghost, and it was a fond memory.

His eyes then wandered to the shop next to the toy store. He was sure there was a butcher there just a few days ago, but now in its place was another shop. It had a dark, old brick façade like all the others on the street. Above the door, painted in golden letters, were the words 'It's Time...'. There were mostly clocks inside, all sorts of clocks and pocket watches, as well as a few random items displayed in the window. One of them was a tarot deck. Stanley leaned forward and observed it carefully. The printed card on the box was not one of those he had seen in his dream, but it was drawn in the same style. It was the Sun card. On a whim, he decided to enter the shop and inquire about it, so he pushed the door open and walked inside. The shop, of course, smelled like the wood most clocks were made of, but also of woodfire smoke. The shopkeeper, a young woman with long black hair tied back in a ponytail and magnifying spectacles, was working on a clock. She was wearing a cream-colored blouse and a purple skirt that day, but he instantly recognized her. She was the odd woman who did not want to work with him because he was too 'human'. She noticed him too and removed her spectacles.

"You?" she said, frowning.

"Is this your shop?" he asked.

"Yes," she said, returning to her work. "I don't need your services," she then said.

"I didn't come for that. What do you do here?" he asked.

"I'm a horologist," she said, paying little attention to him.

"A what?"

She lifted her gaze again and stared at him like the obvious dimwit he probably was in her world.

"A clockmaker," she translated into language he might understand. "Did you come here to buy a clock?"

"No, actually I was interested in that tarot deck in the window," he said, trying to sound pleasant.

"Oh... sure, you can take a look at it. I don't mind," she said.

So he went to the window and picked up the tarot deck to examine it. Another client then entered the shop, a tall man in an elegant black suit under a long black cape. He wore a black top hat over his short brown hair. He too smelled like woodfire smoke, but many people still heated their homes with wood in a fireplace, not everyone used coal. Stanley ignored him. He heard him walk up to the counter and whisper something, and then he heard his and the young woman's footsteps as they retreated into a back room. After a few minutes, he turned around and saw them in the darkness. They were obviously having an argument, and he was clutching her arm firmly.

"Hey!" he immediately shouted, dropping the tarot deck.

He rushed over to the back room.

"Let go of her or I'm calling the police!" he shouted.

The man let go of her arm and stared at him, perplexed.

"The police?" he repeated, before bursting into laughter.

"There are police constables around every street corner at this hour. I wouldn't try anything if I were you," Stanley warned him. He carried no weapons, but he was ready to fight if necessary.

But as he observed the two of them, he noticed a similarity between them. It was not exactly something he could put in words; they did not look related, they just had a different aura or presence than the people he usually interacted with. Their features were a little more perfect, as though they had been etched by the hand of a fairy, and their eyes deeper. There was a cool and detached atmosphere about them, and they both stood very straight like ghosts sometimes did, except they were not ghosts.

"Please go now," the young woman told the man in a low voice.

He tipped his hat and left the shop, and she returned behind her counter, followed by Stanley.

"Are you alright? Did he hurt you?" he asked her.

"No, he didn't hurt me," she said calmly.

"Has he been here before? Do you want me to call the police?" he insisted.

"He is the police... our police," she said in a sad voice.

"Is that why you were looking for help? Has this man been harassing you?"

"It's... complicated," she said, running her hand through her hair.

"Give me a try," he offered again. "So, what is he? Some kind of ghost who can materialize and interact with this world?"

She smirked as though she found him funny.

"Mister Suspect..."

"Please call me Stanley."

"Stanley," she then said. "This is not your world. You should go home."

He straightened himself and frowned.

"Because I'm too 'human', is that it?"

"Yes, that's exactly it," she said.

"And you're not?"

She seemed disconcerted for a moment, then said: "Are you going to stay in my shop when I asked you to leave? Are you like him?"

"No," he said. "I will go now."

He quickly walked out of the shop and made his way back to his office, furious. This girl was cute, but she was getting on his nerves. Why did she keep saying he was 'too human' when they were both human?

He threw open the front door and nearly stepped on the mail that lay on the floor. There was a letter there. He picked it up and examined it, but the envelope was blank. He did not remember any of his clients owing him money and he had no friends except Cornelius and William. He stepped inside the office and removed his hat. William was there, slouching on the dusty chair, as usual. Where did he even come from, with his seventeenth century doublet and breeches and his bald head? He looked like Shakespeare having a bad periwig day.

"What are you staring at?" he snapped at him and the poor William looked dramatically shocked.

"Well, excuse me for living in this house..." he said.

Stanley let out a loud sigh and went to sit at his desk. He opened the letter. It contained money – a lot of it – and a brief note: *'Forget what you saw today. Callie'*

He read it again, wondering who this 'Callie' was, until he realized she had to be the clockmaker. How and when did she slip past him and drop this off in his mailbox before he returned? She had to be lightning fast. Or not human...

CHAPTER 3

DECEMBER SIXTEENTH, 1886. STANLEY gazed anxiously at the small envelope the mysterious woman had dropped off in his letter box a few days ago. The money was very welcome, of course, but he just couldn't forget about her. For one thing, she appeared to be harassed by a strange man, and then, though she remained vague, she had suggested that Stanley couldn't help her because he was human and she was not. He had retraced his footsteps the next day and returned to her shop, but it was gone. Beside the toy store was just an empty building that seemed like it had not been occupied for a long time. He asked Sam about it since he lived on the same street, but he told him he did not remember that shop being there.

"Perhaps she just took a shortcut to your office the other day," William said from his chair.

"I was already taking the only shortcut," Stanley pointed out. "No, there's something uncanny about her and her shop, and I'm going to find out what."

"But didn't she tell you to leave her alone?" Cornelius said.

"After wanting to solicit my services if I were not human," Stanley said. "She's not a ghost, so what could she be?"

He flipped the pages of different esoteric books laid out on his desk, but he simply could not find anything about clock-makers who could travel faster than anyone on Earth. Unless she could travel *through time*... He returned to Madame Chauvin's book for its precise descriptions of creatures of the underworld but found there nothing about creatures capable of traveling through time.

"Time travel..." he whispered to himself, as he scratched his chin.

"Even if she is capable of such a thing, she doesn't want your help," Cornelius reminded him.

"Cornelius, you almost sound like you want to keep me away from her. Why?" Stanley asked, turning to him with suspicion, and Cornelius suddenly looked guilty.

"What did you do?" Stanley asked him, raising an eyebrow.

"Nothing, I just want you to have friends, and she was mean to you," Cornelius said, shaking his head.

"She was not mean, she politely brushed me off," Stanley said, returning to his books.

"There are more polite ways to turn down a man than telling him he's not human," William remarked.

Stanley rolled his eyes.

"First of all, she's not my sweetheart. Secondly, this was not a date but an impromptu meeting, and she did not turn me down. She just told me to leave her alone."

"Same thing," William said, raising his shoulders.

Stanley let out an exasperated sigh.

"Listen, both of you," he said. "I don't want a sweetheart. I just want to know what other sort of creatures than ghosts live in this city so I can better perform my job."

Since he could not find any answers in his books and his ghosts were not being helpful either, he decided to go out and investigate on his own. So he got up, put on his coat and hat, and left.

William turned to Cornelius and said: "I think he likes her."

"No! I don't want him to like her, I want him to like Madame Chauvin!" Cornelius protested.

"Why? Isn't she old anyway?"

"But she believes in ghosts!" Cornelius said. "If Stanley has a sweetheart who is afraid of ghosts, then he will have to choose between us and her!"

"Oh dear..." William said, who had not thought about that prospect.

The days were getting colder and colder, and that morning small snowflakes fell softly from the sky, but not enough to cover the ground yet. The streets of the East End were busy as usual, and the carolers annoying, but Stanley had something else on his mind. William was not entirely wrong. Callie was not his sweetheart, but he liked her. He was not even thinking about courting her, but he wanted to see her again, perhaps under the pretense of investigating a potential creature from the underworld. But he had no clue where to find her now that she had moved, so he walked aimlessly down the streets, looking for a face that resembled hers.

After some time, he left the meat and vegetable markets and turned onto a street he had never explored before. It was a small, mostly empty street except for a few laundresses chatting around their heavy baskets. But a woman in a lavender dress caught his attention. She was far away, but her long, curly black hair tied into a braid resembled Callie's, so he began following her. She walked down the street at a brisk pace, then turned on the corner. Not wanting to lose her, he quickened his pace and emerged onto another, busier street, with many shops, and barely caught a glimpse of her as she entered one of them. He did not want to look like a stalker, so he slowed down until he reached the shop and discreetly peeked through the window. He was right; it was Callie. Just catching a glimpse of her made his heart race. He lit himself a cigarette and waited. There was no reason to be nervous: after all, this was just another chance encounter. But apparently not for her. She walked out of the shop, carrying a small packet, a frown on her face.

"Are you stalking me?" she immediately asked him when she saw him.

"Oh, hey there, what a surprise," he said, tipping his hat.

She ignored him and began to walk. He came up beside her and realized that the dress she was wearing was very similar to the one the woman in his dream wore.

"That dress... where did you get it?" he asked.

"At the department store... Everyone has one these days," she answered, looking dumbfounded.

"Of course," he said. He was getting nervous again. "Did you find what you wanted at the shop?"

"Yes... soap. Do you also want to see the contents of my purse?" she asked him. She stopped and stared at him with angry eyes.

"Sorry, I didn't mean to sound rude," he said.

"But you are rude," she said. "Didn't I tell you to leave me alone?"

"You did, but you revealed what you are when you dropped off that envelope in my mailbox."

"I didn't reveal anything," she stated.

She began to walk again, and he followed her.

"You can travel through time, am I right?" he said, aware that he sounded way too excited about it.

"Don't be ridiculous," she said. "Besides, why would I reveal anything about myself to a liar like you?"

"A liar? Me?" he said, offended.

"You're not Indian, and you're not the descendant of a soldier by the name of 'Sachdev', because Sachdev is an Arora surname derived from the Sanskrit 'Sachdeva', who were priests. The Arora caste are traditionally traders and businessmen, so I doubt your ancestor was a soldier," she said, turning suspicious eyes to him.

He had not expected her to investigate every word he said, but the fact that she did somehow thrilled him. It meant she, too, had been thinking about him.

"I guess I'm busted," he admitted. "I'm just a boring Suspect from Kensington."

She stopped and began to laugh.

"What?" he said.

"Sorry, it's just the way you said it..."

He smiled.

"Callie, whatever you are, you can tell me," he said. "I work with ghosts all the time. I live with three of them."

"Three ghosts? That must be tough."

They resumed walking, but this time she was not trying to distance him.

"I have to confess, I returned to your shop even though you told me not to, but it was... gone," he said.

"I had planned to move for a while."

"Who are you hiding from?" he asked, but she did not answer.

They soon arrived in front of her new shop. Like she said, it had simply moved - arguably overnight. The sign was the same, and all her clocks were inside.

"Callie..." he said. "If you didn't want my help, why investigate me?"

"I didn't investigate you. I just like to educate myself, so I looked up your supposed ancestor's name."

"That's what I would call investigating," he remarked.

She sighed and shook her head.

"Stanley, you really are... something else."

"I'll take it as a compliment," he said. "So, are you safe here? Does that man know where you've moved?"

She lost her smile and lowered her eyes sadly.

"Of course he knows. He will never let me live the way I want. But it's my destiny, I guess."

"There is no such thing as destiny. You can be whatever you want."

"Are you a paranormal investigator by choice or because you were born with the ability to communicate with ghosts?" she asked, putting him on the spot.

"I guess I chose this profession because I was born with the ability."

"Then it was your destiny, just like mine is..."

"Is what?"

She looked around her anxiously.

"Stanley, I appreciate your concern for me, but I have to open up my shop," she said. "I don't mind if you come by, but please don't follow me again. I don't appreciate being stalked, nor would any woman."

She climbed up the steps to her shop and turned around. Stanley pursed his lips and lowered his gaze.

"I'm sorry Callie. You're right, I should leave you alone," he said.

He was about to leave, but she called out to him one last time: "Stanley!"

He turned around and gazed at her. All excitement had left him now, and the few thrilling minutes he had spent with her already seemed like nothing more than a distant dream since she now thought of him as a stalker – and he probably was.

"Yes?" he said mechanically.

"My real name is Calcedonia," she said with shining eyes, before going inside.

Calcedonia. An unusual name for sure, but what difference should it make to him? Unless she was giving him
some sort of hint. As he slowly walked away from her shop,
he began to wonder if they were being watched, and the
more he thought about it, the more their whole conversation
made sense. Someone – probably that man – was watching
her, and she could not talk to him freely, but she had given
him a hint in the form of her name. Could it have any
connection with what she was? It sounded Spanish or Italian.

He walked into a bookstore further down the street and
asked if they had any Spanish or Italian dictionaries he might
be able to consult, and the puzzled shopkeeper brought out
a dusty Italian dictionary for him.

"Don't study too hard. Christmas is right around the
corner, boy," the man said, assuming he was a student who
had returned home in this poor neighborhood only for the
holidays.

"Thanks, I'll keep that in mind," Stanley said, and the man
left him to attend to other customers.

He quickly found the word. It was Italian for chalcedony,
a microcrystalline form of quartz. It made for a romantic
girl's name, but still gave him no clue as to what Callie
might be. She was not human, and she obviously wanted
him to find out what she was without telling him because
she was being watched. But he had enough materials at
home to, hopefully, meet her expectations and help her out of
whatever situation she was caught up in. With the renewed
excitement of a teenager, he rushed back to his office.

There, he barely took the time to remove his coat and hat
in the hallway and burst into the office saying: "Guess what
happened!"

As he had expected, William and Cornelius were waiting for him, but Cornelius had the biggest smile on his face. Stanley did not think he had ever seen him smile.

"What's that smile for? Are you feeling sick?" Stanley asked him, frowning, but the child ghost did not answer.

Stanley ignored him and went over to his desk, where he found a letter. He picked it up and read the name and address of the sender: 'Mademoiselle Eve Chauvin, 38 Rue Berthe, Paris'.

"What the hell?" he said. He turned to his two friends. "Who did this? I thought I threw away that letter..."

But it was not hard to guess which one of his friends had been up to no good.

"Cornelius!" he snapped, and the child hid behind William.

"I just wanted you to have a friend who believes in us!" he said in his defense.

"We didn't think she would reply," William added.

"So you helped him?" Stanley said. He rolled his eyes and sat down.

How embarrassing. One simply could not have any privacy with spirits around. But the deed was done now, so he thought he might as well read what she had to say. He checked her name again. 'Mademoiselle' meant she was unmarried. An old spinster kitchen witch?

He opened the letter and William and Cornelius flew over to him.

"Can I at least read my own mail alone?" he grunted, and they backed away, looking guilty.

This Mademoiselle Chauvin had one of the most beautiful cursives he had ever seen, and her English was perfect. He again felt embarrassed at the thought of his own handwriting. She must have thought of some prank when she received his crumpled letter filled with ink stains and mistakes. He began to read quietly:

'Dear Ernest,

I received and read your letter with great pleasure and could not wait to answer you. I hope you won't mind, but I took the liberty of calculating your natal chart in order to better understand you. Your Sun sign is Sagittarius with Scorpio rising. You are assertive and ambitious, but secretive. Your clairvoyant abilities come from your Moon in Cancer; many people like you share this combination. Mercury in Scorpio explains your general interest in the occult and dark subjects. With Mars in Sagittarius and Venus in Capricorn however, you may be quick to get angry and come off to others as oppositional. You long for mature interactions and relationships and will withdraw from anything shallow.'

Stanley smirked. She might as well have looked into her crystal ball and could not have described him better. He had never had much of an interest in astrology, but either it worked, or she truly was a witch.

"That sounds just like you," William commented, who had crept up behind him again.

"It sure does," Stanley said. There was no point in trying to stop the two nosy ghosts anyway, so he continued reading:

'I am a Pisces with Pisces rising and the Moon in Gemini, so I rely on intellect to explain my intuitions, whereas someone like you will tend to rely on their intuitions to explain the world around them. I am not a clairvoyant, but I do tarot readings and sometimes unwillingly perform astral traveling while asleep. And I shall now tell you why your letter intrigued me. I recently drew the exact four tarot cards you saw in your dream, but, at the time, I did not understand the meaning of the reading. Then, on the night you reportedly dreamed of a child coming out of a grave, I had the exact same dream - an unusual dream for me. I believe I somehow ended up in your dream that night.

In my dream, I was the one laying on the ground. By my head was a tombstone with the name 'Giselle'. The air was cold and it was raining outside. I looked up and saw a young man in a brown suit, with brown hair. He was wearing a mask and carrying a pitchfork. I looked up to him, and he put the pitchfork through my throat! I fell back on the ground and bled to death... Now you probably think I am a deranged woman who reads too many dark romance novels, but I believe you and I both dreamed we were 'Giselle'. I believe she died in the exact spot we saw, and she is desperately trying to reach out to someone with a message. As a clairvoyant, perhaps if you find her grave you will be able to connect with her and help her on to the other side. I hope this will help you make sense of your dreams, and I do look forward to hearing from you again after you find out who Giselle was.'

"A murder mystery... and in Stanley's backyard. How interesting!" William said.

But Stanley put down the letter with trembling hands.

"What's wrong?" Cornelius asked.

"You don't understand," Stanley said, turning to them. "The man she described... It was me! But I never killed anyone, and certainly not a child!"

He pursed his lips and frowned.

"It can't be... It's not possible!" he repeated. "This is just a coincidence. There's no way some old lady in France could have had the same dream as me!"

"But isn't the place she described the same you saw? Isn't it your old home?" Cornelius insisted.

"That's exactly why you shouldn't have sent her that letter!" Stanley snapped at him. He got out of his chair, furious. "This lady is a fraud! She lures weak-minded people with all her astrology and tarot crap. She gains their trust and then asks them for money for an astral soul cleansing or whatever it is she does!"

"She wrote about astral traveling," William corrected him.

"It doesn't mean a damn thing, it's all hogwash!"

"But she didn't ask you for money. It sounds like she just wants to help Giselle's spirit find peace," Cornelius said.

Stanley paced around the room nervously.

"Did your father also have brown hair?" William then asked.

"Yes."

"Then it could have been him. Perhaps he murdered someone when he was younger?"

"My father? He was a bloody old asshead, but I can't imagine him murdering a child..." Stanley said, perplexed.

"How do you know that? Many a respectable man end up behind bars when a corpse is found in their backyard or underneath the floorboards of their house," William said.

"There's no way to know unless the spirit of Giselle manifests itself to me," Stanley said. "But it just doesn't make sense. If she had remained in our house, why did she not try to make contact with me? And if she's gone, then why did both I and Eve dream of her?"

"I think you should go back to your old house," Cornelius said. "I will come with you."

"What makes you think Giselle's spirit would even be there?" William said.

"No, he's right," Stanley said, calmer now. "I don't believe that old lady and her astral projections, but sometimes spirits manifest themselves through dreams, do they not? Perhaps she too is a clairvoyant, but in her dreams... Giselle may still be in my old home, but afraid to come out."

"It was pretty crowded in the walls..." Cornelius agreed.

"But she will show up if we call her," Stanley said.

"But aren't you afraid of that house?" William said.

"Terrified. But it's my job, this is what I do. I rid old houses of revenants."

He drew in a deep breath and turned to his friends.

"Ready for a little nighttime trip to the underworld?" he said.

Stanley was only brave when necessary, and he would rather not have dealt with frightening entities from the other world at all. But, perhaps because of his gifts, he also felt compassion for the spirits who were stuck in this realm, and he felt compelled to help them. So that night he returned to his old house in Kensington, intent on finding out who Giselle was and if and by whom she was murdered in the backyard. He brought with him a small suitcase in which he carried all the tools he might need to call a stubborn spirit or perform an exorcism.

Because his house was on a quiet street and breaking in through the front door would certainly get him in trouble, he went down the stairs to the kitchen, where Annie had lived and worked for the Suspects for so many years. Cornelius appeared beside him and nodded. He went through the wall and opened the door from within for him, and Stanley entered the kitchen. He lit an oil lamp that had a little oil left in it. Though he had already been to the kitchen many times, it was the first time he saw it at night. It was equipped with a nice cookstove, a table and a sink fit for a child to use because Annie came into their home at the age of twelve to replace Ida, the older maid, who was getting married. On the other side of the small room was a little bed that looked hard and uncomfortable, and the only light that came in was through a narrow, barred window at the street level. It was almost like a prison cell. He noticed small spots on the floor tile that could have been blood, or wine, or any other red thing that stained. He took the oil lamp with him and went up the stairs to the first floor. He had not seen it in years, nor did he miss its vulgar, flamboyant wallpaper and carpets. His parents liked 'too much' of everything everywhere, too much color, too many paintings and ornaments. Every room in the damned house was an eyesore to him who liked everything plain. He explored the entire first floor and found nothing there but dust and cobwebs.

"Are there any spirits here with us?" he asked aloud. "If you're here and you have a message for the living, you can come to me."

No answer. He then went on to the backyard, which was, as he had expected, covered in weeds and thorn bushes. But the tool shed their gardener had used when he came once a week was still accessible, and there he found a shovel. He used it to clear a way through the bushes until he found the exact spot he had seen in his dream, but it was covered by the heavy stones of the stone path.

"Cornelius, can you get underneath the stones and check if there is a corpse there?" he asked.

"You mean you want me to go down into the dirt?" Cornelius asked, unsure.

"Well I certainly can't. Hurry up!" Stanley said.

Cornelius seemed unhappy, but he did as he was told and soon reemerged, shaking his head frantically.

"What happened? What did you see?" Stanley pressed him.

"An earthworm went up my nostril!" Cornelius complained.

"But did you see anything?" Stanley insisted.

"No, there was nothing but dirt and bugs…"

"The body could have been buried somewhere else…" Stanley said.

Since they could not dig up the entire backyard, they returned inside and decided to investigate the second floor, which had a parlor, a drawing room, and the master bedroom. Nothing interesting there either.

On the third floor, the nursery where Stanley used to play as a child had been remodeled into an office and was left in disarray, as though his father had to leave the house in a hurry. Mary, the governess' bedroom, and his bedroom were left mostly untouched. He noticed that some windows had been boarded up from within. Strange. As he was looking around, though, he again began to feel a presence upstairs, in the attic.

"Do you feel something?" he whispered to Cornelius.

"I do... but it's not a ghost," Cornelius said.

"Can you go up there and see what it is?"

Cornelius stared at him with big eyes.

"You're the paranormal investigator, I'm just a child!" he said in a whisper.

Stanley tried to gather his courage. He had never been up in the attic alone as a child, and the idea terrified him. But there was something up there, and perhaps not a ghost.

"Alright, I'm going up there," he said.

He slowly walked out of Mary's old bedroom. The door to the staircase was right before him, at the end of the hallway.

"I'm here with you," Cornelius said, who sounded just as frightened as he was.

The flame of the oil lamp suddenly went out. It was out of oil, and they would have to continue in the dark. Stanley walked up to the door and, with trembling hands, opened it. The house was perfectly quiet, as though not even a mouse moved. And like in his memories and his dreams, the presence in the staircase was so heavy it was almost suffocating.

The door to the attic suddenly opened a crack at the top of the stairs, scaring the two of them. Stanley's heart was racing with fear, but still he went up the stairs, one after another, until he got to the attic. He pushed the door open. The window was not boarded up, and the soft blue moonlight provided better visibility than in the other rooms.

"Is someone here? Giselle?" he asked aloud, but no answer came.

He looked around the attic: it was filled with boxes, old pieces of furniture, and everything was covered with a thick layer of dust. A small table near the window caught his eye. He went to it and examined it: it was a sort of altar, with various objects and gemstones scattered atop. He picked up one of the stones, but he did not know much about gemstones and could not tell what it was.

"Looks like Father Dearest was performing some sort of ritual here," he said.

"We should try to call Giselle now," Cornelius said.

Stanley looked over his shoulder: the door was still open a crack. No moving objects and no orbs flying across the room. He would have to call Giselle or she would never come out.

He put down his suitcase, opened it, and pulled out a Ouija board. The board game had been created to entertain bored middle-class people who wanted to give themselves a little fright at parties, but it was also an excellent tool to communicate with the dead for those who actually could, because, just like there were shy people, there were shy ghosts. With its help, a bashful spirit could spell out words or sentences using the letters and numbers, or answer questions by moving the planchette to the words 'YES' or 'NO'.

Stanley sat down on the floor and set up the board, and Cornelius stood beside him, on the lookout for any paranormal activity.

"Whoever is here, I would like to talk to you," Stanley said aloud. "If you are here, please manifest yourself. You can talk to me using this board."

He put his fingertips on the planchette and waited.

"I know you're here, and I'm here to help you," he said.

A cold chill ran down his spine and he thought he saw a shadow move across an old mirror, but when he turned his gaze there, it was already gone.

"My name is Stanley. Can you please tell me your name?" he asked. He was not polite in everyday life, but he had learned that, like the living, spirits did not answer rude individuals, especially those intruding on their dwelling places. Introducing oneself, saying 'please' and 'thank you' were the best ways to establish a peaceful contact with a ghost.

He waited, and this time the planchette began to move, slowly at first. It spelled out the name 'GISELLE'. Stanley and Cornelius exchanged a quick glance.

"Giselle, are you stuck here?" Stanley asked.

The planchette moved to the word 'NO'.

"What do you want, Giselle?" he asked.

The planchette moved quickly this time and spelled out: 'HURT SOPHIE'. Stanley quivered. Cornelius looked around the room, but he, too, seemed like he could not find her.

"Why do you want to hurt Sophie?" Stanley asked.

The planchette moved quickly under his fingers again and spelled out: 'SOPHIE KILLED ME'.

"That's not true!" Stanley shouted, getting up, and suddenly the door slammed shut.

Cornelius moved in front of him, ready to protect him, and Stanley slipped his arm around him. All around them, the air filled with the scent of woodfire smoke. Stanley quickly reached into his suitcase and pulled out a small phial of salt and a bundle of sage. With a match, he lit the sage.

"Giselle, I don't know what you are, but I know you're not a ghost! You'd better show yourself now or I will have to exorcise you!" he said loudly.

Challenging an angry spirit while alone in a room without an exit was a bad idea, but now he knew Giselle was hostile. He saw a shadow move again in the mirror; it was spiraling around them. And on the Ouija board on the floor, the planchette spelled out the word 'DIE'.

"Giselle?" Stanley called out again as a warning.

But the voice that answered him had nothing of a child.

"Stanley..." it said in a cold, eerie whisper. "You are a murd erer..."

"No I'm not!" Stanley shouted. "What are you? Show yourself, you coward!"

Before the creature of darkness could answer, though, someone appeared before Stanley and he heard a woman's voice saying: "No!"

Everything around him disappeared in the blink of an eye, and the next moment he found himself in his office again, with a frightened Cornelius by his side. And before him stood Callie. She was wearing her black dress again, and her hair was loose over her shoulders. She held a tiny golden pocket watch in her hand that shimmered with green light, which she quickly put away in a pocket on her breast.

"Callie? What are you doing here? What am I doing here?" Stanley asked, astounded.

He looked around him: it was his office alright, but the clock said six thirty.

"Six thirty? I thought I left at seven..." he said.

"You did, but I had to bring you back," she said.

"Bring me back? In time?" he said, turning to her.

"Yes," she said. Her voice was unfriendly.

"You can travel through time?" he said, excited and amazed at the same time. "But why bring me back here?"

"It was a trap, Stanley. That creature lured you to the attic to get you."

"Wait, you mean you know what was up there? Are you involved with ghosts?" he said.

"Not with ghosts. With demons."

"With demons? How?"

"I am a demon," she said.

She stood before him with her arms crossed now, as though she was pondering what to do with him next, and he stared at her in disbelief.

"Stanley, that must be it! The thing in the attic was a demon!" Cornelius said by his side, and Stanley turned to him.

"You think so?" he said.

"Who are you talking to?" Callie asked, confused.

"Oh, one of my ghosts. There are two here with us, Cornelius and William," he said.

"Oh..." she said, surprised. "Um, nice to meet you," she said, looking around the room.

"Looks like there was no reason to worry after all. She's not afraid of ghosts since she is a demon. You have our blessing to court her," William said.

"Oh, shush!" Stanley told him.

"Well then, I'd better leave now," she said.

"Wait! Now you have to tell me more!" Stanley begged her. "Why is there a demon in my attic? Was he summoned by my father? And who is Giselle?"

"Unfortunately, I cannot reveal those things to you, but please don't return there. It's dangerous," she said, and with this she left his office and he soon heard the front door closing.

CHAPTER 4

STANLEY HAD HAD ENOUGH of mystery and unanswered questions, so he decided to confront the one person who most likely held the answers: his father. He hated the old man and never wanted to interact with him again, so he had avoided confronting him all this time about whatever still tied him to this world. But now he was sure that he had done something to a child named Giselle, and that it involved demons. So he went to the spare room in his new house where he most often heard him rattling. He was a poltergeist who did not appear before him nor speak with words, so he would have to find another way to communicate with him. He sat at the small desk in a corner of the room and placed an oil lamp on the dusty surface. Cornelius appeared and posted himself behind him, and William, as usual, slouched in an old chair. They were both used to his father's presence and were not afraid of him.

"Father," Stanley said, trying to remain calm. "I need you to talk to me."

Of course there was no answer; the old man was such a nuisance.

"Come out, you old bastard, and make some noise!" Stanley then shouted, and he heard the rattling of chains inside the wall. At least the old man still responded when provoked.

"Alright, you old geezer. I want the truth now," Stanley said. "I'm going to ask you questions. Knock once for 'yes', twice for 'no', and don't you dare try to lie or I'll exorcise you!"

He waited and finally heard one knock. Good. He was cooperating.

"Do you know of a child named Giselle?" Stanley asked.

One knock.

"Did you kill her?"

Two knocks. Stanley turned to his ghosts, who also seemed perplexed.

"Did you summon a demon in our home?" he asked, but his father did not answer.

He let out an exasperated sigh. With a knocking spirit, he had to figure out the exact questions, or he would not get precise answers.

"Was anyone murdered in our backyard?" he asked.

One knock came in response.

"Was it Giselle?"

One knock.

"Was she murdered using a pitchfork?" he asked, aware that his voice trembled.

One knock came, followed by two knocks. Yes and no? He hesitated, then decided to ask the burning question on his mind.

"Did Sophie murder Giselle?"

His father's spirit knocked once. Yes.

"I didn't murder anyone!" Stanley cried out, but of course no answer came.

"You should try to stay calm," Cornelius said. "Maybe it was another Sophie..."

Indeed, it could just be another child by the same name. He had not thought about it.

"Was this 'Sophie'... me?" he asked, holding his breath, and the answer came in a terrible single knock.

"B–But... that's not possible!" he said. "I... I..."

He was beginning to stutter again. William got up and joined Cornelius by his side.

"Am I... a murderer?" Stanley asked, almost in a whisper.

A pile of books on an old crate began to move, slowly at first, then one of the books in the middle of the pile flew across the room and fell open on the floor. Stanley got up and hesitantly walked over to it. He picked it up. It was a book of poetry by Edgar Allan Poe.

"The gentleman in the wall must be trying to tell you something," William said.

"That I'm a murderer?" Stanley said in a dark voice.

"He didn't, technically, answer that question," William remarked.

"What does the book say? Is the answer on the page?" Cornelius asked.

"It's just a poem, 'The Raven'," Stanley said, confused, then he noticed a scratch on the page. He read the verse: "'Prophet!' said I, 'thing of evil!–prophet still, if bird or devil!'"

"What does it mean?" Cornelius asked.

"In this poem, a grief-stricken man mourning the loss of his love Lenore starts talking to a raven, hoping he can ease his sorrow, but the raven just responds 'Nevermore'..." Stanley explained to the child ghost.

"How would that answer Stanley's question, though?" William said, scratching his goatee.

"There is a scratch on the page, under 'thing of evil'..." Stanley said. "Are you calling me evil?" he then shouted to his father, and all of them heard a very loud, single knock.

Stanley closed the book and hurled it at the wall in the direction from which the knock came.

"Liar! How would you know anything about me? You never even wanted me around! You were far too busy running around London and looking fashionable!"

No answer.

"Listen, you sick man!" Stanley continued. "I know you summoned a demon into our home, and for all I know, you murdered Giselle! You're trying to blame me because no one else can hear you, but I know I never killed anyone!"

Again, his father did not answer, but they heard the rattling of chains, and it seemed more and more distant, as though he was retreating.

"Right, get out of here, you old bastard!" Stanley shouted.

He left the room, agitated, and went into his bedroom across the hallway.

"Spirits can lie," William reminded him, having just flown in. Cornelius followed him.

"I know..." Stanley said.

He sat down on his bed and took his head in his hands.

"It's still early, you two could return to your old home," William suggested, but Cornelius shook his head.

"What we encountered up there was not a ghost," he said.

"He's right, and if it truly was a demon, there's not much I can do on my own," Stanley said. "I wish... If only my dreams could bring me answers instead of just giving me all these vague clues."

"You could ask Mademoiselle Chauvin..." Cornelius said.

"I couldn't possibly bother her again," Stanley said. "And she wouldn't even be involved if you two hadn't sent that letter."

"But because we did, we now know who was murdered," William said.

"And now everything is much more complicated," Stanley pointed out.

He lay back on his bed and gazed at the ceiling.

"So a child named Giselle was murdered in my backyard, my father summoned something in the attic, and that thing wanted me to come up there all along, that was why I was so afraid of the attic as a child. There was a demon up there waiting for me. But what could a demon want from a child?" he wondered aloud.

"Shouldn't you ask Callie about that?" William said.

"No! He should ask Mademoiselle Chauvin!" Cornelius said.

"Why? She's not a demon," William said.

"But I like her..." Cornelius said in a small voice.

Stanley sat up.

"William is right. Only Callie can tell me what sort of demon is up there and what it wants," he said. "I will talk to her tomorrow morning."

"Why not now?" William wondered.

"Because her shop will probably be closed, and I don't want her to think I'm a stalker," Stanley said with a sigh. "Also, I need some sleep."

It had been a long night, and he was exhausted, both emotionally and physically. If he knew he would not be in a better mood the next morning, at least he would have more energy. So he changed into his nightshirt and went to bed.

He had not measured exactly how early it was when he arrived in front of Callie's new shop at seven thirty in the morning. The dark streets were mostly empty, except for one man. He, too, seemed to be waiting in front of the mysterious shop, but he was not the man Stanley had previously seen with Callie. This one had much friendlier features, shoulder-length blond hair, and his general lack of facial hair made him look younger than his build suggested. He wore a blue suit and tie under a long black raincoat, and the ribbon on his top hat was also blue. He tipped his hat when he saw Stanley, and the young man came and stood beside him, gazing at the shop's closed door. There was light inside. Callie was awake, but she would probably not be opening just yet. Stanley's heartbeat quickened at the thought of seeing her again.

After a good night of sleep – and no nightmares for once – he had awakened with a clearer mind. Now everything made more sense. Of only two things he was sure: a child named Giselle was murdered, since both he and Eve had concordant dreams about it, and there was a demon living in the attic of his old home – Callie said so. He suspected that it had been summoned by his father but could not confirm it. Also, his father knew who had murdered Giselle and was trying to make him believe it was him, perhaps at the guidance of this demon. So far, apart from demons being involved, this was not so different from any other paranormal investigation. It was common for ghosts to deliver vague messages to the living, for example, by moving objects or opening books at a certain page, but those messages were not necessarily truthful, and even when interrogated, spirits could lie. What Stanley needed to know was why a demon would be interested in him, to the point of waiting for him in his attic. He had again gone through all his books of demonology, and they generally agreed that, unless one summoned a demon themselves, demons did not seek them out. And if his father had indeed summoned it, then there would be no reason for the demon to even know Stanley's name, let alone try to use his clairvoyant abilities to trick him with a child ghost to save. As for Callie – Calcedonia – he still did not know very much about her, except that she could travel through time and wanted to protect him. And, in order to protect himself, he needed more information from her. He couldn't fool himself: he knew very well that once he obtained that information, he would continue his investigation until he could exorcise or banish that demon. After all, it could be dangerous to any other humans who took possession of the house when someday it would end up being sold.

"You seem nervous... present?" the man by his side said, breaking the silence.

"What?" Stanley said, turning to him.

"You look eager to get inside and buy a present for someone," the man said, pointing in the shop's direction with his head.

"Oh... uh, no," Stanley said. "I just want to buy a clock."

"It must be a very important clock then..." the man said with a grin.

Stanley then realized that this man also smelled like woodfire smoke.

"Do you..." he said.

"What?"

"Do you heat your home with wood or coal?" Stanley asked.

The man stared at him for a moment.

"Well... I'm old-school, I guess. I have a fireplace," he said.

"Oh," Stanley said, nodding. It made sense then that he might smell like smoke then. He discreetly checked the collar of his own coat, and it did have a light smoky scent to it too.

"If you're selling coal stoves, I might be interested," the man said, leaning over to him as his eyes remained on the shop's door.

"Oh... No, I'm not selling anything," Stanley said.

Callie finally flipped the 'CLOSED' sign on the back of the door to 'OPEN'. She then came out and stared at the two men, looking surprised.

"Good morning, Callie," the man in blue said in a smooth voice. He tipped his hat.

Callie was beautiful every time Stanley saw her, but somehow she looked even more so in the shadows of the night. He was still trying to come to terms with the fact that she was a demon, and what it meant. The books described them as ugly creatures, who sometimes adopted an attractive shape to lure humans and trick them into forming a pact with them. But if that was her intent, why waste time trying to keep him away? She might as well have come in the first time she knocked on his door and he would probably have given her anything she wanted, just because she was beautiful. Granted, that was both stupid and unprofessional on his part. But she had been good to him, whether she liked him or not; she was obviously not the sort of demon described in the books.

"The shop opens in ten minutes," she told Stanley in a cold voice. Then, through some sort of silent agreement, the man in blue followed her inside. She closed the door and flipped the sign again, and Stanley waited.

After a good twenty minutes, the man in blue finally opened the door. Stanley walked up to him, but he immediately darted off to the right, avoiding him.

"Oh, Sir!" Stanley said.

The man turned around.

"Yes?"

He no longer looked so friendly. Whatever their secret conversation, it had obviously not gone the way he wanted.

Stanley walked up to him.

"I think you dropped a coin," he said, handing him a coin.

"Well, you could just have left it there for the needy," the man muttered as he took it.

"Have a good day, Sir," Stanley said with a smile.

He then headed into the shop, the sign now saying 'OPEN'. He found Callie there, dusting the window and rearranging the items. She ignored him.

"Good morning," he said, tipping his hat, nevertheless.

"Why did you come back?" she asked in a somewhat angry voice, before returning behind her counter.

"Was that man also harassing you?" he asked.

He walked over to her. She gazed at him and sighed.

"Stanley... I don't know what to do to keep you safe. You seem to be looking for danger," she said.

"I'm not, but how can I be safe if I don't know what I'm up against?" he said.

He sat on a tall stool and leaned over the counter.

"I know that a little girl named Giselle was murdered in the backyard of my old home, any idea who she might be?" he asked.

"No," she said. She picked up a clock and began working on it.

"But you know something about the demon living in my attic," he said.

"Only that it is a demon. If you expect me to know the name of every demon living in someone's attic or basement in London, I don't."

"But you used some device to travel through time and save me. Why? And how did you know where I would be?" he insisted.

She lifted her gaze and observed him for some time. Even when she was displeased, her black eyes were absolutely beautiful.

"I followed you, like you followed me. Fair enough?" she said.

"Indeed," he said with a smile.

"I followed you and I arrived too late. You were already dead. So I turned back time and saved you before the demon killed you," she continued.

He lost his smile and grew silent. Dead. So the demon was after his life...

"I don't know what sort of demon lives in your attic, but I know how demons usually enter human spaces," she went on. "They cannot enter on their own, they must be summoned. How or why this demon was summoned to your attic, I do not know."

"I have an idea..." he said. "But you said you could turn back time... How do you do it? Does it have something to do with that pocket watch?"

She nodded and lowered her eyes.

"I am a succubus – the lowest class of demon. We have no special powers, we just seduce men."

"So how did you get that pocket watch?" he asked, more and more intrigued.

"I made it," she said. "I am a real clockmaker, it's my hobby as well as my cover in the human world."

"Then could we not use the pocket watch to defeat that demon?" he asked. "You know, if it remains there, it could attack other humans eventually."

She shook her head sadly.

"I no longer have the watch. The man you just saw took it from me."

"Is he also part of the demon police?" he asked.

"His name is Belphegor. He is a major demon of sloth, but he also controls the gates of time," she explained, looking uneasy. "What I did was a taboo; no one is allowed to make a device to travel through time. My overseer, the man you saw the other day, was suspicious of me, but now I actually used it they sent me Belphegor himself. I will be punished after they complete their investigation..."

"And how will they punish you?"

"Death," she said, and her eyes filled with tears.

He reached for her hand on the counter and took it. It was the first time he felt bold enough to hold a woman's hand.

"I'm sorry, this is all my fault," he said. "There must be something I can do to help you."

"No, you can't do anything," she said, wiping away a tear. "I knew what I was doing was wrong, but I thought I could save lives using it. I wanted to be something more than just a demon in this world..."

She suddenly burst into tears and covered her eyes. He got up and went around the counter to her.

"Callie, please let me help you," he said.

"How?" she sobbed. "I'm a criminal..."

He looked around them.

"What if I could substitute that pocket watch for another one without any powers?" he said. "Then they would have no evidence against you."

She looked at him with surprise.

"Yes, I suppose, I have similar pocket watches around my shop. But how would you manage to substitute it?"

"Do you know where he took the watch?"

"Probably to his office for now. It's just down the street. But, Stanley, you can't go there, it's too dangerous!" she said.

"I may have a good reason to go there," he said with a grin.

He reached into his coat pocket and pulled out the mysterious man's wallet. He didn't like him, so he had stolen it while distracting him earlier.

"Stanley! You didn't...!" she said, turning pale.

"I was sure this man was also harassing you, so I stole his wallet. I was going to use it to find out where he lived and report him to the police, but now I think I can make a better use of it," he said with a wide grin. "See, I can help you."

"Stanley! You're doing it again - getting yourself in trouble!" she protested.

"I'm already in serious trouble if a demon wants to kill me. How much worse can it get?" he joked.

She sighed again. He moved closer and hesitantly reached out to her, and she let him wipe away her tears. Demon tears... They were as beautiful as she was. His heart was racing again, but not because of the tangled situation he had unwillingly got himself into: it was because of her. She gazed at him with gratitude now, as though all she ever wanted from him was his help after all.

"Can you give me a pocket watch that looks identical to the one he took?" he asked.

"Yes, of course," she said. She dug into a drawer and pulled out a miniature pocket watch. "This is the model it is based on. It looks identical, but it has no powers."

"Thanks," he said, taking it. "And where can I find this Belphegor?"

"His office is two blocks down the street, number 35. He works as a notary public," she said.

"A notary public? Do all demons have common jobs?" he asked.

"The more common, the better," she said. "We can have any profession in the human world, but we tend to choose one according to our interests, and major demons' interests always lie in handling or signing contracts with humans, be they legal or demonic."

"It makes sense," he said. "Alright, I'll be back in no time with your watch."

He winked at her and walked out the shop's door, and his heart was filled with a new courage – and perhaps recklessness. He was playing a dangerous game now, with demons, but she had endangered her life for him, he owed her the same.

He presented himself at the demonic notary's office around nine o'clock and gazed at the large wooden door. A golden sign on it read 'Christian Baal & Associates, Notary Services'. Another sign on the side of it read 'Ring the bell and enter'. It seemed like a very ordinary place, on a clean street. He rang the bell and entered. Like many other similar buildings, it had several offices. He did not know which one was Belphegor's, but he was likely to be the big boss here too, so he knocked on the door to Christian Baal's office.

"Come in," a man's voice said, and he recognized it.

He pushed the door open and found the man sitting at his desk, working on some paperwork. Nothing seemed strange about his office, except perhaps the fact that no fire burned in the fireplace.

"You?" he said, seeming surprised. "Do you need a notary?"

Stanley pulled out the wallet from his pocket and placed it on his desk.

"You dropped this on the street. I found it after leaving the clockmaker's shop. Luckily, no one stole it," he said with a polite smile.

The man took it and looked through it. He seemed pleased that none of the money had been stolen.

"Thank you," he said. "I guess I didn't realize I had dropped it."

Of course he didn't, because a demon wouldn't care how much money he was carrying, Stanley thought.

"My pleasure," he said. "So you're a notary?"

"I am. Did you find your dream clock?" Belphegor said.

"I didn't. I had to place a special order," Stanley said.

The demon seemed amused by his answer.

"Well then... Is there anything else I can do for you?" he asked.

"Now that you mention it, since you are a notary public, might I ask you a question of a legal nature?"

"Of course. Is this regarding an estate?" Belphegor said, inviting him to sit down.

Stanley sat down and crossed his arms. His eyes quickly moved around the office: apart from a small bookshelf containing books of law, a desk, and a few chairs, the demon had a collection of valuable antiques on the walls and side tables. His eyes stopped on a samurai sword on the wall.

"Antiques?"

Belphegor smiled.

"I'm a collector," he said. "So what's your name?"

"Robert Witherspoon," Stanley said.

"And what is your situation?"

"I have an uncle in the Americas who passed away recently, and I know I am his only heir, but they won't let me claim my inheritance because of an issue with the paperwork," Stanley said.

"What sort of issue?" Belphegor asked.

"Can you guess?" Stanley asked him with a grin.

"Mister Witherspoon, I am a notary, not an investigator," Belphegor said, always smiling. "But I do have an idea... Is it because the name on your birth certificate is not 'Robert'?"

"You're smart. I like that," Stanley said.

He saw Cornelius appear behind the demon – finally. He needed to get the man out of the room so he could search it, but he was not going to get very far alone. He pretended to look around the room again.

"Nice office. Aren't you afraid of burglars, though? The front door is unlocked," he said.

Belphegor laughed.

"No, I am not worried that anyone would try to burglarize this place."

Cornelius understood and disappeared, and soon the two men heard a noise upstairs. Belphegor seemed puzzled.

"Oh... I do hope I didn't jinx you," Stanley said innocently.

"Wait right here for a moment," Belphegor said.

He got up and left the room, and Stanley immediately jumped from his chair and went to the other side of the desk. He pulled open each drawer and quickly searched them: no trace of the pocket watch. He then turned to the bookcase, when a firm hand caught his wrist. He was quite sure he had not heard anyone coming back down the stairs, but the demon was right there beside him again, an angry look on his face.

"Well, well, Mister Witherspoon," he said. "Are you just a nosy boy or a kleptomaniac?"

"Let go of me! I didn't take anything!" Stanley shouted to alert Cornelius, who immediately appeared on the other side of the room. He no longer looked like the frail, sweet child he usually was, but like a vengeful spirit.

"You think I don't know you took my wallet this morning? You're not the first pickpocket I come across," Belphegor said, and with this he pushed Stanley against the wall with incredible strength.

"Cornelius!" Stanley called out, and as he did, the desk came crashing into the demon, pushing him against the other wall. The Japanese sword then came flying in his direction and stuck into the wall right beside his head.

"Let's go!" Stanley cried, rushing out of the office with Cornelius.

He ran as fast as he could down the streets, which were now crowded. A good thing: he would be able to lose his pursuer easily. But he did not go back to his place: first, he had to get Callie to safety. He stormed into her shop – which, luckily, was empty – and flipped the sign on the door.

"Stanley? What's going on?" she asked in a panic.

"We need to go now. I'll explain later!" he said. "Does the shop have a back door?"

"Y–Yes, of course," she said.

She took him to the back, and they left through the small door. They ran together through the darker alleyways until they came to Stanley's place. They also entered it through the back door, and only once they were inside did Stanley remember to breathe.

"Stanley, what happened with Belphegor? What did he do to you?" she asked, grabbing both his arms. She, too, was a lot stronger than him.

"I distracted him and went through his things, but he caught me," Stanley said, trying to catch his breath. "I'm sorry, I didn't find the watch."

"He caught you? And you made it out of there alive? You must be the luckiest human ever!" she said. "But are we safe here?"

"I gave him a fake name," he said. "Even if he does find us, it will take him some time."

"We are in so much trouble…" she repeated, shaking her head anxiously. "What are we going to do?"

"Let's just sit down and think about it for now," he said.

He took her to his office and ushered William out of the sofa he liked to slouch on, and he and Callie sat down.

"Was one of your ghosts there? I don't want to steal anyone's favorite seat," she said, making him laugh.

"That's alright, William doesn't mind," he said.

"So you say!" William said, standing before him with his arms crossed. "And what sort of trouble did you get yourself into this time to come running in through the back door?"

"Demon trouble," Stanley said.

Cornelius appeared beside William and tugged at the sleeve of his shirt.

"I think he would like us to leave him alone," he said.

"He didn't say that," William responded, but Stanley gave him a look that meant: "Yes, I want to be left alone."

His two friends disappeared.

"So that was William?" Callie asked, looking in the general direction where he had stood, although she could not see him.

"Yes, William is attached to this house. He died in 1610," Stanley said. "Cornelius is a child ghost who lived in the wardrobe of my old home. He attached himself to me when I was a child. And somewhere in the walls is my father's ghost. He just follows me around to annoy me."

"What is it like, living with so many spirits?" she asked him.

"I don't know what it's like not to live with spirits," he shrugged. "What is it like being a succubus? What do you do?"

"It's the lowest position in the demon hierarchy," she said as her eyes browsed through the office.

The morning sun filtered through the light curtains on the old windows; the heavy green portieres around them were open. Stanley preferred to live in the dark, but now and then he liked a little sunlight. He suddenly realized that the fire was out in the chimney.

"Oh, you must be freezing," he said, getting up.

"It is a bit cold in here," she said, rubbing her arms. In their haste, she had not even grabbed a coat.

He went to the fireplace and started a fire, then removed his coat and carefully wrapped it around her shoulders. He had always wanted to do so with a woman, but he'd never had the opportunity - and most women would not want his old patched-up coat, anyway. But she seemed happy and smiled somewhat.

"Is there anything else I can get you? Tea?" he offered.

"Yes, that would be nice, thank you," she said.

He noticed her discomfort, despite her smile. Her lips trembled, and she suddenly burst into tears and covered her face with her hands. He hesitantly slipped his arm around her shoulders.

"Oh, Callie, don't worry, everything will be alright," he said, but she shook her head.

"I'm scared..." she sobbed.

"I know, but you have me now, and two friendly ghosts who will protect you," he said in a soothing voice.

She turned her moist eyes to him. He smiled and wiped away her tears once again.

"Don't worry, we'll figure out something," he promised her. "Wait for me here. I'll fix us some tea. You'll feel better once you're warmed up."

Not wanting to waste a second of this precious time with her, he rushed out into the hallway and down the stairs to the kitchen to make them a pot of tea. There, he found William and Cornelius sitting around the small table and looking at him with mischief.

"What?" he asked them.

"So, how is the romance going?" William asked.

"It's not romance," Stanley said, annoyed. "I'm in trouble, she's in trouble, and now we're both in even bigger trouble with the demons because of me. I need to figure out what to do next."

"Around a cup of tea?" William said. "Would you like some flowers with that?"

Stanley ignored him and put a kettle on the cookstove.

"Is he blushing?" Cornelius whispered to William.

"If that's not love, then I do not know what is," William commented. "I hope he doesn't forget us. I'm terrified of leaving this world alone."

Stanley turned to them, surprised. Of course, he knew that they were both stuck in this world because they had unfinished business, and he knew the light would come for them sooner or later, but he had not given it much thought until then. He came to sit at the table with them.

"Do you really think I would let you cross over alone?" he asked William, serious. "How could I ever do such a thing to my friend?"

William shrugged as though he did not care that much after all.

"Are you afraid of the light? Is that why you stay with me?" Stanley asked both of them, and they immediately nodded.

"But we also want you to be happy..." Cornelius said in a sad voice.

"I couldn't be happy without my best friends..." Stanley said, lowering his eyes.

The kettle whistling startled them. He got up and put some fresh tea leaves in the teapot, then poured the boiling water atop them. He did not like milk and sugar in his tea so he had none, nor did he have any real food to offer Callie. He stared at the teapot for a moment, then put it on a tray with two cups and left.

"Are we his best friends?" Cornelius asked William anxiously.

"The boy has no friends apart from us," William said.

"What do you think of this female demon?" Cornelius asked.

"She looks like a charming young woman, and she saved the two of you last night."

"But isn't it strange that she even knew where to find us, and that we would be in danger?"

"I suppose there is a logical explanation. Stanley doesn't seem too worried about it," William said, raising his shoulders. "Do you not like her now? You're the one who begged me to leave them alone."

"I know," Cornelius said, lowering his eyes. "But it seems like, since she knocked on Stanley's door that one day, suddenly he's getting in trouble with demons."

"But Mademoiselle Chauvin's letter was what made him decide to return to his house," William said. "You could also say she is responsible for whatever situation he got himself into. And, ultimately, all of this might just be his destiny."

Cornelius shifted on his chair and began to swing his little legs underneath the table.

"I wish Stanley had never grown up..." he said in a small voice.

When Stanley returned to his office, he found Callie standing by his desk and looking at the mail on it.

"Oh, sorry, I was not going through your mail," she said, startled. "I was just..."

"Going through my mail," he said, laughing. "I don't mind. You won't find anything interesting there though. Mostly bills I'm afraid."

He brought the tray to the desk and set it on it since he did not own a coffee table. With the back of his hand, he pushed away the unopened letters and books to make some room.

"Who is Sophie? Your sister?" she asked.

She had obviously seen Mister Scarborough's letters.

"That would be me. On the paper," Stanley said as he poured her a cup of tea. "I'm afraid I don't have any milk or sugar," he then said.

"So you're not a man?" she asked him, curious.

He lost his smile and looked around him nervously.

"I am a man, just in the wrong body," he answered. "Those letters are from the administrator of my father's estate. Because of the way I dress and identify, he refused to meet me and is still searching for 'Sophie Suspect'. So I can't inherit my own house. But even if I did, I couldn't pay the property taxes on it, so the city will eventually take possession of it either way – demon and all."

"Couldn't you just put on a dress and a wig once and go claim your inheritance, and then work to pay the taxes?" she wondered as she took a sip from the very bitter black tea. She cringed slightly and sat down on the chair.

"Is it too bitter?" he asked.

"Just a bit," she said, but she laughed softly, and he laughed with her. "So why can't you get your inheritance?" she asked again.

"Do you have any idea how much it costs to own a house in Kensington?" he said.

"I wouldn't know. As a succubus, I belong to my overseers. I'm not allowed to own anything. I can only have my shop as long as they let me."

He brought another chair near the desk and sat with her. He did not like talking about 'Sophie' with anyone, but he could see that she meant no harm, she was just curious about him. She wanted to know him better, like he wanted to know her better.

"I know that some women crossdress so they can work among men and earn a living, but I'm not like them," he explained while averting his gaze from her. "As far as I can remember, I was always a boy. And when my body started growing into a woman's, I didn't understand what was happening. The governess and the maid tried to tell me that I was a girl, and that this was just how girls naturally became women, but I felt completely different from them. When they put dresses on me, it felt so wrong, I couldn't stand it... I only feel good in men's clothes, and when people call me 'Stanley' and interact with me as a man. I know this is probably difficult to understand for someone like you..."

He lifted his gaze to meet hers, and this time her eyes were filled with compassion.

"On the contrary, I understand you," she said. "My situation is different, of course, but also somewhat similar. I see myself as an ordinary woman - a human. Succubi compete to seduce men, it's the very purpose of our existence, but I want to be an ordinary woman. I want to work in a shop, and sometimes go shopping for a new dress. I want to fall in love someday and have children." She lowered her eyes sadly. "Well, children are out of the question, I suppose, since I could only mate with an incubus and produce demon offspring... Our mates don't stay with us. Demons don't raise their offspring. They drop them off in a coven of their kind and the young ones are expected to raise themselves. There is no such thing as being a 'mother' in my world."

His heart filled with warmth as he listened to her, and he took her hand and held it again. This time, she held his hand too.

"Don't give up on who you are," he said. "Besides, you could always adopt a human child."

She smiled softly.

"You make everything sound easier than it is."

"There are as many different people in this world as there are people, and yet the ones who govern us would want us all to be just one thing. Why should their narrow vision rule over our lives?" he said.

Her smile widened, and the black diamonds of her eyes sparkled now.

"How did I ever meet someone like you?" she said.

"I believe you came knocking on my door," he said, and they both laughed.

CHAPTER 5

STANLEY SPENT THE REST of the afternoon talking with Callie as though they had always been friends. She told him about life as a succubus, and what she liked and disliked about it. As a demon, of course, she did not abide by the same laws as humans, and female demons enjoyed greater freedom. Sex was not a taboo for them; it did not tarnish their reputation, on the contrary. A female demon with many lovers was considered dominant over the others and was respected. On the other hand, succubi were expected to be available to their male and female overseers whenever they requested sexual favors from them, and sleeping with your boss was, in their world, a status symbol. But Callie was different. While, as a healthy demon, she also enjoyed sex, it was not the sole purpose of her existence. She liked reading, making clocks, as well as shopping for beautiful things. She had romantic dreams, and wanted to get married and have children, even if those things were impossible in her world.

"When I was a young demon, I didn't think about anything, really. Succubi are not raised to believe they are intelligent. It would serve no purpose," she explained while enjoying another cup of the bitter tea. "And I played my part without questioning anything until I met a different sort of prey." A 'prey' was anyone a demon preyed on, whether as food – because some fed on humans – or to form a pact. In the case of succubi and incubi, their prey were the humans they seduced, and all that ever happened to them was an enjoyable night in which all their wildest dreams got fulfilled.

"How was he different?" Stanley asked, who had been listening eagerly to her every word.

Callie smiled to herself and seemed lost in thought for a moment.

"He asked me what my name was. He wanted to see me again after that one night," she said. "We're not supposed to ever see our prey again, but I made an exception for him. We met again and talked... He convinced me that I was intelligent, and that I could be much more than what I was. Of course, my overseer came to know of it and put an end to our affair. But something had changed inside me... I wanted to be someone in this world, not just an anonymous succubus. So I started educating myself, and I eventually became a clockmaker."

"That man... did you love him?" Stanley asked, sipping on his third cup of black tea.

She looked away in a nostalgic manner, and he realized that, whether she loved him or not, he was the one who had first made her dream of love. He was a little jealous of him.

"I wanted him to teach me love... but we never got a chance," she said.

"If you met him again, would you fall in love with him?" he asked.

Her eyes lost that beautiful spark that had lit them up when she talked about him.

"I never will... he died," she said.

"I'm... so sorry," he said.

She sighed.

"Demons live longer than humans. It was bound to happen, anyway."

"But still..."

"What about you? Won't you tell me about Kensington and growing up as a human child?" she asked, returning her eyes to him, but a knock on the front door startled both of them.

Stanley looked over his shoulder: the sky was dark outside already. Had they been talking that long? He turned to Callie, who looked terrified, and gestured to her to remain quiet. He then walked over to the front door and peeked through the keyhole. Nobody. He opened the door a crack, then looked outside. The sunny morning had turned into a cold night, and a thin layer of snow covered the ground. Suddenly, five children jumped out of nowhere in front of him and began singing carols.

"Oh no, you've got to be kidding me!" he muttered, but they went on singing as loudly as they possibly could, hurting his sensitive ears.

"Alright, here you go," he said, giving them a few coins from his pockets. "Get lost now!"

"Thank you! Merry Christmas, Sir!" they chanted as they walked away to go bother another person.

He shut the door and locked it, then returned to the office, where Callie anxiously awaited him.

"Who was it? Demons?" she asked.

"Worse than that... carolers," he said with such a funny frown she couldn't help but laugh.

He laughed along with her and went to close the shutters on the windows. They would be safe here for the night. He was about to sit down with her again when they both heard another knock on the front door, followed by one on the back door. Stanley did not like that. Carolers would not knock on the back door.

"Cornelius! William!" he called out in a whisper.

Callie's fingers tightened around the arms of her chair. The two spirits soon appeared before them.

"Who's knocking on the door? Demons?" Stanley asked them.

"We don't know, we didn't see anybody," Cornelius said.

All were scared now. Stanley got up and listened, and they heard more knocking on both doors.

"Cornelius, do you feel the same sort of presence as in my attic?" he whispered.

"Yes..." Cornelius said.

"Don't worry, it can only hurt the living. You two will be alright," Stanley told his ghosts.

"What about you?" William asked.

"We need to get out of here," Stanley said.

"What's going on? Did the demons find us?" Callie asked him. She could not hear Cornelius and William.

"Looks like whatever was in my attic found us first," Stanley told her, while trying not to sound alarming. "We need to get out of here through the rooftops."

She nodded and followed him upstairs as quietly as she could, and the knocking became more insistent. They went up to the third floor, which also had an attic, but not a frightening one. There, Stanley grabbed a dusty old coat and hat since Callie was wearing his, and he opened the window. He led the way and they climbed onto the roof. It was a little slick, but they somehow managed to make it to the roof of the next building, and then the next, until they reached an alleyway. They could not jump across it and safely land on the next roof, so Stanley began to climb down the gutter, and Callie, who was apparently an acrobat as well as a clockmaker, simply jumped off the roof and landed on the ground with the precision of a cat.

"Can all demons do that?" he asked her, surprised.

"The Greek philosopher Thales said: 'A sound mind in a sound body'. I don't just educate my mind, I'm also part of a women's gymnastics club," she said with a grin.

"I wish I could say the same," Stanley said, whose back and hips would be sore the next day. "Alright, follow me!"

They ran down the street, dodging people and children playing outside in the snow, and Stanley was aware of something following them at a distance. He took Callie's hand and made a sharp turn, and they ran into a restaurant. He peeked out the snow-covered glass of the window for some time, until he saw a shadow move across the street and past them.

"Uh... Stanley," Callie whispered.

"What?" he said, turning around.

The restaurant they had just entered would have seemed like any other restaurant, if not for the odd crowd dining there. All of them looked different, of course, but their skin seemed awfully pale, and, while some had black eyes, most of them had ruby red eyes. Only the restaurant owner seemed like a normal human being.

"Will you be dining with us tonight?" he asked, sounding uncomfortable.

Stanley's eyes moved again around the crowd and their plates. Not a single vegetable on any plate. They sure loved their meat.

"Perhaps another night, thank you," Callie said, sounding more frightened than she ought to. She took Stanley's hand and pulled him outside.

On the street, he looked around them but saw nothing suspicious, and the ghastly shadow following them was gone.

"We could have stayed there for dinner," he remarked.

"Sure, if you want to become *their* dinner," she said, frowning. "That was a vampire restaurant, Stanley!"

"V–Vampire?" he said, astounded. "Wait, were they eating what I think they were eating then?"

"You probably don't want to know," she said, and she began walking. He followed her.

"Do vampires also eat demons?" he asked.

"I'd rather not find out," she said. "Demons have their own territory, vampires have theirs. We leave each other alone."

"So we're in vampire territory now? What could happen to us?" Stanley asked.

He claimed to believe only in what he saw, but now that he had encountered demons and vampires, he was ready to believe in anything. And though he did not know just how dangerous vampires might be, he was sure they were nothing like the demon in his attic, so he was more excited than scared.

"We could get killed if they think I'm stealing a prey from them," she said. "Oh, Stanley, where can we go?"

She stopped in the middle of the street and looked around her. People were going home now, and the streets were almost deserted. If demons were roaming, they would be spotted easily. A cab came down the street and Stanley called it.

"Where to Sir?" the coachman said. He looked rather rough and possibly drunk, but he was the only cab around.

"King's Cross Station," Stanley said.

The man shook his head.

"Too far! Too far!"

"I'll give you a sovereign, two if you get us there before the last train leaves," Stanley said, showing him the coin.

"Alright, come on in. But you'd better hurry up if you wanna make the nine o'clock train. That's the last one!"

Stanley and Callie got inside and the cab took off. The man really wanted to earn his sovereign. His horse was galloping through the snow and the whole cab jumped off the ground more than once. The two fugitives both held on tightly and laughed, and finally they came to a halt near King's Cross Station. They got off with a few bumps and bruises, paid the coachman, and he tipped his hat and left.

"Quick, we need to get onto a train!" Stanley said, taking Callie's hand, and they rushed through the crowd.

There were three trains in the station that appeared ready to leave, so they climbed onto the last wagon of the first one and it took off less than a minute later. Stanley closed the door behind them and they both let out a deep sigh of relief. But the wagon's other door immediately opened and the ticket controller apprehended them. Apparently, he was used to people sneaking onto the trains as they departed.

"Hey! You! No beggars on this train!" the man said under his black peaked cap and thick black mustache.

Stanley had not realized that, in their mix-and-match attire, they probably both looked like beggars and not respectable people.

"Oh, thank goodness you're here!" he told the man in a pleasant voice. "We were just dining in a restaurant across the street before boarding our train, and thieves managed to steal our luggage – even our coats and the tickets I had in my pocket! Luckily, they didn't get my wallet, which I always carry on me, and the restaurant owner was able to provide us with some old coats so we wouldn't freeze to death. Anyway... how much for two tickets?" he said, pulling out his thick wallet, which still contained most of the money Callie had given him.

The man observed them both with suspicion for a moment, then shrugged and said: "Where are you going?"

"To the terminus," Stanley said.

"Five pounds and two shillings for two people."

"Must be pretty far, huh?" Stanley said, counting the money.

"You're on the Special Scotch Express to Edinburgh. Five and a half hours, one three hour stop in York. Might take a little longer. There was an incident due to the snowfall; they're working on it now. I hope you weren't heading to Liverpool, or you're on the wrong train!" the man said, tipping his hat, and he left them.

Stanley turned to Callie, who looked surprised but relieved.

"Edinburgh... That's really far away," she said.

"I've always wanted to see Scotland anyway," Stanley said, offering her his arm. "Well then, we'd better find seats."

The night train was not very crowded, and they quickly found four empty spots and were able to sit comfortably - as comfortably as one could on the hard seats of the North Eastern Railway trains. It was a fairly new train, with a powerful steam engine, and the interior of the narrow wagons was a warm red color with gold-plated trims around the windows. It was mostly clean, except for a few cigarette butts on the ground. With the always increasing volume of passengers, the line was obviously struggling to keep it pristine, and Stanley did not think the first-class seats were any better. Blankets had been laid out on the seats for the travelers, as the half-empty train was quite cold. Callie wrapped a blanket around her shoulders, and Stanley covered himself with another.

"Warm enough?" he asked.

"I'm alright," she said.

She turned her absent gaze to the window, and, with the train's speed, the white snowflakes upon the night sky made it seem like they were going through a blizzard.

"Don't worry Callie, we'll be in Edinburgh tomorrow morning, and no demon will come looking for us there," Stanley said. "You won't have to be a succubus anymore, you can be whoever you want to be."

She turned to him and smiled softly.

"Yes, I suppose so."

"Let's think about what we will do there," he said cheerfully.

"What about your friends? Will they follow us?" she asked him.

He lost his smile and looked away.

"William is attached to my office in London... But the good news is he can't go anywhere, so whenever I return, he will still be there."

He turned to her with a smile again – a forced one this time. He had never traveled outside of London; he had never been anywhere really, and never without his ghosts. Cornelius would probably follow them at a distance, but he hated having to leave William behind. He had never realized how he, who thought himself so solitary, had grown so fond of his friends from the other world, and leaving even one behind meant leaving 'home' behind.

"You look like you're about to cry," she remarked.

"It's just the cold air," he said, wiping his eyes.

"You can cry if you want. The last few days and nights must have been very scary for you," she said.

"Just the usual for a paranormal investigator."

"Is it alright if I cry a little then? I just want to be human tonight and I'm scared," she said softly.

"Of course you can cry," he said, and she lay her head on his shoulder and let out a few tears. He wrapped his arm around her shoulders and pulled her closer, repeating: "Everything will be alright, I promise."

The train wagon was beginning to warm up and some of the passengers were already asleep. Everything was quiet except for the distant sound of the locomotive, and the muffled 'clickety-clack' of the wheels on the snow-covered tracks. Stanley gazed out the window at the darkness surrounding them and wondering whether they were actually traveling to Edinburgh or to another world. If they were indeed headed into another world, he hoped it was one in which he and Callie could both live as themselves, without having to fear vengeful spirits, demons, or even humans. He could hear his friend's soft and steady breathing on his shoulder: she had fallen asleep. He too was feeling sleepy, but somehow he could not close his eyes. He wanted to remain awake, for fear that all of this, as frightening as it had been, might disappear.

The train rocked slowly back and forth, and despite his efforts, Stanley's eyes were beginning to close. He thought he blinked only once, but when he opened his eyes, he noticed that all the empty seats were occupied. None of their occupants looked human, but they were not ghosts, and not demons. They all were short, with rounded faces, and looked more or less like children. Their clothes were as diverse as their looks, but none of them were dressed like the humans asleep around them. Their presence was eerie, but peaceful, and they chatted informally while enjoying the ride. Stanley was not surprised when another one of them materialized in the seat facing his and Callie's. He could not tell, at first, whether the creature was a little boy or girl in its world - it could have been either. It had short, black hair, and the piercing green eyes of a cat. Its skin had an ethereal pallor to it, but not quite like that of the vampires Stanley had just seen for the first time, and its ears were pointed and covered with black fur. The creature wore an intricate blend of men's and women's clothes, with wine-colored trousers, a white baroque blouse with wide sleeves, and a green paisley vest and matching tie. It wore an oversized black silk top hat over its messy hair, of which the ribbon was decorated with a small bird feather - not the sort one would usually wear on a hat, but rather a chicken feather. It smiled when Stanley noticed it, revealing sharp white teeth.

"Good evening, traveler who does not sleep," it said in such a soft whisper Callie never stirred.

Stanley nodded to acknowledge the peculiar creature.

"Are you also traveling somewhere?" he asked in a whisper.

"I'm going home to Scotland after vising my cousin in France. What about you?"

"I'm going far away from home. It's become too dangerous there," Stanley said sadly.

The creature did not seem cold, but it did not have a coat like the others, so Stanley removed the blanket covering him and held it out.

"You will catch a cold dressed like that," he said, and the mysterious creature's smile widened. It took the blanket, wrapped it around its frail shoulders, and rubbed its cheek against it with a purring sound.

"You gave the cat-sìth a present; you shall therefore receive a blessing," the creature said.

"Cat-sìth? Is that what you are?" Stanley asked.

The cat-sìth nodded.

"When you are lost in the darkness, traveler, call upon me and I will guide your footsteps," it said, before vanishing.

Stanley opened his eyes again as the rising sun's first rays pierced through the window of the train. He had fallen asleep, resting his head against Callie's. He looked around him: the train was again half-empty, and all the fairy-like creatures he had seen during the night were gone. Another dream? The blanket he had given to the cat-sìth was covering him again, but he noticed the small feather stuck on it. He smiled, took it, and slipped it into his vest pocket. It was not every day he received a token from a magical creature.

The snow had stopped falling outside, and now the train was passing through white hills and small villages. Callie began to stir and opened her eyes.

"Oh... I must have fallen asleep," she said, sitting up. "What time is it?"

Stanley checked his pockets and found the pocket watch he had taken from her shop. It had no powers, but at least it could give them the time.

"Looks like it's eight thirty-four. We should be arriving soon. I don't know how long the train stopped in York, I was asleep."

"So we're in Scotland now?"

She wiped her sleepy eyes and looked out the window.

"I would assume so," he said.

The ticket collector came into the wagon and said: "Good morning, ladies and gentlemen! It's a beautiful day outside, and our train is expected to reach Edinburgh by nine o'clock. You will find many restaurants near the station where you can enjoy a Full Scottish breakfast, but make sure to try out Callum's haggis! And don't forget to grab a buttery from the bakery!"

"I'm not sure what a buttery is, but haggis sounds amazing..." Stanley told Callie.

"A buttery is a bread roll that tastes like a croissant, and *that* sounds amazing!" she said, turning to him with a smile.

"Alright, then a Full Scottish with butteries it is!" he said.

The train arrived in Waverley Station a little early, and the sleepy passengers began to disembark. Like everyone else, Stanley and Callie were a little sore from the seats and stiff from the cold, but the excitement of being on a new journey soon took over. Stanley had never traveled by train before, and he had barely got a chance to see King's Cross Station in London. Stepping out into Waverley Station was like entering a brand-new world, one filled with mystery and magic. Of course, now he believed in all creatures of the underworld, but the magic he sensed here was very different, and it had something to do with the creatures he met that night. Callie staggered for a moment on the platform, her eyes marveling in the architecture of the covered train shed, and beyond it, the vast station bustling with people. With the holidays just around the corner, a tall Christmas tree had been erected in the center of the station, and children with their parents flocked around it, already dreaming about Santa Claus coming to their homes in a few days. Stanley gazed at them quietly, and he remembered why he hated Christmas so much.

Despite growing up in a wealthy home and having a nursery full of toys all to himself, he had no memory of ever going out with his parents to see a Christmas tree in London. They were socialites, only interested in their status, and, with his stuttering problems and general lack of manners, he was an embarrassment to them. His parents never once told him about Father Christmas or Santa Claus, only his governess did, and Christmas Eve was just another lonely night. He did not see his parents that night, as they were always attending a party somewhere. Mary, the governess, put him to bed and told him that when he awakened in the morning, Santa Claus would have come. But he did not care about Santa Claus and whatever new toy he would find in the nursery the next morning; he wanted his parents to sit around a table with him, like the families in the picture books, and spend the evening together. He wanted to put his stockings up near the chimney and sit on his father's lap and listen to stories and feel warmth in his home. Instead, he only got the sounds of ghosts in the attic and a present to open alone in the nursery the next morning. Later in the day, he was dressed up in the most ridiculous frilly dress Annie and Mary could find, and they pulled his hair and burned his scalp with curling irons, trying to make him look like a doll, then sent him downstairs to greet his relatives who came over in the afternoon. He dreaded that moment. None of them were very fond of him, but his grandmother was especially judgmental, and he knew the moment he opened his mouth and started stuttering, she would comment on his lack of intelligence and blame his parents.

Things changed after his mother died when he was six. His father no longer showed any interest in his disappointing child and refused to see him at all. He became interested in the occult – not like Stanley who could actually interact with that world, but like bored middle-class people who liked the thrilling experience of holding a séance at a salon with their friends. He did not believe in ghosts, only in seducing women with his supposed psychic powers. He once held a séance at his home, and Stanley and Cornelius watched the adults from the top of the staircase, along with a few other curious spirits.

"What are they doing?" Cornelius asked.

"I think they're trying to talk with spirits," Stanley said.

His father and his friends held hands around the table and called upon the spirit of Sir Francis Drake, who would, of course, not answer them because he did not live in this house.

"I think they are expecting someone to answer them," said Oliver, the ghost of a soldier who lived in the wall of the first-floor hallway.

"But they didn't call any of us," Molly said. She was the ghost of a jolly maid from the beginning of the century who had remained in the Suspect household because it was the only home she knew.

"We should play a prank on them!" Stanley said, turning to them with a mischievous smile.

And so he went up to the nursery and wrote the following message on a piece of paper: *'I am the spirit of Sir Frances Drak, and I banesh thou from this home'*.

He turned to Cornelius and said: "That's how it's spelled, right?"

"I think so," Cornelius said.

The child ghost then delivered the message by flying across the room and dropping it on the table around which the adults were seated. Of course, with his poor spelling, Stanley's prank was discovered and his father punished him, but somehow even his father's scorn was better than his complete indifference.

"You look sad," Callie remarked, bringing him back to reality.

They had stopped in front of the Christmas tree.

"Oh, it's nothing," he said, shaking his head. "I just never had a real Christmas at home, I guess."

"Neither did I. Demons don't celebrate human holidays," she said sadly. "Would you like to celebrate Christmas with me?"

"I don't know. Do you want to?" he said.

She offered him the loveliest of her smiles.

"I want to live as a human," she said. "And what is more human than celebrating a holiday? Let's make it the way we've always wanted it!"

He also broke into a smile. Indeed, to celebrate Christmas, he did not need blood relatives, only people who wanted to celebrate it with him, like Callie.

They then headed out onto Princes Street and gazed at the tall stone buildings, so different from those in most of London. Even the snow-covered paved streets, which had retained their medieval layout, seemed different. Everything in this old city breathed freedom and might, as though the city itself stood like a brave warrior, towering over the northern lands and the sea. The great Scott Monument dedicated to Sir Walter Scott stood solemnly at the end of the street, and locals told the pair they ought to visit it while they were in town. And there would be much, much more to see and do here.

They quickly found the restaurant recommended by the ticket collector and ordered a Full Scottish. He had not lied: the food was excellent, and Stanley, who was used to eating mostly bread and a real meal perhaps once or twice a week, threw himself on the food and finished his plate in a few minutes while Callie slowly chewed on a piece of buttery, closing her eyes, and savoring every bite. It was the first time in many years Stanley shared a meal with anyone, and it changed the ritual of eating from just the necessity of filling one's stomach to one of sharing and enjoying time together. Was he going to become sociable now? He had to be coming down with something...

"You really like the food... not what demons usually have for breakfast, I assume?" he said with a smile.

"Demons typically feed once a week on raw meat," she explained with her mouth still full. "I do like fresh meat, but I also like sweets and pastries. I would probably eat only sweets if I could."

There was not only a new glow in her eyes, but her cheeks were all rosy too, as though she was coming back to life after a long slumber in the cold London fog, much like Stanley.

"Well then, we'll have to make sure to feed you sweets every day," he said, smiling as he gazed at her.

"What about you?" she asked, looking at the plate he had just finished.

"Me? I'm very plain – meat and potatoes... I don't really care for vegetables and I hate anything sweet," he said.

She laughed softly.

"You sound more demon than I am!"

"Maybe," he said, laughing with her.

After eating, since they still had plenty of money, they went shopping on Market Street and Stanley finally got to buy himself his dream brown and black cutaway morning suit, while Callie picked out her dream outfit, a crimson bustle dress with a neat black lace-trimmed collar. Stanley gazed at her with wonder as she tried on different pre-made dresses in a small shop and finally picked the one in her favorite colors. The grace in her moves, her natural femininity, the small dimples on her cheeks when she smiled, and the sparkle in her innocent black eyes were mesmerizing. It was not a succubus thing, it was a Callie thing, and it was her sharp, lively, and vivacious spirit that made her shine so much brighter than all the other women. Cinderella herself could not have been more beautiful under her fairy godmother's spell.

They both then purchased coats and hats, and now they looked like any other respectable young married couple.

"Perhaps we should think about new names," Callie suggested as they exited the last shop.

"Good idea," he said. "Who do you want to be?"

"It will be easier for us to find a place to stay as a married couple. How about Mr. and Mrs. Jones?"

"That sounds good enough," he said.

"Well, dear husband, shall we start looking for a flat?" she said, and they smiled at each other.

They stayed overnight in Cockburn Hotel, at the foot of Cockburn Street, and Stanley loved its tall stone buildings with their steep roofs all in perfect rows, crossed here and there by a small close, and all their little shops. He loved them so much, in fact, they decided to rent an apartment there. The rents were not cheap, but much more affordable than in a similar neighborhood in London. Their new apartment was on the third floor, with a view of the busy street underneath. It was already furnished and had a small living and dining room, a bedroom, and an office too small to install an additional bed. They would have to share one bed. They moved in on the morning of Christmas Eve, after purchasing the various items they would need, and that included a Christmas tree, to be delivered in the afternoon. As he put down the last packages on the old red velvet sofa in the dining room, Stanley noticed Cornelius sitting on the windowsill, a sad look on his face.

"There you are! I was wondering why you didn't follow me," Stanley said happily, and he began to unpack.

Cornelius observed him silently.

"Why so quiet?" Stanley laughed. "Don't you like our new home?"

"Do you mean your new home with me or your new home with Callie?" Cornelius asked.

Stanley put down the box he was holding and stared at him.

"Cornelius, I had no choice but to leave London! That demon is after me, and Belphegor is after both of us!" he said.

"Then why did you not call upon me sooner? I was right there, beside you in the train... but you didn't see me," Cornelius said, and he looked up to Stanley with tear-filled eyes.

Indeed, if he was right there, then why did Stanley not see him? Because he didn't want to? Or because all his attention was focused on Callie and this new adventure?

"You were my best friend..." Cornelius said, and he began to cry.

"I'm still your best friend, am I not?" Stanley replied with a mixture of anger and sadness.

"Now you want to be Callie's friend... and her beau," Cornelius said.

"Where did you ever get such an idea?" Stanley said. "Besides, you're just a child, what would you know about grown-ups' feelings?"

"That's the problem... you grew up, and I can't grow up," Cornelius said.

Stanley's throat felt tight, and he, too, wanted to cry. Was this the end of their friendship? Because he was finally growing up and going out into the world? What did Cornelius expect?

"Yes, I grew up, and I will grow old and die someday. I'm human, Cornelius," he said in a trembling voice. "But I still want you by my side. I still need you."

Cornelius shook his head.

"No, you don't need me anymore. You don't even miss me. If I hadn't appeared, would you have called upon me?"

"Of course I would have! I was just very busy..."

"With Callie..."

"No!"

But Cornelius shook his head again.

"I'm going home. You don't want me here," he said.

"That's not true! I want you to spend Christmas with us!" Stanley said, and he rushed over to him, but Cornelius had already vanished.

"Since when do you even celebrate Christmas, Stanley?" he heard his accusing voice say before it too faded away.

"Cornelius!" he cried out, but no answer ever came.

A profound sadness suddenly gripped his heart, and the pain of it was so intense he sat down on the windowsill where Cornelius had been just moments before. He wrapped his arms around himself as this new loneliness crept inside his body, underneath his clothes, his skin, and it was colder and more bitter than the chilling wind outside. Across the room, he could see his reflection in the old mirror hanging over the fireplace, in which burned a warm fire. He looked like a gentleman now, in these nice clothes, and he had a home with Callie, even though they were just pretending to be a married couple. His once empty life would have seemed perfectly full now to any outside observer, and though he had to agree that he was better off now, and safer, he missed the days when he lived alone with his three ghosts, when he yelled at carolers on the street and investigated haunted homes for a living.

Callie walked into the room, breathless and rosy-cheeked, and her arms full of ribbons and tinsel to decorate their tree.

"What's the matter Stanley?" she asked, as she noticed the sad look on his face. She immediately put down the decorations and went to him.

"It's nothing," he said, trying to sound cheerful.

She sat beside him and took his hand.

"Tell me what happened..."

"Cornelius came... and left. He's going home."

"Your ghost friend? Doesn't he want to spend Christmas here with us?" she asked.

"No. And I don't think he wants to be my friend anymore," he said in a defeated voice.

"Why?" she asked, surprised.

"I grew up... I think he expected me to be a little boy forever with him," he said.

He took his head in his hands. He did not want to cry in front of her, not on Christmas Eve, but now he really needed to. She slipped her arm around his shoulders and rubbed his back in a soothing manner, like he thought a mother would.

"That's not fair of him. You're human, of course you're going to grow up. What did he expect?" she said.

"I know, but... he was my friend for so many years. Now I'm alone..."

"You're not alone. You're with me," she said, moving closer to him, and the soft fragrance of her long black hair, the warmth of her body against his, were comforting. They had not spent that much time together, but he had gotten used to her presence, her laughter, her friendship very quickly, and now he did not know how he could live without them ever again. Was this not how people fell in love in all the stupid romance novels he used to laugh at? Now he was just like one of their characters, staring all day long at the siren whose sweet laughter put him under a spell, longing for a chance to be close to her or touch her. All day, every day, she was the one on his mind, playfully ignoring the stolen glances, the times their fingers brushed against each other's, the hints he gave her of his feelings. His mind was poisoned with love, and he had forgotten his friends, but he did not want to be saved from this sweet sickness of the heart, for it was more beautiful than anything else he had ever experienced before. Cornelius had not asked him to choose between her and them, but if he had, Stanley knew he would have chosen Callie, and he hated himself for it...

The Christmas tree arrived mid-afternoon and they deco-rated it, even if Stanley's heart was not really into the holiday anymore. And because they had spent so much on the apartment and moving in comfortably, they had agreed they would only exchange small presents that night. After a hearty dinner in a nearby restaurant, they walked back home in the snow, admir-ing the decorations people had put up on their doors and around their windows, and even the cold northern wind whipping their faces could not bother them. They greeted other couples out for a night stroll and returned to their warm apartment, where they sat on a rug in front of the fireplace and the tree. They drank wine and talked until midnight, then began exchanging presents. Stanley had never in his life received a present meant for him – something he really wanted. But Callie, with the magic in her heart, knew exactly what he wanted. She had purchased for him a new tie, a woolen scarf, and gloves, all in earth tones, and he was delighted to receive them. For her, he had purchased small, beautiful objects she liked, such as a golden comb for her hair and a miniature perfume bottle she could wear as a necklace. She laughed with the joy of a child when she opened it, and immediately tried it on. Just seeing the joy in her eyes as she celebrated her first Christmas as a human was enough for him, but she had yet another present for him.

"Another one? Where?" he asked. He thought they had opened them all.

"Close your eyes!" she said.

"Alright," he said.

He closed his eyes, smiling, and waited. But she did not place a present in his hands. Instead, her lips came upon his and she slowly kissed him. He opened his eyes, surprised, but she smiled and kissed him again, and he let her. He had never been kissed before, and the succubus' kiss was sweeter and softer than a dream. It had the flavor of adolescence and mischief, all the feelings Stanley thought young people experienced when meeting secretly behind a tree, or when a boy and a girl played, chasing each other, until the call of their blooming feelings brought their lips together. It was young and joyful, but also lasting and stable, like the eternity two adults could enjoy together freely. Stanley's heart was pounding in his chest when their lips parted, and he knew he had made the right choice by coming here with her. It was worth it – if only to experience love with her for the first time.

"Merry Christmas, Stanley," she said with shining eyes.

He blushed and gazed at her, not knowing how to respond.

"Is that all you have to say?" she laughed.

"No..." he said. "I... I love you Callie, and I would like to call you my wife..."

She never lost her smile, but he thought he saw a shadow of doubt flash through her sparkling eyes, only for a second. Of course, this life was all new to her, as it was for him.

"Y-You don't have to decide anything now," he quickly said, backing away slightly, but her smile grew wider and her cheeks reddened, and she lowered her eyes shyly.

"I would love to call you my husband, Stanley," she said, and his young heart swelled with pride and love like never before.

He pulled her into a tight embrace and kissed her again, with passion this time, and she responded with the same. And that night he surrendered to her in the quiet darkness of the bedroom. He who had never had a lover before and would not have felt confident showing his body to anyone, somehow was ready to trust a demon - of all women. But Callie was special. She was not bothered by the details of his anatomy; she liked him for who he was, and though he could see the burning desire in her black eyes, she let him take his time. She helped him undress slowly while covering his lips in tender kisses, and she let him undress her and discover her voluptuous body with his hands and his eager lips. Women were a forbidden fruit he had so longed to taste... He never told his family - his father would probably have lectured him about how he was supposed to naturally be attracted to square jaws, beards, and hairy chests, without being able to explain to him what was attractive about them. But since he was a teenager, Stanley had been looking at Annie, the little maid, instead. At twenty, her sweet lips, her rounded waist and hips, and her small breasts, of which he occasionally got a glimpse while she was scrubbing the floors, were the things that ignited fires in his loins. His skin quivered with delight when she helped him undress, to take baths, and sometimes he thought she wanted to get into the tub with him. But Callie was his now, by her own choice. He was allowed to touch and kiss every part of her body, and so he did, and she let out soft cries of delight when his fingers and lips found her most sensitive parts. Not only her lips were wet that night, she was wet for him in every way, and when his lips found her and tasted her, he thought there could be no greater ecstasy in this world. But there was: the one that she gave him with her warm lips and tongue in return. He who had always felt so shy about touching himself now experienced a deluge of pleasure, coming wave after wave under the expert strokes of her tongue and her fingers, that left him like a puppet in her hands, ready to let her do as she pleased with him. She then climbed atop him like a queen, riding his hips, rubbing, and rocking herself on him, and she guided his fingers to where she wanted to be pleasured and he obliged. She gazed into his eyes like a conqueress claiming her prize, and he was that prize. Except in this race to ecstasy together, she intended for both of them to win. And so they did, again and again, until their bodies, their hearts and souls were contented at last.

CHAPTER 6

STANLEY OPENED HIS EYES, and he was standing again on the staircase leading to the attic in his old home. He had not had that dream since he left London, and he thought that, since he now knew what was up there, it would go away. But he was there again, in the darkness, facing the old, twisted stairs. He could hear the clock ticking upstairs, and the black mold on the walls began to shift into eyeballs again. He tried the door to his right: it was locked. But he was not going to let this dream frighten him. It was only a dream after all, and therefore, he could decide the outcome. So he kicked open the door leading back to the hallway. Simple enough. Why had he not thought of it before? But instead of his home, he found himself in a forest at night. The air was cold and crisp, and smelled like the tall pine trees surrounding him. He was in the mountains somewhere. A golden thread was tied to his finger, which seemed to be tied to something else in the darkness. He tugged at it, but whatever was on the other side was not moving, so he began to follow it, stepping over branches and snow-covered leaves. A branch hit something on his forehead and he realized he was wearing a mask. He felt its contours with his fingers, surprised. Why would he wear a mask in the forest? But it was a dream, and dreams could be odd.

He went deeper and deeper into the forest, following the golden thread, until a young woman emerged from behind a large rock. He came to a sudden halt, startled, and gazed at her. She was petite and looked somewhat fragile. Her worn-out clothing looked like peasant's hand-me-downs, and she went barefoot. Her long black hair fell loosely over her frail shoulders, and she too wore a mask - a black one decorated with feathers. Attached to her finger was the other end of the golden thread. He smiled. She was younger and thinner, but he recognized Callie under the mask. She had told him she was born in a demon coven, but she never told him when and where. Perhaps it was in this forest. And it didn't matter to him that she went barefoot. She was his Cinderella, whatever she wore. So he offered her his hand and she took it, looking unsure at first. The forest around them then disappeared, and in its place was a ballroom. They were both still wearing masks, but she had traded her hand-me-down clothes for a beautiful, lavender-colored eighteenth century pannier dress, and she wore a tall, curly black wig decorated with pink ribbons over her thin natural hair. She smiled beautifully and they danced together, spinning around the other masked dancers in this masquerade ball from another era, until the clock struck midnight. The clock chime came crashing upon Stanley like the roar of a lion, followed by the scream he usually heard in the attic in his dream, and he woke up.

March twentieth, 1887. Stanley and Callie had been living in Edinburgh for three months now, and their life had been peaceful. The city, they learned, belonged to the *sìth*, who were fairy folk. Vampires and demons lived there too, but they were a minority, and not under Belphegor's jurisdiction, so they would be safe there as long as they did not offend the fairies.

Stanley had found himself a job as a sales clerk in a fashionable women's clothing store, and though he hated working around petticoats and dresses, the customers all fawned over this 'handsome Ephebus' and the shopkeeper loved him. Stanley did not think he had become that much handsomer overnight, but something had changed in his features. They were friendlier now, less tense, and he even thought the crease between his eyebrows from his constant frowning was disappearing. Callie naturally wanted to work as a clockmaker, but it could expose them both to danger, so she found work instead as a seamstress, and, once a week, she wrote a feminist column for a local newspaper. She was following her dreams, living as an ordinary woman, and fighting for their rights, and she seemed happy. And Stanley wanted to make all her dreams come true. As a man, he earned double her wages, and on her own she could probably not support herself. While he was happy to provide for both of them, he agreed that it was unfair and discriminatory, and he supported her and her new feminist friends. As for him, though he followed the news about men's labor unions and their progress, he still shied away from them. For one thing, he did not work in a factory like most of them, but he was also reluctant to make himself too visible, because he could still be arrested for crossdressing. It was a risk he had to live with every day if he wanted to be free.

When they were not working, Stanley and Callie lived the normal life of a newlywed couple, even though they were not legally married. They had purchased rings and called themselves Mr. and Mrs. Jones, from Nottingham. They spent their first few weeks in Edinburgh finding work and furnishing their apartment, and then Callie started pursuing her hobbies again. Stanley quickly realized that he knew little about her interests and what sort of person she was in everyday life. But wasn't it the same with any young man and young woman? One could only learn so much about the other while courting; and they learned to live together after getting married. Callie was by no means difficult to live with, on the contrary. She was always smiling and helpful, and around Stanley she played the perfect housewife, but he had also caught her slouching on the sofa with her spectacles on, reading a book, or doing her gymnastics in front of the mirror in their bedroom in nothing but her chemise, and he had seen the light black mustache she spent so much time and effort tweezing each week. He did not understand why she tried to be perfect around him - he never asked her to - and he thought she was adorable with her spectacles and even her mustache, but she didn't. They got along well and never argued, but she was a high-energy woman, who wanted to go out and meet people, and be politically involved. He liked to stay at home and watch the outside world from his window, and sometimes have tea with Freddy and Lila, the two spirits who lived in the walls of their apartment - a charming couple, victims of the Black Death a few centuries back. So, most of the time, he just let Callie go to her feminist meetings alone, and he remained in their apartment, missing the ghost friends he left in London.

Since Cornelius had left him, he had sent letters back home to him and William in the hope that they would read them and not forget about him. He promised them he would return someday, but even he did not know whether he could. Perhaps Cornelius was right, and he had outgrown his life as Stanley the recluse. Now he was Stanley the almost married man, with a home and a spouse to look after, but even if going out with Callie on his arm filled his heart with pride, he sometimes felt like he was missing something. It had nothing to do with her; it was him.

That morning, when he woke up, he found the bed empty beside him. He opened his eyes and reached out to the spot where Callie usually lay. It was still warm; she had just gotten up.

"Sweetheart?" he said, and she soon came back into the bedroom, fully dressed.

"Good morning, Stanley," she said, as she finished buttoning up the collar of her dark purple dress. She smelled like bergamot and lemon that morning, not like the rose fragrance he had purchased for her for Christmas, but she owned just about every fragrance one could find on the market and, she said, there was a perfect cologne for every dress she owned. He preferred her without anything – dress or fragrance.

"Where are you going?" he asked, rolling over in the bed and rubbing his eyes.

She laughed.

"To work, of course. It's Saturday morning, darling."

Her voice was always like the cheerful song of a little bird to his ears, and just listening to it made him happy. He wished she would have a Saturday morning off for once, as he only worked in the afternoon that day, but she had her job and it made her happy, and when she was happy, he was happy. He sat up in the bed.

"Do I get a kiss at least before you leave?" he said, stretching out his arms to her.

She laughed again, danced her way over to him, kissed him on the cheek, and then she was gone. It was not the romantic kiss he was hoping for, but she was like that. Romance with her happened more often at night, under the sheets, and when they were naked. He could not blame her: it was in her nature as a succubus to be sexual. And he was too, just not as much as she was, and he would have preferred long romantic walks and conversation and sharing the depths of their souls with each other before passionate lovemaking, but, after all, everyone was different, and one had to accept the little things in their partner's character they did not necessarily like or understand.

He stretched out and got out of bed, washed, and dressed as usual, and then he noticed that Callie had left a folder of papers on the dresser. It contained flyers for a feminist meeting she intended to give away after work that day. She was always in such a hurry; she was bound to forget something, eventually. He smiled, thinking of her and all her adorable little flaws.

Since she was gone already, he took the time to sit down with his new ghost neighbors for a cup of tea before leaving. The sky outside the window was gray that morning. Winter was almost over, but the air was still cold. Stanley did not know what the spring and summer looked like in Scotland, but he looked forward to seeing them with Callie and doing with her all the normal things people enjoyed in the warmer seasons. Perhaps he could even learn to play tennis with her, even though he was not very athletic.

After finishing his tea, he put on his coat and hat, and the scarf Callie had given him for Christmas. He treasured it because she had handpicked it for him, and it was the present she gave him on the night they became lovers. How could he ever forget that night? He remembered every moment of it and replayed it in his mind over and over when he was alone. He had never imagined someone would want him as he was, much less love him. But Callie was used to sleeping with men and women and had no problem with what he was. She let him express himself as a man in bed, and with her, his confidence grew. She was the best partner he could have hoped for.

With a bright smile on his lips and the folder tucked under his shoulder, he walked down the winding streets until he reached

Miss Martha's shop, where Callie worked. The owner knew him well as he came to pick up his love as often as he could, so she wouldn't have to walk alone and potentially encounter another demon.

"Good morning Martha!" he said, tipping his hat. "I just came to give my wife something. Is she here?"

"Oh, good morning Mister Jones," Martha said. "Yes, Callie is in the back, working on a dress."

She gestured to the back room in which Callie worked, and he headed there. He had expected to find her busy at work, working her magic on a new dress with her clever fingers, but he found her instead sitting in front of her sewing machine, her work left undone. She was holding a small locket in her hands and gazing at the photograph inside with the saddest expression he had ever seen on her beautiful face. He could not clearly see the photograph, but it appeared to be that of a young man. After a few silent seconds, she noticed him and put away the locket, looking startled.

"Stanley! What are you doing here?" she said with a smile, but it was not genuine.

"What's this locket?" he asked in an empty voice.

"It's nothing," she said.

He walked over to her.

"What's this locket? Show it to me," he said.

"It's just a piece of jewelry," she said.

Since she would not show him, he grabbed the hand she was hiding behind her back, but she was physically stronger than him and disengaged herself. She got up, looking furious.

"What are you trying to do? Hurt me?" she said in an angry whisper.

"Who is he? Who is that man?" he asked.

He could feel anger and jealousy rushing through him now, like never before. He did not think she was cheating on him - it was not possible since they were always together. But if, in her heart, she was untrue, he would never forgive her.

"What are you accusing me of?" she said defiantly.

He stared at her for some time, saying nothing, then he turned around and left. He swung the shop's door open so hard it almost fell off its hinges, and began to walk down the street, but Callie soon caught up with him, breathless. She grabbed his arm and forced him to stop.

"Stanley!"

"Who is that man?" he all but shouted as he turned around to face her.

She gazed at him coldly, and for the first time, he felt like she was distancing herself from him.

"The man I loved. You know about him. He died," she responded.

"I thought you loved me!" he said.

"I do!" she said.

"Then why did you keep a photograph of him in a locket?" he snapped at her.

"Because it's all I have left of him!" she said. "Are you going to be jealous of a man from the past?"

"I will if he still has your heart!" he said. "You're my wife now, you belong to me!"

"Oh, I *belong* to you?" she said. "Well excuse me for having had a life before I met you! Not everyone is an outcast like you, Stanley."

Her words hurt him more than the blade of a knife would have. Yes, she belonged to him. That was what he expected of love: to belong to her and her to him. He did not want to have only half of her heart, or three quarters. He wanted all of it to himself. And yes, he was jealous, even of a dead man. Terribly jealous. But, not wanting to argue in the street anymore, he turned around and began to walk.

"Stanley! Where are you going?" he heard Callie say.

"I'm going for a walk. We'll talk later," he replied.

Stanley knew he was an ass sometimes, but he did not know just how hateful and angry he could become until he fell in love. He would never hurt Callie, but for a moment, when he thought the man in the picture was alive, he had thought about finding him and getting into a fight with him. He was ready to go that far – even further. He was ready to *kill* anyone that stood between him and Callie. He shook his head and sat down on a bench in the park where he had wandered. All around him, couples and families strolled peacefully. They were not at each other's throats, ready to commit murder over a photograph. What was wrong with him? He breathed in and gazed at the gray sky and the trees. He had left his dark and sordid life in London to come to Edinburgh, and the old stone city, the strong northern wind, the cold, the strength of nature here and its magic had brought him back to life. He was not going to lose it all now over this misplaced jealousy. Callie had done nothing wrong. She had the right to remember someone she had loved, and he had no right to interfere. He could not erase her past just because it made him jealous. He brought his hands together and gazed at the ring he was wearing. They wore rings, but they were not actually married. She did not *belong* to him legally, nor did her life and her decisions. She was a free and independent woman, and he could not keep her captive.

He returned home late that night after spending hours pondering how he would apologize to her, and he had expected to find her angry and feisty, but she wasn't. He found her sitting on a chair in their living room, holding her head in her hands and crying. She had not even bothered to light a fire in the fireplace, and she sat alone in the dark, lost in her own sorrow. He rushed over to her.

"Callie!" he said, falling to his knees by her side. "Callie, I'm sorry I got so angry..."

She did not answer and kept on crying, and her despair was heartbreaking. This was not some feminine ruse destined to appease him: they were the tears of someone who had lost everything, even hope. He wrapped his arms around her and held her tightly and stroked her hair.

"Callie... Callie..." he said. "Please forgive me... I should never have raised my voice like that. Of course you have the right to have a past and to think about someone you loved. How selfish of me to tell you not to!"

"I'm so tired of pretending..." she sobbed.

"Pretending?" he repeated, surprised, and once again, only for a second, he found himself doubting her.

"I'm not strong... I'm not perfect..." she then said, and he understood what she meant, what she could not tell him.

She was a strong, independent woman, but at times she was also weak and vulnerable. And, for some reason, she thought she could not show him that side of her.

He cupped her moist cheeks with his hands and caressed them softly.

"Callie, you don't have to be perfect for me. Did I make you feel like you had to be?" he said in a gentle voice.

"Sometimes, yes," she said.

"Oh, no, Callie, sweetheart, I never expected perfection from you," he said, kissing her forehead.

She gazed at him with sad and uncertain eyes, as though she was the one now having doubts about their relationship.

"Stanley," she said. "You wanted to be a prince, to discover a poor Cinderella who had never been noticed or loved before and transform her into a princess with the magic of your love, but real women are not like that. I fought my own battles before meeting you. I loved and lost love..."

He had not realized how well she could see through him. Indeed, he had rather naïve views about love. He wanted to be her one and only, and for her to live up to his expectations of purity and perfection like Cinderella. And perhaps he did see her as a trophy he should guard jealously to flatter his fragile male ego, but he didn't want to be that sort of man.

"You're right. Everything you said is right. I'm a complete ass," he said. "But I want to change. I don't own you, and I don't want my love to become a prison for you. So teach me how to love you and let you be imperfect and free at the same time, and I will learn for you."

She smiled sadly and lowered her gaze, and he delicately wiped away her tears.

"I just want to be me," she said. "I'm not always sweet and feminine. Sometimes I just want to be myself, to slouch around in a chemise and read a book, to play sports and mess up my hair and makeup. Sometimes I also want to think about the past, otherwise it will be like it never happened. I can't just give up everything for fear of losing you."

"No, of course not! You will never lose me!" he said, kissing her again.

He brought another chair and sat beside her and took her hands.

"Would you tell me this man's name... so I can accept him and the part he has played in your past?" he asked, looking into her eyes.

"His name was Elmer," she said, and her fingers tightened around his.

He took her hands and kissed them, then he kissed the ring he had given her.

"Thank you. I will cherish his memory with you," he said.

She smiled and leaned forward and kissed him. They were both still learning about each other and about love, and what it meant to live together. Falling in love had happened so quickly and easily; now they were facing the hardest part about love: keeping it, with all its imperfections. It was the end of a dream for Stanley, but he was sure it just meant the beginning of a new one, one in which they would no longer be a prince and princess, but a man and a woman.

Callie's moods, Stanley learned, were like the sky, and storm clouds never lingered too long in her heart. After a few uncomfortable days during which they both felt hesitant to show the other affection, love soon returned to their home, and with the coming of spring, Callie was very busy organizing and attending suffragette meetings.

"Are you coming tomorrow night, darling?" she asked him one evening while sitting in front of the vanity and putting on her favorite cosmetics. She looked just like a summer fairy in her light, sleeveless chemise, her curly hair loosely held by silver combs, and with all her perfumes and creams, she smelled like a flower garden - one with roses, gardenias, lilacs, and mimosas. Stanley didn't like smelling every flower at the same time on her, but it was what she liked, and in her feminist meetings, all the women were apparently competing to wear the most potent perfume. He had to open the windows when she came home smelling like a whole flower shop, and she laughed every time.

"Where to?" he asked.

He sat in the bed under the blankets, smoking a cigarette. The rumors were right: nothing beat a cigarette after a few hours of mind-blowing sex, especially with a succubus. He needed an emotional release, and so did she, and hers was making herself pretty.

"The suffragette meeting," she said, turning to him with a frown because he had forgotten. "I told you about it. It will be very interesting, and a speaker will come to talk about gender and identity."

"Who?" he asked lazily.

"Eve Chauvin. She's amazing!" she said with a bright smile.

"Oh, Eve Chauvin? I've read one of her books."

"She's fabulous, isn't she?" Callie said, excited. "She has her own herbalist shop in Paris, where she sells cosmetics and does tarot readings, but it's also a safe home. Battered women can come to her with their children, and she will find a safe place for them. She has presented several petitions to the French government for women's suffrage. They've all been rejected so far, but she never gives up!"

"Impressive," he said, barely paying attention to her. His body was still tingling from all the things she did to it.

"So, tomorrow night at eight o'clock, I want you ready and looking your best," she said.

"I always try to look my best for you," he remarked, and she laughed softly.

"I meant 'please wear a black suit', my love."

"A black suit? What's wrong with the brown one?"

"Nothing, I just want to show off my very own Prince Charming," she said, and her smile was irresistible.

So, the next evening, he put on his best black morning suit, just for her, and even colored the light hairs on his upper lip and chin with her mascara. This meeting was very important to her, and she wore her favorite crimson dress with black lace trims, and a matching black hat. Before leaving, she slipped several soap bars in her purse.

"Why are you carrying soap?" he asked her as they walked down the street.

"Eve taught us to always carry something heavy in our purses, so we can use them as a weapon," she explained. "Do you know why women's clothing doesn't have as many pockets as men's?"

"Because women carry purses?" he said.

She rolled her eyes.

"Women carry purses because the clothing we buy never have any," she said. "The only way a woman can have pockets in her clothes is to make all her dresses herself, and who has time for that nowadays? It's just another way to make us helpless by keeping one of our hands busy carrying a purse all the time. It's much harder to run in high heels and carrying a purse."

"So why don't you just wear flat heels?" he asked. "Not all women's shoes have high heels."

"Because I like high heels," she said, straightening herself.

He would probably never understand women, but as long as their world made sense to them, it was all that mattered.

They arrived at the venue early and it was not too crowded, so they went inside. The building was a small theater, usually hosting plays, but it was sometimes used by the suffragettes and the labor unions for meetings. Small groups of women were gathering and talking informally - some of them dressed in men's clothes. One of them noticed them and walked over to them.

"Callie! Good evening, sweetie," she said, and they kissed on the cheeks.

"Hi Victoria," Callie said. "This is my partner," she then said, turning to Stanley.

"Oh, hi there. Are you also an Amazon?" Victoria asked, offering him a handshake.

"A what?" he said, frowning.

"Uh, let's go sit down, darling," Callie told him, and she pulled him away.

They sat at a distance from the other groups, and Stanley gazed at all the different faces. As far as he could tell, he was the only man in the room – or at least the only one identifying as a man. The women in tuxedos were not actually trying to pass as men, just affirming their freedom through their clothes, and some of them had long hair, while others even wore eyeliner.

"What are the Amazons?" he asked Callie.

"They are a select lesbian society. Some wear men's clothes, some women's clothes, but they all identify as women. They're not like you," she said.

"Is there anyone in this world like me?" he said, cynically.

"I'm sure there is," she said.

"You seem quite confident about it."

Once everyone was seated, the meeting began. Several women stepped onto the stage and spoke about the female condition and suffrage. They were organizing and rallying more and more women, and even Stanley believed that soon women would have the right to vote like men. As for fully equal rights and wages, he did not foresee it happening in his lifetime. He wanted it, of course, but he knew men would never let it happen because they were not ready to lose their privilege, just like the French nobility was not ready to lose their privilege and have to compete with commoners on equal economic grounds before the Revolution. And, judging by the voices of men cussing behind the door and banging on it, they were not even going to let this meeting happen.

"Men are gathering behind the door," he told Callie in a low voice.

"Oh, it happens all the time. But don't worry, we're always a larger crowd," she said.

He looked around the room again. Indeed they were numerous, but he did not know how many men awaited them outside. And then he saw the fairy folk appear in the room, one after another. Like the last time he saw them, all of them were different, some had cat ears, some dog ears, and some did not look human at all, but all of them had in common their childlike and genderless appearance, and their presence was peaceful. They were watching over the women in the room.

"Can you see spirits?" Callie asked him in a whisper.

"The sìth are here. They will protect us," he said, and she smiled.

"Oh, look, here she comes!" she then said as her idol stepped onto the stage.

After reading her book and her letter, Stanley imagined this Eve Chauvin as an eccentric old lady clad in a witch's robe, with three different colored shawls over her shoulders, a pointed hat, and perhaps carrying a broomstick, but she was nothing like that. She was in fact young, and quite pretty. She was petite, even perched on high heels, and had the slender frame of a teenager. She wore a tasteful but sober lavender-colored dress and a matching hat and wore her long black hair shoulder-length and loose. Like most of the women in the room, her makeup was flawless, except she did not wear rouge on her lips, but a daring purple tint. There was something odd about her, but Stanley could not quite pinpoint what. Perhaps it was in the way she walked, or stood perfectly still before the crowd, or perhaps it was in the deep black of her eyes. She began to speak and her soothing mezzo voice seemed to carry a spell of its own. Her English was perfect, and her French accent lovely. A green halo, invisible to ordinary human eyes, then formed around her, as in response to that of the sìth around the room.

"Can you guess what she is?" Callie whispered to him.

"A sìth?" he said, curious.

She turned to him and frowned.

"No, Stanley, look at her teeth."

He had not even paid attention to her teeth, but now, as she spoke, he noticed that her canines were slightly protruding and longer that a human's.

"A vampire?" he whispered to Callie, and she nodded.

Now he was confused. He knew little about vampires, except that they preyed on humans, so why would this one be fighting for women's rights? But it was not all he noticed about her.

"And now I would like to share a very personal story with you," Eve said. "It's the story of a little girl. Like all little girls, she dreamed of fairy godmothers and princesses."

The crowd smiled: many could relate. Eve smiled at them and continued.

"But not all little girls are born girls, and not all little boys are born boys," she said. "The little girl's name was 'Paul', and her father did not want her to be a princess, so he beat her every day, and he beat her mother when she tried to protect her. Then, the people in their village heard about her, and they wanted to kill her... simply for wanting to be herself." She paused and lowered her eyes sadly, then continued. "The little girl grew up sad and lonely, and then she fell in love with men who abused her emotionally and used her body. Because she was born in a male body, she could have a profession and make a living on her own, but only if she wore men's clothes and pretended to be 'Paul'. Society did not give women and people like her any options. In her case, she could not even marry a man and have rights through him. She often thought she would be better off dead. But death came for her quicker than she thought. She became very sick and died within a few days, in the safe home of a friend like her, knowing that she would not have a grave in her name, and that the only person in this world who would remember her was her friend. She lived her life unwanted and hated, and she would die anonymously, as though her existence never mattered in the end."

Women in the crowd began to cry as they listened to her, and even Callie pulled out her handkerchief. Most people in the room probably thought Eve was telling them the story of a close friend, and that she was the one who watched her die, but Stanley thought she was in fact the girl in the story, and that she was telling them of her life as a human, before she became a vampire. They were the same, she and him. They faced the same rejection and had to live with the constant fear of being arrested or even murdered for what they were. And yet they still had to live in this world and somehow find their own hope and dreams in it. Eve was a powerful and very charismatic speaker, and yet she also possessed the sweet candor of a child in the way she saw hope for herself and the other women in the room, whoever they were and however they identified. As for Stanley, she also brought tears to his eyes because she was telling his story, or what could have been his story if he had not met Callie. He would have lived and died with his ghosts and no living person would have remembered him as 'Stanley'. Perhaps he too would have felt like his existence never mattered in the end. Eve's words moved something inside him; they were opening doors he had long closed, and now he hoped he could meet her in person and talk to her more after the event.

"Feminism is not only about women," Eve continued. "Patriarchy teaches us that we can only be one of two things – a strong, aggressive, and emotionally absent 'manly' man, or a weak, passive, and emotional woman – and each person is assigned clothing and a behavior based on their genitalia. And because they have predetermined that all people with female genitalia are weak and emotional, they are prevented from voting, from receiving livable wages, and from being independent. On the other hand, all people with male genitalia are expected to be virile breadwinners, providing for passive, helpless women. Does anybody in this room feel passive or dependent on a man?"

"No!" all the women unanimously shouted.

"That's right!" Eve said. "Everyone in this room is perfectly capable of living alone and making their own decisions. Our fight to be recognized as equal human beings begins with the right to vote but doesn't end there. We must continue to fight for complete equality, and for everyone to have the right to live as their true, authentic self. The fight begins in your own homes. Educate your husbands and sons. Talk to your mothers, your sisters, your neighbors. Let them know we will never back down! I am proud to lead a coalition between the French and the British suffragettes, and your French sisters are just as tough as you all are. We beheaded monarchy, now I want to behead patriarchy!"

"Yes!" the crowd shouted, and they gave her a standing ovation.

She stood before them in a powerful stance, her fist in the air like the figure of Marianne leading the French Revolution, except she was leading another kind of revolution. And Stanley also felt like he had just been empowered and revolutionized from within by this woman with incredible confidence. It was hard to believe the old eccentric kitchen witch who had written him was also this warrior defending all women, and more so that she was also a vampire. She was a lot of things, but what kept him staring at her in a sort of daze was the fact that she was like him, he knew it, and his heart raced with the excitement of a child at the thought that he would get to talk to her soon.

"Aren't you going to stand up?" Callie told him cheerfully.

But before he could even answer, the men outside suddenly broke down the door, shouting: "Harlots! Degenerates!"

"You're the degenerates!" Eve shouted right back at them.

And, without wasting a second, she picked up her purse, which apparently contained soap bars, or perhaps bricks, and hurled it at them with inhuman strength. It crashed against the wall beside them, leaving a large hole in it, and several of the men fell to the ground, terrified.

"Ladies! Get ready to fight!" Eve then said, jumping off the stage, and all the women cheered and began throwing their purses in the men's direction. The men, who had not expected any reaction on their part, scattered and ran away, and several of the Amazons rushed over to the doors and blocked them.

"Eve! They're going to return! They won't let us out!" one of them said.

And suddenly a brick came crashing through a small window near the back of the room, which was used to air out the theater. It was not large enough for a man to get in, but a burning torch was then thrown inside. Some women screamed and retreated near the stage, while Eve and others tried to put out the torch with their shawls. Stanley and Callie were also pushed toward the stage, and he saw the sìth disappear. Were they not here to protect them after all?

More bricks flew inside, followed by more torches. The small theater with its wooden floors was on fire now, and it was already creeping up the curtains near the stage. The women were crying and screaming, but Eve knew what to do. She stepped in front of them.

"Calm down, everything will be alright," she assured them in a compassionate but firm voice. "Now I want you all to head to the back door in a single file, holding the hand of the woman in front of you. Walk quickly but don't run. No one must be left behind or trampled."

They all nodded, but part of the ceiling then collapsed and they started running to the back door in a frenzy. Stanley and Callie ran with them. They somehow made it through the back door and out onto the street, where the rain was beginning to fall. Stanley turned his gaze to the sky, and the green halo around the clouds let him know that this was the work of the sìth. They did not like conflicts and violence between humans, and they were bringing the rain to extinguish the fire. The rain soon turned into a downpour, but nobody would leave before Eve came out of the theater, and she eventually did, coughing and struggling to breathe. Two of the Amazons went to her.

"How... how many people are here?" she asked them.

"Forty-two, you included," one of the Amazons said.

"I counted forty-three heads. One of us is still inside!" Eve said, before rushing back into the flames.

"Eve! No!" the women shouted.

All held their breath for a few long minutes, but she soon returned, holding up the last woman. Their clothing was partly burned, but they would both be alright.

"Alright, you all need to scatter now. The police will come and they are not on our side," she said. "Take the back streets and alleyways, and don't leave your girlfriends alone!"

"Yes!" they said.

The small crowd separated, and all went in different directions, and, amidst the confusion, Stanley had not noticed that

he and Callie were being followed. And when they acciden-
tally turned into a close which led to a dead end, they found
themselves surrounded. Behind them was a group of five men
armed with clubs and hatchets, and before them and all around
were tall stone walls. Callie prepared to fight in her demon way
– whatever that was – and Stanley stepped in front of her. He
did not know how he could fight so many men without any
weapons and without his ghosts, but he would not let them
touch Callie. Following some new instinct he did not know
he possessed, he crouched, and his vision changed. Where the
shadows of the men against the light of the street lamps were
before, he now saw their souls instead, or perhaps their aura. It
was red, angry, and violent. The scene before his eyes flickered
from red to black to red again, and he said just one word: "DIE!"

He did not know why he had said it, nor what was happening
to him. Was he losing his mind? But Eve suddenly appeared
between them and the men, seemingly out of thin air. She stood
like a statue again, and the green halo around her took the shape
of an ethereal woman and came out of her body.

"Witchcraft!" one of the men shouted, but he struggled to
move as though he was paralyzed. In fact, they all appeared to
be paralyzed.

"It's not witchcraft. It's the *Fae*," Eve said, her hands resting
on her hips.

The spirit that had just come out of her body then lunged at
the men with a piercing shriek, and they cried out in terror.

"You! Take your girlfriend and run!" Eve then shouted, turning back to Stanley and Callie, and they both did as she said.

They ran as fast as they could, not wanting to know what
would happen to those men, but more importantly, not wanting
to draw the attention of the underworld.

CHAPTER 7

"WHAT THE HELL WAS that?" Stanley asked Callie as they rushed back home through the downpour.

"Not our problem!" Callie said.

They ran as fast as they could because of the rain, their potential pursuers, and Eve. If they had both seen vampires and other supernatural creatures before, neither had ever seen anything like what she just did. There were things in the underworld that were better left in the underworld, and no matter how kind and impassioned Eve might be, she was first and foremost a supernatural creature - a dangerous one - and Stanley did not want to know just how dangerous she could be.

They finally reached Cockburn Street and slowed down their pace, certain now that no one had followed them. Stanley stopped and leaned against the wall of a house to catch his breath. Being with a demon was exhausting. Not only could Callie outlast him in bed, but she could outrun him anytime, and he knew she'd had to slow down in order not to lose him along the way.

"Are you alright?" she asked, placing her hand on his shoulder.

"I'll be fine in a minute..." he said. "What do you think happened to those men?"

"We'll find out in the newspapers tomorrow..." she said.

"Did you know Eve could do something like that... whatever it was?" he asked.

"I had no idea. I only suspected she was a vampire because she never appears in the daylight, and tonight, when I saw her up close, it was obvious."

"Do the women who admire her know?"

She raised her shoulders.

"I don't think it would make a difference to them."

"I think it would make a difference to me if I knew a public speaker I admired might bite my neck and drink my blood when I asked them for an autograph," he said.

The rain gradually stopped, but they were soaked now and needed to get home, so they started walking again.

"Anyway, everyone is safe now... all the innocent," Callie said, gazing at the wet, paved street underneath her feet.

She seemed somewhat sad or anxious that night, so Stanley wrapped his arm around her shoulders.

"You don't need to think about those men," he told her gently. "They tried to murder us all, and they got what they deserved."

"Oh, I would have done much worse to them if I was powerful like Eve," she said, turning to him. "I was just thinking that... I could have lost you tonight."

"But you didn't. I'm fine; not even a scratch!" he told her with a smile.

"But you're human," she said. "Sooner or later we will encounter creatures more dangerous than a mob of angry men. How will I protect you from them? Blow them a kiss? I'm a succubus; I can't do anything."

She lowered her eyes sadly, but he smiled and cupped her sweet chin with his hand.

"Being by my side is how you protect me," he said. "Besides, should only the most powerful creatures in this world be allowed to love someone? What about ordinary – or mostly ordinary – people like us?"

His response made her smile again.

"Mostly ordinary? I wouldn't say that," she laughed.

"Somewhat ordinary," he said.

"Not even close."

They laughed together and she took his arm.

"I thought we could live a normal life here, but it looks like we just jumped from one supernatural place to another," she sighed.

"I don't think so. I think the supernatural world is all around us, wherever we go," he said, gazing at the tall stone facades around them and the ghosts beginning to come out again after the rain to enjoy an ethereal midnight stroll. He noticed the cat-sìth standing in an alleyway and gazing at the two of them as they walked by. It looked like it wanted Stanley to stray away from the light of the street and follow it into the darkness, and while Stanley did not sense any hostility in its eyes, he preferred to ignore the creature.

He returned home with Callie and they changed their clothes and warmed themselves by the fireplace, and Callie gazed absently at the dancing flames before them.

"A penny for your thoughts?" Stanley said.

He had brought out the woolen blanket from their bed. He sat on the sofa with her and wrapped the blanket around their shoulders. She rested her head on his shoulder and sighed.

"The demons will forget about you eventually and you can open another shop," he told her with a kiss in her hair, thinking she was missing the job she liked so much.

"I don't think I even want a shop anymore..." she said softly.

"Then what do you want, darling? Whatever it is, we can make happen," he said.

Well, not everything. He could not give her a baby if that was what she wanted, and neither could any other human, because she was a demon. But it was not that. She did not want to share with him what she truly wanted, and what made her so sad that night, and he did not understand why.

"I want to stay here forever with you – even if we encounter a vampire now and then," he said, stroking her long black hair, and he could truly picture the two of them growing old here, in the old stone city with its winding streets and mystery. The memory of William and Cornelius back in London then crossed his mind. They were alone in his former house unless it had been rented out to someone else. Perhaps his father's ghost had remained there too – he had not sensed or heard him since he left London. Was there a warm fireplace they could sit around, or was the old building always cold and dark? Now that all the adrenaline of the night was leaving his body, Stanley's mood was growing darker, and he could not quite tell why. Was it because of Callie? She had her moods, and they did not always affect his, but lately she had seemed more and more distant. He knew she sometimes still thought about Elmer and he would not intrude on the privacy of her memories with him. It irked him, but he needed to give her time to move on – however much time she needed.

A cold chill ran down his spine. He looked over his shoulder. The room was lit only by the fire in the fireplace, and everything seemed normal. Nothing had moved. And then he heard a sound in a bedroom – a small one, like that of a light object falling.

"Callie?" he whispered, but she had fallen asleep on his shoulder.

Gently, very gently, he lifted her up and lay her on the sofa while he got up. It was probably just Freddy or Lila who had bumped into something as they moved around the apartment, but he wanted to be sure. So he quietly walked over to the dark bedroom and lit the oil lamp on the dresser. He picked it up and moved around the room, looking for the object that had fallen, but everything was just as usual, except for the growing uneasiness inside him.

"Freddy? Lila?" he whispered as to not awaken Callie, but they did not answer.

Something then caught his eye, in the tall mirror in a corner of the room. He walked over to it and gazed at his reflection, but saw nothing special in it. But there was something else, something his eyes could not see with the light. So he placed the oil lamp on the nightstand and returned to the mirror, and there it was: right behind him. He could not tell what it was at first: it was dark and shapeless, like a shadow floating mid-air, and the more he gazed at it, the more petrified he became. Then, slowly, a face emerged from the shadow. Not the face of a human, more like that of a lion with a thick black and purple mane and piercing red eyes. Stanley was paralyzed with fear now, but he remembered Callie in the living room. He had to protect her, by all means. He noticed a book on the nightstand. A book? Was that really all he could ever find to defend himself against supernatural creatures? Yes, it was. So, in a sudden move, he picked up the book, spun around, and hurled it at the demon before running out of the room.

"Callie!" he shouted, but as he entered the living room, he found himself in another place. It still looked like their home, except everything was the opposite of what it had been. The warm yellow of the wallpaper was now purple, the fire burned upside down in the chimney, all the furniture was backward, and, more frightening than anything else, Callie was gone.

"Callie! Callie!" he cried out.

He walked around the room in circles, calling out her name, but she did not respond. He then went to the window, but now it only opened from the outside. And what he saw through its foggy glass was just as bizarre as the interior of his apartment: where the street had once been were clouds, slowly passing by, and when he looked up to the place where the sky used to be, he could see the city of Edinburgh upside down.

The creature in their bedroom crept into the room, its large paws as quiet as those of a cat, and Stanley turned around to face it. It was a monster, with the size and shape of a bison, a hunched back, large paws like a tiger, the face of a lion, and a long tail. It was covered in black and purple fur and its smell was the most putrid Stanley had ever smelled. This was his first encounter with a demon in its true form, and he did not need to ask what it wanted: he recognized the presence, the darkness of the demon in his attic.

"So you found me now. You've got what you wanted," he said in an angry and trembling voice.

The demon opened its mouth and a long, thin pink tongue came rolling out almost to the floor.

"Stanley... why fear me?" it said, seemingly without moving its lips.

Its voice was eerie and feminine, clashing with its appearance.

"Where is Callie?" Stanley asked.

"Callie is in your living room... but you are not," the demon said.

"I noticed that. So what is this place? Your realm?" Stanley asked, frowning.

"This is *your* realm," the creature said, moving closer to him.

Stanley backed up against the window, terrified, but there was nowhere he could escape.

"Are you afraid of what is inside your mind?" the creature asked.

"My mind is not upside down and backwards, you stupid fool!" Stanley retorted. "If you've come to kill me, then why bother with all this masquerade? Just do it quickly."

The creature seemed to laugh.

"I did not come to kill you, only to show you who you really are," it said.

"This is who I truly am. Callie and I are living a normal life now. She will not return to her life as a demon and you won't get anything from me," Stanley warned the creature. "Now, if you're not going to kill me, take me back to reality and Callie!"

"Reality... which one?" the creature laughed softly.

"The real world, you nincompoop!" Stanley shouted.

His entire body was shaking now, both with fear and anger. Just because he sometimes read backwards and mixed up words did not mean his mind was upside down. It only meant he used it differently.

"Stanley's reality... yes, I can take you there," the creature said with seeming satisfaction.

Stanley was not sure what happened next, but it felt very much like his soul was flying across time and space. It flew out the window and across the land, the clouds and city and hills rotating around him. Night became day and day became night, and the sun was spinning around the world with maddening speed. And finally he crashed into his body again, somewhere else.

He blinked his eyes, and he was now sitting at a desk in the old nursery of his childhood home. Before him on the desk was a pile of papers and books. He gazed out the window to his right: the sun was shining brightly outside. He then looked down at his hands and they were different, larger. He brought them to his face and felt a real beard around his chin.

"What the hell?" he whispered, confused, and his voice pitch was now that of a man born in a male body. It surprised him so much he touched his neck, wondering how his vocal cords could have changed so much in a second.

Callie then walked into the room through the door to his left. She was dressed like a proper, elegant lady, in a white and blue striped bustle dress, her long black hair gathered in a neat bun. She was carrying a tray with a cup of tea and smiling.

"So how is the new chapter going, darling?" she asked in the sweetest voice.

She walked over to him and placed the cup of tea on the desk beside him.

"Callie? Where am I?" he asked.

"Why, at home, of course," she laughed. "It must be a fascinating chapter to make you forget everything. I can't wait to read it!"

"Chapter?" he said, curious.

He looked down at the pages before him, and on them he had written the story of everything that had just happened to them, from their first encounter in London to meeting the cat-sìth in Scotland.

A child then came running into the room, saying: "Papa! Papa! Look!"

Stanley stared at him for a moment. It was Cornelius, except he was not a ghost. He was a human child, and with his curly black hair and hazel eyes, he looked just like Callie and him. He was carrying two toy soldiers and showing them to him.

"Look at them fighting! Look!"

"Cornelius! Your father is busy, you can play with him later," Callie told him with all the gentleness of a mother. "Off you go now."

Cornelius looked disappointed, but left the room and ran down the stairs.

"Don't forget your sister is coming this afternoon," Callie then said, before leaving the room.

"My sister? What?" he said, but she did not answer.

He slowly got up and gazed around the room. It was the old nursery indeed, and his old home, except it was different, quieter, and bathed in sunlight. There were no ghosts living there. He went into the hallway and opened the door to what had been Mary's bedroom: it was still a bedroom, with the old wooden bed and the wardrobe he remembered there, but the bedding was different.

"Can I help you Mister Suspect?" a young woman's voice asked behind him.

He turned around and found himself facing Eve. She wore a sober black dress and little makeup, like his governess Mary when he was a child.

"Who are you?" he asked, frowning.

She seemed puzzled.

"Miss Chauvin, the governess..." she said with a French accent.

"Oh, please excuse me. I guess this is your room," he said, apologetically.

"Were you looking for something?" she asked.

She stood perfectly still before him, and the bright sunlight coming in through all the windows was not hurting her. Therefore, she could not possibly be a vampire. A black cat came up the stairs and began to rub against her legs. She picked it up and began to pet its head, and it purred happily.

"It looks like Cat-Sìth is hungry. I will go get him some milk," she said, and with this she turned around and went down the stairs.

Stanley stared at her for some time, then shook his head. Was he losing his mind? Was he a writer, living in his family home in London with his wife Callie, their son Cornelius, their governess Miss Chauvin, and a cat named Cat-Sìth? Had he just imagined another life for himself, one in which he was born in a different body with supernatural abilities, and he had turned the people in his household into the characters of a story?

He went down the stairs to the parlor on the second floor. The wallpaper in it was the one he remembered, but the furniture was different, less colorful. It was decorated according to his and Callie's taste. He then examined his father's old bedroom, which was the one he now shared with his wife. Nothing unusual in either room; it was an ordinary middle-class home.

"Darling!" Callie called from downstairs.

"Yes?" he said.

"Could you please go up to the attic and bring down the box with your grandmother's tea set? I need to start setting the table for tea," she said.

"The attic? Yes, of course," he said.

His body quivered at the thought of going up there, but after all, if he had only imagined the ghosts and demons, there was no reason not to go there. Yes, it was all just his wild imagination as a writer. So he went up to the third floor, and then up to the attic. He hesitantly opened the door and found himself again in a perfectly ordinary room, only a little dusty. He looked around it and found a box containing a lovely tea set with flowers. It had to be the one Callie wanted to use. He was about to pick up the box when he heard footsteps behind him. He turned around, ready to defend himself against whatever creature from the underworld might appear, but it was just Miss Chauvin. She looked much less reserved and smiled brightly.

"Stanley!" she said in a whisper, closing the door behind her.

She then came to him and wrapped her arms around his neck and kissed him. He took a step back, startled.

"Miss Chauvin!" he gasped.

"Don't worry, she can't hear us," she said. "I've been missing you all day!"

He removed her arms from around his neck and gently pushed her away.

"What's wrong?" she asked.

"Are we... lovers?" he asked, frowning, and she lost her smile.

"Stanley?"

"Did we do something together?" he asked again.

"Oh, so you're going to pretend you forgot everything?" she said, spiteful now. "How convenient now that I'm carrying your child!"

"M–My child?" he repeated, astounded.

Her eyes filled with tears, and she pursed her lips.

"So I guess you were lying when you said we would elope together and raise our child in the countryside?"

"I... I'm sorry, but... I don't remember any of this," he said, shaking his head.

She turned around and stared at the floor for a moment, then she walked out of the room, slamming the door behind her.

Stanley looked down at his hands once more. Who was he and what sort of trouble had he gotten himself into? But Callie – his real-life wife – was waiting downstairs, so he picked up the box with the tea set and returned to her. She welcomed him into the dining room with an angelic smile and took the box from him.

"Thank you darling," she said. "You should get ready now. Sophie will be arriving soon."

"Sophie?" he said.

"Your sister."

She frowned slightly and walked over to him. She seemed to be looking for something on his face, like a sore, then she whispered: "How is your treatment going?"

"What treatment?" he asked.

"Your mercury ointment. For the... disease," she said, looking uneasy.

Mercury ointment was commonly used to treat syphilis, and one of the symptoms of the disease was sores. The treatment could also cause memory loss.

"Wait, do I have syphilis?" he whispered, in case their son or the governess were listening.

Callie moved her gaze away from him.

"Oh please, Stanley, do we have to talk about this now? Don't you think it's bad enough that my husband can't even be faithful to me and started visiting prostitutes the moment I got pregnant?" she said in a choked voice.

"Darling..." he said.

He tried to embrace her, but she would not let him.

"I need to set the table," she said coldly.

Someone knocked on the front door, but he ignored it. He watched Callie set the table sadly, wondering how he could cheat on a woman he loved so much and who tried so hard to be a perfect housewife for him and a perfect mother for their son.

"The door is not going to open itself, Stanley," Callie said.

So this was what their marriage actually was? Was this why he had tried to embellish it in his novel, by making her a demonic temptress on the run and himself the hero who could save her?

He left the room and walked to the front door and opened it. And there, standing before him, was himself. Stanley. The one he knew, who was not born in a male body. He was wearing his habitual, worn-out brown suit and the usual frown on his face.

"You?" he said, confused.

"You sure take your time to open the door," the other snapped at him. "The least you could do after throwing me out on the streets is not let me wait outside in the cold."

"Is it cold?" Stanley asked.

It seemed quite warm out there in the sunshine.

"You nincompoop!" the other muttered as he walked past him.

Callie came out into the hallway, looking overjoyed.

"Sophie! I'm so glad you came!" she said, and she threw her arms around the other Stanley's neck and kissed him on the cheek. He turned his head back to the Stanley at the door with a cunning smile. They were having an affair. Stanley - the husband - was sure of it, and he felt helpless as he watched them walk together into the dining room. He shut the door and stood there, in the hallway, wondering what was going on. His life seemed normal, and yet everything was upside down. Upside down. The image of his apartment in Edinburgh and the upside-down fire burning in the chimney flashed before his eyes. This was not real, it was an illusion created by the demon. But how could he get out of it? The attic. The gateway had to be there.

He rushed up the three flights of stairs, past Miss Chauvin and the cat, and burst into the attic.

"Come on out, you monster!" he shouted. "I'm not falling for your tricks! This is not real!"

He waited, but nothing moved or even stirred. Nothing except him. Something hit him with the force of a shockwave and when he looked at his hands again, they were the thin hands with twisted fingers he remembered. He was back in his old body. It was disappointing, but it meant he was right, and this was all an illusion.

"You're not coming out?" he warned the demon. "Fine then, I'm going to find you!"

He grabbed an old sword that was leaning against the wall and rushed back down to the third floor. He checked all the rooms, but they were empty. He did the same on the second floor and found no one there, but when he got to the first floor, he stopped. There, in the middle of the dining room, was Callie. She appeared to be standing, but her eyes were closed, her skin pale, and her hair undone. She was still wearing the same white and blue striped dress, only it was now stained with something. Tea? Stanley took a step closer, then another, then he walked slowly around her. She was not exactly standing. She appeared to be held up from the shoulders by invisible strings, like a puppet. He then noticed Cornelius on the other side of the room, he too pale and with his eyes closed, and invisible strings also held him up. The room had not changed, but the colors seemed to have faded on the walls, the furniture. The table was not completely set yet, but one of the teacups had already tipped over and spilled on the floor and Callie.

"It looks like the upside-down tea party did not go as planned," a childlike voice said, and when Stanley turned around, he was facing the cat-sìth.

"D-Did you do this? Are you with that thing?" Stanley said, picking up the sword.

"Me? I was not invited," it said nonchalantly.

It began to walk around the room, looking at the furniture and the portraits on the wall. Stanley had not even noticed them before, but all of them were upside down except one, the one the cat-sìth had stopped in front of. Stanley walked over to it and gazed at it: it was a photograph of two young children - twins. One was him, 'Sophie', and the other was also him, except he did not remember having a twin.

"Who is that child?" he wondered.

"I wonder if this is the same child I just saw in the backyard..." the cat-sìth said.

"You saw her?" Stanley gasped.

"Of course. I can show you."

Stanley hesitated before the creature's feline grin, but he somehow wanted to trust it.

"The paths in this world can be treacherous and one can easily get lost. Let me guide you, traveler of the upside-down and inside-out realms," it said. "By the way, you can call me Cat."

They went out into the hallway and opened the door leading to the backyard. It was, like the last time Stanley had seen it, overgrown with thorn bushes, but covered in a thick fog. Cat stepped forward assuredly on the stone path before them, its hands in its pockets.

"Do you even know where we're going, Cat?" Stanley asked, suspicious.

"I have found that the best way to find one's way back to a certain spot is to retrace one's footsteps," Cat replied.

They soon came to a crossing. Three stone paths converged there, and in the middle was a wooden sign with directions. One arrow pointed toward the house and said: 'Happiness'. Another said: 'Memory Lane', and it pointed toward the thorn bushes. The last one pointed upward, to the sky, and said: 'Not an option'.

"Why is the sky not an option?" Stanley asked Cat, who seemed to know its way around here - better than him, at least.

Cat turned around and grinned.

"Because you can't fly. Even you know that, Stanley," it said.

"What's going on? Is this just an illusion or have I lost my mind?" Stanley said, who was beginning to doubt himself again.

"People believe they are mad when reality as they know it changes. If you acknowledge that reality is an ever-changing thing, then you are never mad," Cat said. It then returned to the signs.

Stanley looked at the sign saying 'Happiness', and then to his house again.

"I guess happiness wasn't that happy after all," he said in a sad voice.

"There is no such thing as absolute happiness, nor is there absolute sadness. Reality is a mixture of happiness and sadness," Cat said. "Now let's see... I believe I saw the child down Memory Lane. Shall we go there?"

"Might as well," Stanley said. "And hopefully down there we will find a sign saying: 'The way back to that furry ass with the foul breath and the nasty tongue' so I can put this sword through it!"

Cat chuckled softly.

"Are you not afraid of it?"

"I've lived my whole life with fears beyond my control. Another monster in the darkness makes no difference," Stanley said coldly.

So they went down the stone path to Memory Lane, and it led to another backyard. The same, with the same house in the background.

"Did we just circle back to the same spot?" Stanley asked.

"I don't think so. The clock in the sky says the year is 1866," Cat said, looking up.

Stanley looked up and indeed saw a giant clock in the sky, only it did not show just the hour and minute, but also the exact date: September twelfth, 1866. He would have been five years old then. He then heard the voices of two children arguing. Cat stopped and observed the house. One of the children came running out, holding a small wooden toy horse. Another child then came running out, yelling. Stanley did not need to be told which one he was: he was probably the agitated one.

"Give it back, Giselle!" he shouted, and Giselle, the other one, stuck her tongue out at him and kept running. Apparently, they were equally naughty.

Stanley - then Sophie - caught up to Giselle and tackled her to the ground and took the toy back. Giselle tried to snatch it from him, and they both rolled in the dirt, fighting.

"What naughty children!" Cat commented.

"Well, if I had a twin, I suppose she was like me," Stanley said.

The fight ended with Giselle crying and Stanley holding the toy up defiantly.

"It's not fair. Father gave it to me!" Giselle cried.

"That's not true!" Stanley said.

"Yes it's true! Father said he wished I was his only child, because you're just a tomboy!" Giselle said.

Her words angered the little Stanley, who threw himself on her again and struck her in the mouth, giving her a bloody lip.

"You're so mean! That's why nobody loves you!" Giselle cried. "I'm gonna tell Father, and he'll punish you!"

"If you tell him, I'll strike you again!" Stanley warned her.

"Father! Father! Sophie is hurting me again!" Giselle yelled at the top of her lungs, and little Stanley covered her mouth. He looked into her eyes and said: "I wish you would just die!"

Giselle stopped struggling and stared at him as though she was paralyzed, and then the pupils of her eyes turned white and her body fell limply to the ground. Little Stanley moved back, frightened, then touched her with his finger.

"Giselle?" he said.

She did not answer, and the adult Stanley watched her spirit leave her body. It was immediately pulled into the light and disappeared. She was gone.

"I... I killed Giselle? How?" he whispered in shock.

"What a curious way to die. I wonder what happened," Cat said, bringing its little hand to its chin and scratching it.

"I didn't do anything! I just said those words and she... died!" Stanley repeated.

"If looks could kill, I would say Giselle died just by looking into your eyes," Cat said, turning back to him. There was no accusation in its voice, it was just stating what it had observed.

Stanley brought his trembling hand to his eyes. If they could kill, then why had no one else died? Or had they? Had he murdered other people and forgotten? Was that the reason why he did not want to be looked at?

"Oh, look, the fog is lifting and there are other paths. Shall we explore them?" Cat then said, looking behind them.

Stanley turned around and indeed the path split again, and there was another sign with directions. They went to it and read it. This time, the sign pointing toward the house said: 'The Wrong Way'. Another sign said: 'All The Way', another 'Both Ways', and the last one said: 'The Way Out'.

"What's all this crap?" Stanley said, growing angry.

"There are many ways to be or to do things," Cat commented.

"Then which one is the right way?" Stanley asked.

"It depends where you are going," Cat said, turning back to him.

"I want the path that leads to Callie – the real Callie, not the puppet in that house!" Stanley snapped at him.

"Oh, the path to Callie. One moment," Cat said. It pulled out a brochure from its vest pocket and read it, then said: "According to this, Callie can be found by following the Wrong Way."

"Whatever, let's just find her!" Stanley said, and he rushed past the creature and down that path.

"But that path also leads to..." Cat said, but Stanley was already gone. It sighed, put away the brochure and said: "One can't have it both ways... I was on the way out, but I guess I will just have to go all the way down the wrong way, too."

And it began to walk down the path where Stanley had just disappeared.

Stanley still couldn't believe what he had just witnessed, and yet something inside him told him that this was real and not part of the illusion created by the demon. The child he saw was him. He remembered throwing tantrums with Mary when he did not get his way; he would run away from the nursery, kick the furniture, and slam doors. But to kill his own twin sister? It did not look like he knew what he was doing – in fact, he looked terrified when he realized what had happened. He had very few memories before the age of six, only that it was the age when he began stuttering and seeing and hearing ghosts. Was it all related to the trauma of Giselle's death? He ran down the path until he came to a dead end: a white brick wall at the end of the yard. On it was another sign: 'Point of No Return'. Cat walked up to him.

"It seems like we have reached the point of no return," it said calmly.

"But Callie is beyond it," Stanley said, scrutinizing the sign.

"Once we pass the point of no return, there is..."

"No returning. I know, thanks," Stanley said with irritation.

"We could trace our footsteps back to happiness. Did you not have everything you wanted down that path?" Cat said.

Stanley lowered his eyes. Indeed, in appearance, it was as close to happiness as he could get. And yet, even in a perfect world where he could truly marry Callie and give her a child, he still found a way to mess it all up by cheating on her and she on him. Did it mean there was no happy end for them either way?

"I had everything I wanted with Callie in Edinburgh," he said sadly.

"Did you?" Cat said.

No, he didn't. He did not have all of Callie's heart, and his heart's desires were only met halfway. No matter what he did, Callie always remained distant from him, and he realized that even while living together, he still knew as little about her as he did when they first met. He never asked her about the demon coven where she was born or who were her friends there, and she never asked him about his tastes, what he liked, or just what it was like to be him.

"But there is no such thing as absolute happiness. You said it yourself," he told Cat.

"Indeed," Cat agreed. "Once young people realize this, they are called 'adults', and many of them settle for what they can have rather than what they truly desire."

Stanley did not know why, but when he heard the words 'truly desire', Eve's face flashed before his eyes. He could not deny that he had felt attracted to her the first time he saw her in person, but it was not in a sexual way like Callie. There was something about her that made his heart flutter and feel vulnerable, but also free. But people could experience short-lived infatuations, and they didn't mean a thing. A true relationship was what he had with Callie. It was more than butterflies and sighs; it was living together every day, the good days and the bad, and growing together.

"I guess I was always grown-up then," he said. "I'm not crazy enough to let go of the one love I found just because it's not perfect. I love Callie, and I'm going to save her and make things work out somehow."

"Somehow?" Cat said, lifting its furry eyebrow.

Stanley turned to him and smirked.

"You saw the signs. There are many ways, and none of them seems to be the right way. So why not chose the wrong way and try to make it better?"

"My brochure says you might die if you follow the wrong way. Do you still wish to proceed?" Cat asked.

Stanley shrugged.

"Everyone must die someday; better it be me than Callie. She's in danger, and only I can save her."

"If that is what you want, then go ahead. I prefer not to cross that line," Cat said.

"Chicken..." Stanley said, and he took a step forward, then another, and walked right through the wall.

Cat's ears twitched.

"I am not a chicken. I am a cat," it said.

CHAPTER 8

BEYOND THE POINT OF no return, Stanley found, there was indeed no returning. The moment he crossed the wall, he entered a pitch-black world, and when he turned around, even the wall had disappeared. Wherever he went, whatever direction he walked, he could not tell whether he was actually moving or staying in the same place. It was frightening, but not as much as the thought of what would happen to Callie if he didn't find her soon. He did not know if the demon chasing him was related to Belphegor, but they would certainly know about the succubus who broke their laws, and now she would be handed over to those who oversaw her to be punished.

"Where are you hiding, you fiend? Show yourself now!" he shouted, his fingers tightening on the handle of the sword.

"I am not hiding. You are," the beast's eerie voice suddenly said. It echoed all around him and he couldn't tell where it was coming from.

"Another one of your stupid word puns? Cut out the crap and face me!" Stanley shouted.

"I am facing you," the demon said in response.

Stanley swung his sword around him in the darkness, but it never hit anything. His body was shaking with anger and adrenaline now, and his vision once again began to flicker from black to red. When it was black, he still saw nothing, but when it was red, he saw the giant face of the demon floating in the air all around him. Its piercing red eyes burned like two flames, and its mouth was large enough to swallow Stanley whole. Perhaps it already had, for all he knew. He gasped in terror.

"I am here," the demon said again.

"Who are you, and why are you playing these tricks on me?" Stanley shouted, backing up.

"My name is Beelzebub," the demon said. "I am not playing any tricks on you. This is your mind. You chose to go down the wrong way and find me."

"Liar! You made me come here! You kidnapped Callie and lured me here!" Stanley shouted.

"Calcedonia committed a crime in our world and she was apprehended. It is not any of your concern," Beelzebub said.

"Wanting to save lives is a crime?" Stanley shouted, outraged. "Take me to her now!"

"I cannot," Beelzebub said. "She is in Purgatory, and if you enter it as a human, you will lose your life. Even as a major demon, I am not allowed to take the life of a human for no reason."

"You think I'm going to believe a foul-mouthed, lion-headed demon?" Stanley said. "Take me to Purgatory now!"

"Would you be more willing to talk if my appearance was not so repulsive to you?" Beelzebub said. "I can make that happen..."

The giant face of the demon before his eyes disappeared and in its place appeared a beautiful woman. She was tall and had fine features. Her long, curly blond hair fell loosely around her pale face and onto her shoulders like a cloud. She wore a long black dress with a tall, feathered collar and feathered shoulder pads. In this form, she looked much more like a fallen angel than a beast, if not for her ruby red eyes.

"Better?" she said in a deep, sensuous voice.

He did not answer. She walked over to him slowly, appraising him with her eyes, and grinned.

"I know that Callie committed a crime, but you've been after me since I was a child. You've been lurking in my attic the whole time, terrifying me. Why?" Stanley asked, frowning.

Her grin only widened.

"I was just there. You chose to be afraid of the unknown."

"No, I didn't. Everyone is afraid of the unknown, especially children!"

"You were not afraid of Cornelius. How do you know he was not one of us?"

"I..." he said.

"You made a judgment call," she said. "You decided that the spirit living in your wardrobe was good and the demon living in your attic was evil."

"So you're trying to tell me you were just living there, and I was afraid for no reason?" he said, doubtful.

She laughed.

"Of course not. Demons can only enter human spaces when invited."

"So who invited you? My father?"

"Indeed."

"Why?"

"You already know the answer."

No he did not, and he was getting tired of her tricks. So he lifted the heavy sword he was carrying and swung it across her body, but it went right through it as though she was made of thin air. He tried again and again, but the blade never seemed to touch her.

"What are you made of, you fiend?" he cried.

"I am a major demon. You will only touch me if I allow it," she responded.

He let go of the sword, breathless, and shook his head.

"Fine then," he said. "I'm stuck here. You've got what you wanted. What are you going to do with me?"

"Talk," she said. "You seem tired... I can make you more comfortable."

She waved her long, slender fingers before him, and a chair appeared behind him. He fell into it and shackles immediately closed around his wrists, locking him to the arms of the chair. He struggled to free himself, but the heavy shackles were only digging into his skin.

"You are so agitated, Stanley. Do you ever calm down?" Beelzebub asked.

"You're not really making me want to," he grunted. "Talk then, if that's what you want."

Beelzebub smiled.

"So you want us to drop the charges against Calcedonia and release her... why?" she asked.

"Because I love her," he said.

"And your love for a criminal is a good enough reason to challenge a major demon for her?"

"It is for me."

His answer seemed to amuse her.

"Do you understand the consequences of playing with time?" she said.

"If it's only to save lives, it shouldn't matter," he said.

"Time is made of endless possibilities," Beelzebub told him. "Saving one life one day does not mean that person would live another day. They could still die the very next. And if one found a way to prevent every human being from dying, this world could simply not support them and would self-destruct."

"Don't be silly, of course I know that not everyone can be saved, but if Callie saved just a few lives, would it truly make such a big difference?" he said.

"It would," Beelzebub said. "Unfortunately we cannot make exceptions for any criminal, even if their intentions were noble."

"So that's your conclusion? She's a criminal and you're going to kill her?" he said.

His chest felt tight and his eyes welled up with tears. Memories of her flashed through his mind now: the first time she knocked on his door, the first time he entered her shop, their first kiss... Callie was the love of his life, the great sunshine that had come to save him from his dark place in London, and without her he was nothing. He could not imagine his life without her smile, her sweet voice, her laughter. He needed her, alive and by his side. He let his head fall forward and began to cry.

"You love Calcedonia..." Beelzebub remarked without any emotion.

"Yes... and I would do anything to save her!" he cried.

"But even in the most perfect of worlds, you cheated on her," Beelzebub pointed out to him.

"That was not me! You created that illusion!"

"I did not. You created all of it," the demon said.

"No..." Stanley said.

But though he refused to believe the demon's words, he knew she was not entirely wrong. His 'happiness' with Callie always seemed to be missing something, though he could not tell exactly what. Was that why he cheated on her in the reality his mind supposedly created?

"I don't even know that other woman, and I don't care about her!" he said. "Please... save Callie! I will do anything you want!" he cried.

"Anything?"

"Yes, anything!"

Beelzebub liked his answer and smiled again. She moved closer until she towered over him. He lifted his gaze to her.

"The reason I have followed you since you were a child is because I want to make you one of us," she said.

"By 'one of us', you mean a demon?" he asked.

"We sometimes recruit living beings with exceptional abilities. It is a privilege granted only to a handful."

"So, what? I'm special?" he said, cynical.

"You are," Beelzebub said. "You committed your first murder at the age of five. That is very impressive."

"First? Who else did I murder?" Stanley asked in disbelief.

"Your mother, and later your father," the demon said.

"That's not true!" Stanley shouted, tugging at the shackles again. "My mother died in childbirth, and my father... well, I don't know how he died, but I had long moved out of home!"

"Dear Stanley, would you please calm down? You're only going to hurt yourself," Beelzebub said.

He stopped struggling and glared at the demon, though he was not sure who his anger was directed at. She did not appear to be lying to him, and he had witnessed his child-self murdering his sister with his eyes. But the woman before him was a demon, and he refused to trust her.

"Prove it," he said.

She smiled.

"Shall we look into the past? You may not like what you will see," she said.

"I know what I will see. Your tricks can't fool me," he said, lifting his chin.

"Really? Then let me show you something."

She rubbed her palms together and parted them, and a large oval mirror appeared between them. At first, Stanley saw his reflection in it, but then its surface rippled like water and instead appeared his old bedroom. He could see it as though he was sitting on the dresser, like those cursed china dolls. His eyes opened wide with fear. So the damned things truly were watching him...

The room was dark, and the furniture was different. There were two beds, on either side of the room, and his child-self seemed to walk aimlessly from one to the other as though he could not understand where the missing child, his twin, had gone.

"People with your talent are noticed very early on, and we like to keep track of them. We wouldn't want to let such a marvelous demon candidate escape our sight..." Beelzebub explained. "So after I heard of your sister's murder, I sent your parents a present for you: three dolls you would play with and take everywhere with you. You could say I was your very own dark fairy godmother."

"Well you made a mistake, because I was a boy inside, and I never touched those dolls," Stanley said as his anger and fear grew. He did not remember what she was showing him. Somehow, it had all vanished from his mind.

"Indeed, that was my mistake," Beelzebub said.

"How come I don't remember any of this? I suppose you have another magical explanation," he said, and she laughed softly.

"No, Stanley. That was not my doing. It was you."

"Liar!"

"The human mind is a mysterious thing," Beelzebub said. "Sometimes, it can forget traumatic events. Do you remember a long vacation in the countryside?"

Stanley frowned.

"My parents never took me on a vacation anywhere."

"Wrong again," she said. "And I can prove it to you because they sent one of my dolls with you."

The surface of the mirror rippled again, and this time Stanley saw himself sitting on a chair, in a room he had never seen before. Its walls were all white, and there seemed to be little furniture except for a bed with a white metal frame, like a hospital bed. Bright sunlight filtered through large open windows. He was dressed in a white nightgown and his overgrown brown hair blew softly in the breeze. He gazed absently straight ahead, perhaps at a doll on a dresser.

"Shortly after Giselle, your mother was found dead, sitting in a chair in the dining room," Beelzebub said. "Both deaths were investigated by the police, who suspected your father of poisoning the family. He was arrested, and you were found sitting in your bed in an apparent state of stupor, so you were taken to a sanatorium to be treated. As they found no evidence in your home, the police released your father and ruled that both deaths were natural."

The door opened in the white room, and two men walked in. They appeared to be doctors.

"Sophie... Sophie!" one of them called out, but the child did not seem to hear him.

Seeing no reaction, the other doctor pulled out a toy. It was just a stick, with a paper circle glued to the top of it. On one side, it was black, on the other, white. The doctor rolled the stick between his fingers, making the circle flicker like a black and white ball, and it indeed caught the child's attention. The young Stanley then turned his eyes to the two doctors and said: "W-W-Where am I...?"

Stanley did not remember any of it, only that there was a time when he did not stutter, and a time when he did.

"Your mind went into a state of shock after your mother's death, and you lost the ability to speak," Beelzebub explained. "You remained in the sanatorium for several months, but, as the healthy child you were, you eventually overcame it and began to speak again – with a few issues. You returned home to your father, and since you had forgotten all about Giselle, he decided to pretend that she had never existed."

"What...?" Stanley said, shocked. "You must not be talking about the same man I knew. My father hated me," he said, shaking his head.

"Whoever said he didn't?" Beelzebub said.

The reflection in the mirror changed again, and this time showed the attic. Stanley could see the scene from the angle of a toy laying on the floor – probably one of the dolls after he outgrew them. His father was studying an old book by candlelight, and beside him an altar had been set up.

"After you returned home, your father began to suspect you of being the cause of all these deaths in his home, and he became interested in the occult," Beelzebub said. "He thought he could bring back Giselle from the dead and trade your soul for hers, and he summoned me. Not from that old grimoire like you might think, though; he invited me over for tea. Well, he invited a friend of his, but I came instead."

The next scene showed a young woman sneaking up in the attic. She seemed human and wore an ordinary purple dress and hat. She turned her gaze to the doll on the floor and grinned. She walked over to the old standing mirror against the wall and her fingers moved before it like she was tracing magical characters in the air, and the surface of the glass began to ripple. She then went to the book of spells on the altar and waved her hand above it, and the writing on the page changed, but it was too far away for Stanley to see it clearly. The door then opened and his father entered.

"Caroline? What are you doing up here?" he asked with a frown.

"Oh, Henry, dear, you scared me!" she laughed, placing her hand on her chest. "I just heard some little birds and thought perhaps you had a nest up here."

Stanley's father looked uncomfortable.

"Those items, they're not..." he started.

"Oh, that book of spells? Don't tell me you really believe in love potions and all that..." she said pleasantly.

"No, of course not. I was just doing some research for a novel," he said, and he had that smile again - the one he always had when he liked a woman and was trying to impress her with bigger-than-life stories. He had never written any novels; he was a banker. But because that was apparently not enough in his world, he often told the people he met he was the descendant of some lord, or a world traveler who had seen the Indies and China, and he made up words that sounded like foreign languages, and they believed he truly spoke those languages. Stanley had always thought his interest in the occult was just another trick to impress his friends, but perhaps it was not after all.

"Oh, a novel! How exciting!" the young woman said, walking over to him and taking his hand.

The scene in the mirror changed again, and now his father was alone in the attic at night. On the altar were two black candles and various objects. On the floor, a reverse pentacle had been traced, and in its center, a chicken lay in its own blood as some ritual sacrifice. In his hands, his father held the old grimoire. He read out a spell, and a soft, purple light fell upon the room. Then, the candles were blown out and a black shadow appeared before him. He took a step back and dropped the book. Beelzebub then emerged from the shadow in her true form – the beast with a lion's head and a purple and black mane. She stuck out her long pink tongue and Stanley's father fell backwards on the floor.

"You have summoned Beelzebub into your home... What do you want?" she said in her eerie voice.

"Oh, Great Beelzebub, bringer of death and rebirth, thank you for coming to me!" Stanley's father said like he knew something about how to address a major demon. Even when actually facing one of the most dangerous beings in this world, he remained his egomaniacal self.

"Speak now, human!" Beelzebub hissed at him, and he scrambled to his knees in a veneration posture.

"I want my daughter and my wife back!" he said. "Please bring them back to life!"

"You ask for too much, human," Beelzebub said. "One. Choose one."

Stanley's father looked up at the demon and said: "Giselle, my daughter."

Beelzebub moved slowly across the room, circling around the trembling man, and she finally stopped behind him.

"A life for a life," she said. "I can bring back Giselle in exchange for Sophie. Do you agree to this pact?"

He seemed unhappy about it, but only for a few seconds.

"I agree. Take Sophie," he said.

The demon grinned, exposing her yellow, rotting fangs.

"You would sacrifice one of your daughters for the other?"

"Sophie is a bad omen upon this home. She brought only death to us," he said coldly. "I'd rather she return to the realm she came from."

Beelzebub seemed satisfied with his response.

"Very well then," she said. "The pact is concluded. Tonight, Giselle will rise from her grave, and I will return on Sophie's eighteenth birthday to take her away."

The demon disappeared into the shadows again, and Stanley's father lay on the floor of the attic, his entire body shaking.

Stanley shook his head in disbelief.

"I can't believe he would do that... even as bad as he was..."

"But he did," Beelzebub said. "However, when I returned on your eighteenth birthday to claim you, you were gone, and he was dead."

"I didn't kill him," Stanley said firmly. "I couldn't, because the bastard called the damned doctors on me a few weeks before my birthday. He told them I was deranged, talking to people in the wall, and acting like a lunatic. They came in the middle of the night, threw me into a locked carriage, and took me away. I had to call Cornelius and he helped me break out. I ended up on the streets and had to fend for myself."

"Impressive..." Beelzebub said. She brought her hands back together, and the mirror disappeared. "But your father died in the same way your mother and your sister did."

"So what? It wasn't me. I never set foot in that house again," Stanley repeated.

Beelzebub began to pace around him, a satisfied grin on her blueish lips.

"Alright, you've proven to me that I'm a delusional murderer. What next?" Stanley said, furious.

"I want to make you a demon, and I want you to work for me," Beelzebub said. "We will provide for all your needs, and with us you can express your true nature. It is an honest proposal."

"You want me to become a demon and murder humans for you? Never!" he said.

"Demons are only allowed to take the lives of humans to feed or to execute a contract, but you would not be dealing only with humans," Beelzebub said. "I oversee major demons. I am in charge of investigating and punishing their crimes. If you work for me, you will most often face demons, and now and then a very bad human like your father."

Stanley did not answer.

"You would have been offered a pact either way, by me or another major demon," Beelzebub continued. "I just claimed you first."

Stanley stared at her. Now he knew what was in the attic throughout his childhood and why, but the more he learned, the worse the story got. Beelzebub had wanted him and kept tabs on him since he was only five years old, and because of his stupid father, the wannabe sorcerer, she had legally obtained ownership of him. He had been lucky to manage to escape her for so long; it was only a matter of time before she found him. He lowered his head in defeat and disbelief.

"I don't believe it... It can't be true..." he repeated.

"I will let you think about it then... inside your own memories," Beelzebub said.

She disappeared and so did the darkness surrounding him, the shackles, and the chair, and he was sent back into the maze of his memories, in the upside-down world. He was a child again, dressed in a white, long-sleeved nightgown, his brown hair loose over his shoulders, barefoot, and coming down the stairs in his old house. His heart was racing; he was angry and scared. He looked up at the blue striped wallpaper covered with upside-down portraits and photographs, and in the center of each one of them was an eyeball staring at him and following him as he walked by. He reached the bottom of the stairs, and he entered the dining room on the first floor, where his mother sat on a chair. She wore a black mourning dress and was holding a small framed portrait of Giselle in her hands. She did not even notice him entering the room.

"Mother..." he said, but she did not answer, so he said it louder: "Mother!"

She turned cold eyes to him and said: "What do you want?"

"I'm scared in my room without Giselle. There's noise in the walls..." he said softly.

"Don't be ridiculous. It's well past your bedtime. You go back upstairs and go to sleep," she replied.

"Mother... Can I have a hug? Please?" he pleaded.

"A big girl like you? Come on, Sophie. Obey me now," she said.

He did not remember her or his father ever hugging him, but he saw hugs in picture books. He had seen parents holding their children on their lap and reading them bedtime stories to chase away the monsters they saw underneath their beds. All he ever wanted from his parents was a hug, but they did not seem capable of hugs, or any other display of affection.

He walked up to her anyhow and placed his hands on her lap, forcing her to look at him.

"Mother, please, hold me in your arms just once!" he insisted.

He reached for the portrait she was holding and took it out of her hands so she would forget about Giselle and look at him. She resisted him and it eventually fell on the floor and the glass broke.

"See what you did? Go to bed now," she said in an angry voice.

She picked up the portrait and the glass shards and placed them on the table beside her.

"Mother!" Stanley said, his eyes filling with tears, but this time his mother turned around and slapped him.

"Go to bed! Now!" she ordered him.

He took a step back and his vision began to flicker in black and red, his heart racing faster and faster. His mother's heart was surrounded by a fortress with cold walls he could never breach, no matter what he did or didn't do. Both his parents were like that. They had nothing but praise for Giselle and her good manners, and nothing but scorn for him, the disobedient, hyperactive child who liked to play outdoors, climbing trees, catching bugs in the yard, and, often, fighting with his sister and his cousins when they came over. Giselle was not any better than him though: she was cunning and sly and somehow always found a way to get her twin blamed for all the mischief she got up to, and their parents believed her. After all, why wouldn't they believe that their other, turbulent child broke a vase, or took the fish out of the fishbowl and put it in the oven to see what would happen? Stanley hated his sister, but after she was gone, he missed her. The bedroom they had shared suddenly became cold and frightening, he had nightmares, and he began to hear things moving and talking inside the walls.

Red, black, red, black... red. His heart was in overdrive, his blood pulsing furiously through his veins, and now he had nothing but hatred for the woman before him who just slapped him for asking for love.

"Why did Giselle have to die? You should have been the one!" his mother suddenly snapped at him. "I had an angel and a demon. I lost the angel and now I'm left with you! You're the spawn of Satan – everything you do is wicked!"

He took a step forward, his eyes fixed on her red image, and he began to see fear in her eyes.

"Sophie?" she said in a trembling voice.

He took another step forward and said: "Die!"

Her pupils flickered and turned white, and she stopped moving. He watched her spirit leave her body and fly up to the ceiling, where the light came for it, and then his eyes fell upon her frozen body again. All the time his eyes flickered, he knew exactly what he was doing: he killed, driven by a sort of primal instinct to dominate and subordinate others. He wanted the utmost power over them: that of life or death, and he enjoyed taking their lives. But when his heart slowed down and his thoughts returned to normal, he found himself gazing at his mother's cold body and wondering what had happened to her after looking into his eyes.

"Mother?" he said.

He touched her with his finger and she was cold like Giselle.

Stunned, or perhaps in shock, he turned around and left the room. He stopped in the hallway and there was a new sign on the wall with an arrow pointing up the stairs. It said: 'Back to bed'.

He slowly went up the stairs, pushed the door to his bedroom open and emerged instead in a white room. It was pleasant and soothing, with its white walls and its tall, open windows through which filtered the summer sunshine. It was a hospital room. He went over to the bed and lay down on it and began to suck his thumb, holding on to the blanket. He did not want to hold the doll sitting on the wooden dresser in a corner because it frightened him. It was comfort he needed, but he no longer knew where to find it, not any more than he knew why he was there. Two men in brown suits and a nurse in a gray and white dress entered the room and came to him. He sat up in the bed and let them examine him because he knew it was what they expected of him.

"Sophie, do you recognize us?" one of the men asked. His voice was soothing and musical to a child's ears.

Stanley stared at them. He understood their words and he recognized them, but his mouth seemed disconnected from his brain. He was in a safe place inside, and he knew that if he engaged in conversation with them, he would no longer be, so his lips would not budge, no matter how much he tried to move them. And since he could not speak, his eyes moved away from theirs until they fixed themselves on the soothing brown color of the man's suit.

"Sophie, can you write?" the other man then asked.

Stanley looked up at him, again unable to answer him. The man then presented him with a small slate and a piece of chalk, two items he was used to having at home, in the nursery.

"Can you write your name?" the man asked with a smile.

Stanley took the slate and the piece of chalk and wrote: 'your name'. It was not the answer they expected, but it was, technically, exactly what they had asked him, and they both laughed.

"Do you understand us?" the first man asked, and Stanley erased the slate with the sleeve of his nightgown, then wrote: 'yes'.

"You understand what we are saying, but you can't answer us with your voice?" the other said.

Stanley hesitated, then wrote: 'yes'.

"Do you know why you are here?" the first man asked.

Stanley looked down at the slate. His heart was beginning to race again. Fear, anger, confusion... He did not understand why he was there, but he knew it had something to do with his eyes and his voice. So he began to draw eyes all over the slate, then scribbled all over them and, in small letters in the bottom right corner, he wrote: 'don't look at me'.

He dropped the slate and closed his eyes, covering his face with his hands, and when he opened them again, he was sitting at a small desk in the nursery. He was older, maybe ten or so. Mary, the governess, was there, as well as his evil tutor, Mister Hawthorne. The tall, stringy man with a thin mustache and thin brown hair stood beside him, holding a long stick.

"One more time, Miss Sophie!" he said in a sharp voice.

Stanley looked down at the slate before him on the desk. His handwriting was terrible. No matter what he did, it could never follow a straight line, and when he reached the end of the line, rather than skip to the next line, he would turn the slate sideways and continue writing. He did not like cutting long words because if one line ended with the beginning of the word and another began with the ending, then if he put the two halves together, the word no longer made sense. It made more sense to him to write the ending of the word at the end of the line and the beginning at the beginning of another line. But the adults had decided that if a line ended with 'fruit-' and another began with 'cake', the reader was supposed to picture the two halves of the word flying off the page and switching places mid-air to form the word 'fruitcake' and not 'cakefruit'. Reading was very difficult for him, because not only did he have to follow all these bizarre rules, but he also had trouble reading from left to right and on the same line.

"Focus!" Mister Hawthorne ordered.

"The... a-a...apple... f-falls..." Stanley said, trying hard to keep his eyes on the same line, to remember to read from left to right, and to not stutter.

Whack. The wooden stick struck him in the back of the head. It hurt. He looked up at Mary who smiled peacefully and said: "You can do it, just focus."

But getting struck every time he made a mistake only worsened his reading and stuttering problems. He closed his eyes, and when he opened them again, he was sitting in a chair in his bedroom at nighttime. An oil lamp burned on the dresser beside him, and Cornelius was leaning on the arm of the chair. They were reading a book together – not a picture book, but a big book, with many words. It was 'The Adventures of Tom Sawyer', their favorite. With Cornelius, he never had any stuttering problems; they read books slowly, together, and it was fun.

"What does that word mean?" Cornelius said, pointing to a certain word on the page.

"Let's see..." Stanley said. "*'Tom did play hookey, and he had a very good time'*," he slowly read. "It means Tom didn't go to school when he was supposed to."

"I wonder what school is like..." Cornelius said.

"We'll never know since we never get to leave the house, except to go out in the backyard," Stanley said.

"Is that why you like Tom Sawyer? Because he can go out and have adventures?"

"It's because he's a boy," Stanley said sadly.

"I think you're a boy, too. You're not like my sister was," Cornelius said.

Stanley turned to him and smiled. He then noticed a sign on the wall that said: 'Stanley grows up', and no sooner had he seen it than he felt himself being pulled out of his chair, of his body, and he crashed again into his older body. He was seventeen and a half now, and he had begun wearing the old suits and shirts his father discarded, and smoking. Because no one would let him cut his hair short, he had attempted to do it himself, and the result was an uneven bob around his face, which he combed back behind his ears. He slouched on a sofa in the parlor, a cigarette in one hand and a book in the other. Reading was no longer an issue, thanks to Cornelius, and though now and then he still got distracted and got all the words and letters mixed up, he could bring back his attention to the line and successfully read it.

"What are you reading?" Cornelius asked, appearing on a chair nearby.

"It's a murder mystery, not your type of book," Stanley said, his eyes fixed on the page.

Cornelius cringed. He preferred children's books.

Stanley's father then entered the room, looking displeased. Nowadays, he lived in the darkness. He had boarded up the window in his bedroom and insisted that all curtains and portieres remain closed at all times, except when he was having his friends over, which only happened at night. Why curtains were supposed to be closed in the daytime and open only at night, Stanley would never know, but his father often did not make sense anymore and Stanley even suspected he might be going senile.

"Who are you talking to? Your imaginary friend again?" he asked roughly.

"Good morning... or should I say good evening?" Stanley replied in a sarcastic voice, not even bothering to look at him.

His father walked across the room and snatched the cigarette from his hand and put it out in the ashtray on the side table.

"I told you that you are not allowed to smoke. It's not lady-like," he said.

"And what are you going to do about it? You sleep all day anyway," Stanley shrugged.

He put down his book, pulled out a cigarette case from the pocket of his shirt, and lit himself another one.

His father let out an exasperated sigh.

"Sophie, don't you think it's about time to give up on your imaginary friends and start behaving like a young lady?" he said.

"Don't call me that name!" Stanley replied angrily.

His father leaned over him, equally angry.

"Your name is Sophie, you are a woman, and in a few years you will get married and have children. It is your place in this world, and you will, eventually, find happiness in it."

Stanley stuck out his tongue like he was about to throw up at the idea.

"Stop doing that!" his father said.

"Or what? You're going to have a séance and call the bogeyman to spank me?" Stanley replied, ignoring him.

He got up and was about to pick up the cup of tea Annie had left for him on the table, but his father caught his wrist. Nothing unusual, except for the fact that his hand was ice-cold. Stanley turned to him and observed him, only now realizing how pale he looked, and how black his eyes were.

"What happened to your eyes? They were always hazel, like mine," he said, frowning.

His father let go of his wrist and turned away.

"Father, are you alright? Your hands are awfully cold," Stanley said. "Do you need to see a doctor?"

"You're the one who needs a doctor," he replied without even turning around. "You think you're a boy, you talk to imaginary friends and people in the walls... If you don't change your ways, Hell is what awaits you!"

"I hope it's warmer than London at least," Stanley replied, who was not the least bit concerned about God or demons or Hell. Inculcating religion to children like him who questioned everything and demanded clear and logical answers was a lost cause because Christianity, as it was practiced, was based not on the exact words of the Bible, but on their interpretation and social norms. And since most social norms made no sense to Stanley, neither did religion.

His father grunted and left the room. Stanley shrugged and went to the table to pick up his cup of tea, when he suddenly heard a loud scream downstairs. Annie. She had probably seen a little mouse again.

"Annie?" he said, walking over to the staircase.

Now on the wall, among the upside-down portraits, was a piece of paper. Stanley read it, and it was a menu: 'A Special Dinner for Two. Appetizer: Fingers À La Mode. Main course: Annie Au Jus. Dessert: Sophie.'

Stanley shuddered.

"What the hell?"

He heard another scream, and it was not Annie's usual scream. She was terrified of something. He rushed down the stairs to the first floor, then down to the kitchen in the basement, and he found her there, laying on the floor. She was pale and her lips were blue.

"Annie! Annie!" he said, shaking her body, but she was barely breathing.

A cold hand then closed around his arm and pulled him up with inhuman strength. He spun around and saw his father.

"Father? Did you do this? What did you do to her?" Stanley said, horrified, but his father did not answer. He dragged him up the stairs, kicking and screaming, and threw him in his room and locked the door. Stanley started beating on the door.

"Father! What did you do? What's going on?" he cried.

Cornelius appeared beside him.

"Cornelius, quick, open the door!" Stanley said.

"I'm scared. Something has changed about your father, and I think he might hurt you..." Cornelius said, clinging to his leg.

"Don't be silly, he's the biggest wimp ever!" Stanley said, but indeed something had changed in his father, and he had no idea what. The only thing he knew for sure was that he had murdered the maid.

Hours passed, and he was thinking about how to escape, when someone suddenly unlocked the door, and two men in black suits walked in, followed by his father.

"Help! My father killed the maid!" Stanley immediately said, thinking a neighbor had called the police, but the men both gripped his arms firmly.

"See? My daughter is delusional. She thinks she is a boy named Stanley, she talks to imaginary friends, and now she is saying that the maid I fired five years ago just died in the kitchen," his father said as though he was truly concerned about his child's mental health.

"Don't worry, we'll take care of her. She can have a room all to herself, where she can talk to the walls all day, every day," one of the men said.

"Father! Father!" Stanley cried, terrified.

"It's for your own good, Sophie," his father said coldly.

"Cornelius!" Stanley then shouted, but his friend shook his head helplessly. He did not know how to fight so many grown-ups at once.

"There's no one in this house except us and your father, Miss Sophie," the other man said.

As Stanley still struggled, he was taken outside and thrown into a barred carriage and locked in it.

"Cornelius!" he cried again desperately as the carriage took off, but no response came.

He thought his friend had abandoned him, but something suddenly scared the horses, and the coachman was no longer able to control them. He and the two men in black suits all had to get off the carriage to calm them. Cornelius then appeared outside the carriage's door and handed Stanley a key ring.

Stanley did not need to be told what to do. He immediately stuck his hand out through the bars on the door and tried several keys until he found the right one and the lock opened. Then, as quietly as he could, he slipped out of the carriage and began to run. It was the last night he saw his father alive.

His soul flew back into his body and crashed into it, and he was again sitting in the same chair in the darkness, his hands shackled to the chair.

So it was true – everything Beelzebub said – it was true, and he had simply forgotten it. He had murdered his sister and his mother, and because of the trauma he suffered partial memory loss and developed a speech impediment. But he was not the only evil in his house. His father was too. After summoning a demon and promising her the life of his only child, he had apparently lost his mind, and it resulted in the death of Annie. How could Stanley have forgotten her death? Annie was not the smartest girl, but she was sweet, and if she sometimes teased him about his habit of wearing trousers, she also told him that he looked handsome in them. So this was the story of the Suspect family, the one he thought so ordinary and posh. Murderous children, murderous parents, sorcery... they surely were a cursed lot, all of them.

He shook his head. There was no going back. He had indeed passed the point of no return, and now his two options were either to become a demon of his own free will, or to be turned into one forcefully. He lifted his gaze and looked around him.

"Beelzebub!" he called, and, as he had expected, she was not far and immediately appeared before him.

"So, have you made up your mind?" she asked.

"I have a question for you," he said in response. "Did my father murder Annie or was I delusional?"

"What are you trying to find out?" she asked with a grin.

He could not answer her. Indeed, he forgot even the existence of his twin sister. He cared so little about his parents that he never thought about investigating their deaths, and he could not say he cared very much more about Annie. So what would knowing the answer bring him?

"I will tell you, Stanley," Beelzebub said. "You know how similar you are to your father, and not only in your looks. You both spend your time bluffing and chasing the unknown, even though you fear it. You're cunning, unfaithful, and you trust no one but yourselves. And now you think that finding out if he murdered someone will confirm to you whether or not you are a murderer, but you already have all the answers. They were inside you all along."

"You're wrong," he stated. "If he did murder her, then the next time he starts rattling in the walls of my house, I'll call Annie's spirit and let him deal with her."

Beelzebub burst into laughter and shook her head.

"Stanley Suspect... Do you even realize the position you're in?" she then said. "You're not going to leave this place as a human. You *will* be a demon. All I need to know is whether you prefer to be my employee or my slave."

"Can we negotiate?" he asked.

The demon observed him for a moment then said: "You were promised to me. I can take you by force if I want to."

"Then why haven't you done it yet?" he asked.

"Because there is no need for violence between us. You have no reason to resist becoming a demon, since you are basically already like us. Your talents will be valued in our world, and you can do great things. Why throw away such a great offer and become my slave instead?"

"I'm still the only one who can make that decision," he reminded her. "And I will become a demon under one condition."

"And what is it?"

"Drop the charges against Callie and release her, and I will work for you."

"Are you sure that is still what you desire the most?" she asked. "Think carefully."

"Yes, that is what I desire the most," he immediately said.

She seemed to reflect on it for a moment.

"I suppose I can make it happen," she said. "So do you peacefully agree to form a pact with me?"

"I agree. Make me a demon," he said.

Cat was right: once he passed the point of no return, nothing could ever be the same. But it was the only path for him, because it was the only way to save Callie, and being with her again in their home in Edinburgh was all he wanted.

Beelzebub grinned and leaned over him. Though she now had the appearance of an attractive woman, he could still smell decay all around her, along with the scent of woodfire smoke.

"Open your mouth," she said.

"What are you going to do?" he asked with a disgusted frown.

"I shall place my mark on you, in a place where it will not be seen. Other demons must not know who you work for," she explained.

"To do your dirty work, huh? Alright," he said, and he opened his mouth.

She moved closer, cupped his face with her hands, and kissed him, pushing her tongue deep down his throat. He gasped and struggled to escape her, but her grip on him was too tight. His stomach churned at the thought of her foul tongue penetrating inside him and he could no longer breathe. But, just as he thought he was about to faint or throw up, she released him, leaving only a burning sensation on his tongue. He coughed and gagged, and then the burning sensation spread across his entire body as though he were catching fire. He cried out in pain.

"Sorry. It might hurt a little," she said, laughing softly.

"What did you do to me? I thought we were making a pact?" he cried.

"We are," she said.

The burning sensation only lasted for a few seconds, then it disappeared and he fell forward. His head was spinning and he felt nauseous, but he could also sense that something had changed, not only in his body, but also in his mind. He looked up at the demon and she was no longer so repulsive to him, even with the stench of decay floating all around her. So now he had done it - he had followed the wrong way and become a demon. What would his father say? Probably nothing since he had sold him to Beelzebub. Saving Callie was still his priority, but it was no longer the only thought on his mind. There was another one, much darker. He wanted to go back in time and find his father and kill him. He had apparently killed him either way, so what if he did it again? It should not make any difference.

Beelzebub waved her hand again, and the shackles around his wrists disappeared. He stood before her.

"Where is Callie?" he asked in a cold voice.

"You will see her soon enough. I must take care of the administrative part of our deal," Beelzebub said. "Meanwhile, I shall assign you your first mission."

"Fine. What is it?"

"There is a demon named Berith, in the city of York," she said. "He is a great duke of Hell. I have long suspected him of plotting a coup against me, and he has an accomplice. So far, he has been able to evade our spies. You will find out who his accomplice is and report to me. You can kill Berith."

"So I'm your personal hitman," he said. "Alright. How will I find him?"

"One of our spies will assist you."

"And how do I kill him?"

The demon's grin widened.

"You already know how to kill, Stanley."

Stanley smirked.

"I guess I'll find out if it works on demons. And how do I get back down to Earth?"

"I'm sure you will find a way," she said, before disappearing into the shadows.

"Hey! Wait!" he shouted, but she was already gone.

He looked around him, but even his now-demon eyes could see nothing but absolute darkness. And then he remembered there was another way his eyes could see. He picked a random direction and focused on it, letting his heart beat faster and faster, until his vision flickered in black and red, and when he saw red, he also saw a path on the ground, made of perfect, large squares, like the tile floor of a church. Some squares were solid, and the others were holes. He looked at the path before him, but he did not trust it. If this alternative reality was created by his mind, and in it everything was apparently upside-down and backwards, then going forward would not be the right way. He turned around: the path stopped behind him, and there was nothing but a large black hole there.

"Well then, I guess I'll take the wrong way again," he said, and he jumped into the hole.

CHAPTER 9

IN THE BLINK OF an eye, Stanley found himself standing in a fashionable clothing shop he did not recognize. He was in front of a tall mirror and wearing a very nice suit. It was not his dream brown suit, but he quite liked the way he looked in this black one, with a neat white shirt and a black vest and silk bowtie.

"How do you like it, Mister Knowles?" the shopkeeper, an old but distinguished man with gray hair and a beard, asked.

"It's perfect," Stanley said. "Put it on my company's account."

He hoped the demons had an account, because he did not know whether he was even carrying his wallet.

"Anthracite Incorporated, is that correct?" the man said, opening his book of accounts.

That sounded about right for a demonic shell company.

"That is correct. Where is my old jacket?" Stanley then asked, feeling his empty pockets.

"Oh, right here, Sir," the man said.

He went around the counter and brought back all his old clothing. Stanley went through the pockets and found his wallet, the non-magical pocket watch, and the feather given to him by Cat, which may or may not be magical. He slipped the items in the pockets of his new jacket and smelled the collar. He had not brought with him Beelzebub's stench, but still it seemed to linger in his nostrils. He grabbed the black silk top hat and the cane on a chair beside the mirror.

"Anything else, Mister Knowles?" the shopkeeper said.

"Got any men's cologne?" Stanley asked.

"I certainly do," the man said, and he brought out several elegant bottles.

Stanley smelled each one of them, then said: "This one."

"Shall I box it for you?" the man asked.

"No, there's no need," Stanley said.

He took the bottle and applied some perfume to his neck and wrists, then tucked it in his pocket. At least Beelzebub had not lied about the demons providing everything he would need. He and Callie would live comfortably from now on.

He walked out of the shop into the rainy streets of York, a smile on his face as he already pictured them purchasing a house in Edinburgh. The first floor would be the shop of her dreams, and he would help her by providing for her. And perhaps, when Callie had her clockmaker shop again, she would be truly happy.

He stopped and looked at his reflection in the window of a shop. His appearance had not changed. He was still the same old Stanley. He stuck out his tongue and there was now a mark on it – the mark of Beelzebub. At least it was not visible. But his life would be different now – easier in some ways since now he no longer had to fear demons, but more complicated because now he and Callie would never be able to live as ordinary humans. The only alternative was her death, though. He hoped she would understand the bargain he made.

He then thought of his friends, Cornelius and William. What a surprise they would have when he showed up in front of them in his new form. Speaking of which, he needed to pay his landlord in London to ensure they still had their home. He did not want them to be crowded out, or worse, exorcised if a new family moved into the building. The next stop would therefore be the bank, and he hoped there were funds awaiting him. And there were. He found that, through Anthracite Incorporated's account, he was able to transfer funds to his landlord in London, so he paid him two years' worth of rent in advance. He then withdrew some cash to carry on him and went about finding some accommodations for himself. He did not need grand luxury for a simple mission, so he rented a room in a cheap inn, under the name Albert Knowles. The room he picked had only a bed, a wooden desk, and a chair, but it was warm and had no drafts. He would be comfortable enough, and no major demon would think of looking for him there – if they even suspected Beelzebub would send a hitman after them.

He removed his coat and jacket and lay on the bed, gazing at the ceiling. How many hours or days had passed since Beelzebub found them in Edinburgh? Even he couldn't tell, but now an intense fatigue settled throughout his body and his mind. He needed to sleep. So he pulled the rough, woolen blankets over him and closed his eyes.

He awakened to rattling in the wall. Lovely. The old man was back in his life.

"Oh, shut up, or I'll kill you again!" Stanley warned him, and the noise stopped.

An uneasy feeling gripped him. He was used to yelling and cussing at annoying ghosts, especially his father's, but something was different now. He was a murderer. He had murdered his twin sister and his mother. He had no reason not to believe Beelzebub when she told him he murdered his father too. Now, when he looked down, he could almost see and feel their blood on his hands. He was evil, that was why the demons were so interested in him since he was a child. His throat felt tight and tears welled up in his eyes – not for the loss of his parents, whom he barely remembered at all, but because he was never given a chance to be good. The powers he was apparently born with were bound to claim lives sooner or later, and once he had claimed one, his life became forever tainted. This was his destiny and he never had a chance to escape it. And if, by some miracle, he could go back in time, not in a dream but for real, if he warned his younger self never to use his powers, then would he ever meet Callie when he grew up? As dark as his path might be, he still wanted to follow it, if only to be with her one more day, one more second. He wiped away a tear and looked out the window, of which the curtains had been left open. The sky was cloudy outside and he could not tell whether he had slept only for a few hours or all night. A shadow then flew up to the window and perched itself on the windowsill. A crow. It seemed like it wanted to come in, so Stanley got up and opened the window, and it flew in and landed on his shoulder.

"Who are you?" he asked, sensing some magic at work.

"My name is Calvin," the crow responded in a cawing voice that hurt Stanley's ears.

"Alright, alright, not so loud!" he said, and the bird flew away and landed on the desk.

"Apologies," it said in a sarcastic voice. "Why do they even bother hiring people with such sensitive ears?" it then muttered.

"Why do you have such a loud voice?" Stanley retorted, and the bird cawed back even louder.

"Stinking crow!" Stanley said in a low grunt. "What do you want from me?"

"I'm here to assist you in your assignment," the bird said.

"I don't need your help, stupid bird!" Stanley said.

The crow cawed again twice and coughed up a crumpled piece of paper, then flew out the window.

Stanley picked up the piece of paper with a disgusted frown.

"Why did I ever make a pact with a demon of filth?" he said.

He opened it and read it. It appeared to be a note written by someone to another person: *'Meet me at Leak & Thorp at five. I have something for you. P.S. I can't wait to be inside you again!'*

Stanley frowned again and stared at the paper. It was obviously not intended for him. Did the crow just swallow someone's random love note, or did it have something to do with his investigation? He would have to find out. As a precaution, he dropped the paper into the flame of the oil lamp, which he had left on, and watched it burn until he was sure no one could read it.

He was in a bad mood. He wanted to see Callie now and hold her in his arms, but could he even look her in the eyes after cheating on her in his dreams? He grunted again, picked up his coat, his hat, and his cane, and headed out.

After asking a passerby on the street what the date and time were, he found that six days had elapsed since he entered Beelzebub's dimension, or she his, or whatever had happened, and it was four thirty. He was running late if he wanted to catch the two potential conspirators, so he asked for directions to Leak & Thorp, whatever that was, and he was told to follow Coney Street. It was a large department store, and he was told he could not possibly miss it. And indeed, with the lively crowd gathering outside, he found it easily. He did not know exactly what he was looking for until he spotted a man who stood out - not to the other fashionable shoppers - but to his eyes. To them, he may have looked like any other dandy - neatly combed blond hair, blue eyes, precise shave, yellow striped suit and matching hat - but he possessed a natural grace, an elegance not common among human men. Stanley discreetly followed him inside, shielded by the dense crowd. There, he hid behind a men's accessories stall and pretended to look at bowties while keeping an eye on him. The man met up with another in a similarly elegant purple suit. This one had long black hair tied in a ponytail. He was tall and handsome, with youthful features, and he wore spectacles. He kissed the other on the cheek and slipped his arm around him, and they both headed in the direction of the men's restrooms.

Please let this not be what I think it is, Stanley thought. That crow had better have given him a good tip, or else...

The men's restrooms could be entered from two separate doors, and one was close enough to him that he could sneak inside before them, so he quickly made his way through the crowd and slipped inside. The restrooms were empty. He looked around for a place where he could hide, but the other door was already opening, so he rushed into one of the stalls and hid there. *Terrible hiding place,* he thought. As he had expected, they began opening the stall doors to make sure they were alone. He backed up against the wall and his heartbeat began to slow down. His vision flickered, in gray and black this time, and he could feel his body temperature dropping. Was this part of his new demonic powers or did he always have that ability, like that of killing with his eyes? Whatever the case, he was not sure how his body cooling down would help him face a potential demon, but, to his surprise, when the man opened the door to his stall, he looked right through him as though he was not there. He was invisible. Nice. He would have to use that trick again. The man shut the door and said: "We're alone."

The man's scent lingered for a second or two in the stall, and something about it was unusual. Like other demons, he smelled like woodfire smoke, but not only that. There was also a sweet scent to him, like... candy?

Stanley's heartbeat and vision returned to normal, leaving only a prickly feeling in his limbs that was not unpleasant.

He tried to remain as quiet as possible, and now the two men thought they were alone, they locked themselves in another stall, and he could hear them kissing and sighing.

Oh, please, he thought, rolling his eyes.

The sighs quickly turned into pounding against the walls of the stall, and grunting, and moans, and Stanley waited, uncomfortable. He hated going into the men's restrooms. For one thing, having to use a private stall and not a urinal to pee could trigger suspicion, but also they were just plain disgusting. Men equipped with the right parts seemed to enjoy peeing everywhere except in the hole, and when they went for a number two, they left the toilets looking like they had been through war. For that reason, he never used public restrooms and held it until he got home. But he also knew that men's restrooms were a meetup place for those men who liked a quick pass with a stranger, like these two, apparently. But why do it in such a disgusting place? Luckily, the whole thing lasted only five minutes at most, and then he heard both of them breathing hard and possibly kissing again, then they walked out and washed their hands as though nothing happened. That was fast.

Stanley quietly moved closer to the stall's door and observed them through a crack. Watching them washing their hands and chatting, no one would suspect they just walked out of an intense workout session in the bathroom stall.

"That feels better," the man in the purple suit said, stretching out.

"You were so pent up… were you holding it for me, Jax?" the man in yellow said.

The other grinned and cupped his chin with his fingers.

"You know there's no other like you, Bee."

"I had a hard time coming here at all. I feel like I'm being followed everywhere," the man in yellow – 'Bee' – said.

They were obviously using codenames or pet names, and now Stanley was convinced that Bee was Berith. As for the other, he still had no idea who he might be, but he could still report his findings to Beelzebub.

"Don't worry, even if she suspects something, she can't prove it," Jax said.

He pulled out a miniature, golden pocket watch from his pocket, one identical to the one Callie had made.

"Here, take this. I need you to hold on to it for me for a while. And if things get too dangerous, use it," he then said.

"The Time Key... you know no one but the Gatekeeper is allowed to use it!" Bee said, taking the precious item.

"It will be safer with you," Jax said.

"But if someone other than the Gatekeeper uses it, wouldn't they die?" Bee asked, looking up at him.

"A succubus stole it and used it once, and she survived," Jax said.

Stanley's blood froze. It was indeed the magical pocket watch, but they were saying Callie did not make it, rather that she stole it. Why would she lie about it to him? Was she trying to impress him? Either way, she did not lie about being in trouble with her kind for using the item.

"Are you serious? A succubus? How did she even get her hands on it?" Bee asked, and Jax grinned.

"I helped her. She is an important part of my plans – only she doesn't know it," he said.

He leaned forward and kissed his lover, this time on the cheek.

"Be safe, my love, I will return for you," he said, and Bee gazed upon him with pure adoration.

"Come back soon," he whispered.

Jax kissed his lover again and left the restrooms. Bee remained in front of the mirror, put away the watch in his pocket, pulled out a comb, and began to comb his hair. Stanley observed him quietly, wondering what to do next. He knew his orders, and he was sure he had positively identified Berith and his accomplice, Jax. But the two of them looked no different than himself and Callie. Their relationship was apparently under scrutiny and Jax was trying to protect his love with a magical item, nothing more. And this Berith looked like a very sweet demon, not a great duke of Hell. What sort of conspiracy could he possibly be involved in?

Berith stared at the mirror for a moment, then froze as though he had noticed something. Then, he slowly turned to the stall where Stanley was hiding.

"Who's there?" he asked, frowning.

Stanley thought about pulling the invisibility trick on him again, but this time he did not have to. He had identified the target and his next task was to eliminate him. He looked down at his trembling hands. Could he kill a man - demon or human - just like that? But this was what he had signed up for when he made that pact, and Callie's freedom depended on his cooperation with Beelzebub. Knowing now that in order to kill with his eyes he needed to feel anger, he focused on the memory of his father murdering the maid and trying to get him locked up in an insane asylum. But that memory quickly faded away and was replaced by those of the murders he committed. There was one person he hated more than his father: himself. Fine. That would do.

He let his heartbeat quicken until his vision started flickering in black and red. Berith took one step toward the stall, then another, trying to see through the crack in the door.

Black, red, black, red, black... red. Stanley's heart was racing furiously, and before Berith could open the door, he crashed through it and grabbed him by the throat. He saw his reflection in the mirror behind them: his entire body was flickering from red to black like some creature of nightmare.

"N–No... please!" Berith begged him.

"Are you Berith?" Stanley asked in a distorted voice.

"Yes, it's me," Berith said. "I promise if you let me go, I'll tell you everything. I'll surrender. Please don't hurt me!"

But Stanley looked into his eyes and said: "Die!"

The demon stopped struggling. His limbs were now paralyzed. All color left his blue eyes until his pupils turned white, and then Stanley saw his spirit leave his body and vanish. He dropped the demon's limp body on the floor as the adrenaline still rushed through him and observed it for some time, breathing heavily. Then his heartbeat and vision returned to normal. He looked into the mirror and his body was no longer flickering; he was Stanley again.

Killing his target had proven surprisingly easy and thrilling, and he thought he actually enjoyed taking the demon's life, but as the adrenaline left his body, he began to feel sick to his stomach. He looked around him in case the demon's spirit had lingered and even called out to him: "Berith? Are you still here?"

No answer.

"I–I'm sorry. This was not what I wanted to do!" Stanley said aloud, but he could neither hear nor sense his presence. He was gone to whatever world demons returned to when they died.

He pursed his lips and his eyes were moist again. He went to the sink and turned on the faucet and splashed some cold water onto his face. Drawing in a deep breath, he looked at his reflection in the mirror. *Murderer*, he thought. But there was no time to be sentimental. He needed to get out of here before any other humans or demons walked in. He remembered the pocket watch. Kneeling beside the demon's body, he went through his pockets and found the item. He slipped it inside his vest pocket and slowed his heartbeat until his vision was flickering again, in gray and black this time. And thus he walked out of the restrooms, and no one ever saw him.

Time lapsed, and Stanley found himself standing before Beelzebub again, this time in the comfort of a luxury suite in a hotel. Its walls, furniture, and even the carpet were in her colors - purple and black. She sat in a chair, clad in a black silk ball gown with a feathered collar, a glass of wine in her hand. In a vase on a table to her left was a bouquet of black roses, and on her right shoulder was Calvin the crow. Stanley suddenly remembered that he had returned to his hotel room in York and fallen asleep. His mind was empty and his body crushed by an intense fatigue. When he opened his eyes again, Calvin had let himself in through the open window and perched himself on the foot of his bed. He invited him to climb into a tall, oval mirror that had seemingly appeared out of nowhere in a corner of the room. Stanley did not ask any questions and followed him like an automaton, and he emerged from another mirror in Beelzebub's suite.

"Stanley... you look confused," she remarked as she appraised him with her ruby eyes.

He gazed at her and did not answer. His mind was disconnected from his mouth once again, but Calvin seemed to know how to deal with the issue. He flew up to him, perched himself on his shoulder, and pecked his cheek with his beak.

"Ouch!" Stanley said, startled.

He reached for the vicious bird, but Calvin flew away before he could reach him and cawed.

"Oh... he's alive again!" Beelzebub said in a mocking voice. "So, what do you have for me?"

Stanley frowned.

"Berith is dead. I saw his accomplice. He goes by the name of 'Jax'," he said coldly.

"Interesting," she said. "Can you describe this Jax?"

"Tall, long black hair, spectacles, purple suit. He talked about a Gatekeeper."

He remembered he had stolen the pocket watch from Berith's body. It was in the right pocket of his vest, and in the left one were the non-magical watch and the feather Cat gave him. He reached into that pocket and pulled out the watch.

"Jax gave this to Berith," he said, observing her reaction. He saw anger and astonishment flicker through her eyes, and she lost her smile. She held out her hand, and he gave her the item.

"Thank you Stanley, you have exceeded my expectations, and you will be rewarded. What would you like?" she said.

"Callie... I want to go home and be with her," he said, still in an empty voice.

"Of course, you may go home. Use the mirror behind you," she said.

She rubbed her palms together and the glass on the mirror began to ripple, and behind it Stanley could see his and Callie's apartment in Edinburgh. And she was there, standing by the window. A great weight suddenly lifted from his shoulders, and he stepped into the mirror.

He emerged in his living room, as he had hoped, and Callie turned to him. She was wearing a black dress again, similar to the one she had been wearing the first time she knocked on his door. Her long, black curls were gathered in the back of her head and fell onto her shoulder like soft feathers. Her eyes, her beautiful eyes were still like two black diamonds, except he did not see in them the sparkle that used to live there. She stood solemnly in front of him, holding her hands. The dim sunlight filtering through the window behind her bathed the room in a sort of gray haze, making even the warm wallpaper look dull. But Stanley had only one thought on his mind: he wanted to hold her. So he walked over to her and pulled her into his arms, whispering: "Callie! You're home!"

She timidly wrapped her arms around him, not like a lover, not even like a friend, but like a stranger who did not recognize him.

"Yes, Stanley. We're home," she said.

He noticed how empty her voice was, but he did not want to think about that now. All he wanted was to hold her and love her with all his heart.

"Callie, sweetheart..." he whispered, holding her tighter.

She did not move and instead gazed at the fire burning in the chimney. It had burned through all the logs and was about to die out.

"Callie?" he said, pulling away from her slightly.

She let go of him and went to sit on the sofa, facing the dying fire. He brought a chair and sat facing her.

"So... what happened? Who turned you into a demon?" she asked.

Of course he did not expect her to be thrilled about what he had done: now they were both demons they could no longer live exactly like humans, they would have to make accommodations, but at least she was alive and free.

"I made a pact in exchange for your freedom. All charges against you were dropped," he explained, aware that his voice was filled with guilt.

"A pact with whom?"

"I'm afraid I can't tell you. It was part of the agreement," he said.

"I see. And why would you do such a thing?" she asked him, not the least bit moved by his remorse.

"To save you, of course..." he said. "If I hadn't agreed to it, they would have executed you!"

"So instead, you chose to tie us both forever to the demon world?"

His throat tightened.

"But you are a demon, and I..."

"You... what?" she said, scowling.

"I didn't know it, but I was already claimed by a demon since I was a child," he said, lowering his eyes. "I... murdered my twin sister and my mother. And then my stupid father summoned a major demon, thinking he could bring my sister Giselle back to life, and he promised me to the demon instead. She would have found me sooner or later."

"Well, lucky you... you became what you were meant to be," she said cynically.

"Callie, I know you're not happy about this, but we can still live together. Not quite like ordinary humans, but almost. And we'll have enough of everything," he said, taking her hands.

She let him, but did not hold his hands in return.

"And what about my feelings?" she said.

"What about your life?" he asked in response. His hands tightened around hers. "Would you rather be dead?"

"I don't know," she replied, holding his gaze with her cold eyes.

"Callie, my darling, I did this for you. I left London for you. Everything I did was for you!" he pleaded, but she snatched her hands out of his and got up.

"I have to go now."

"Where to?"

"Work."

"At Martha's?" he asked.

She turned to him, and the sheer anger in her eyes made him want to run and hide.

"No, Stanley," she said. "I'm a succubus. My job is to seduce men. You wanted me to be free, and they released me. Now they want me to get back to work."

She walked over to the door, picked up her hat, and turned to him one last time.

"Thanks a lot," she said, before leaving the apartment.

He stared at the door for a moment, stunned. Why had he not even thought about that? Of course, the fact that they dropped the charges against her did not mean that she was now free to go and open another shop and live as she wanted. The demons would want her to behave like a demon and play her part in their world. Had he ruined their relationship while trying to save her? He reached into his pocket and pulled out the magical pocket watch. It looked like any other pocket watch, except it was the size of a coin. What if he could turn back time and prevent all of this from happening? But how did the object work? And even if he did know how to operate it, how far back should he go? To the time when she stole it? To the time when he committed his first murder? He did not really want to relive his miserable childhood, waiting to grow up to find her again. So he put it back in his pocket and let his head fall into his hands. His heart still ached, and he felt sick to his stomach thinking of the murder he had just committed. He needed his friends now, Cornelius and William, but they were in London.

"Freddy? Lila?" he called out, but the couple did not answer. They sometimes visited other ghosts in the adjacent houses, traveling through the walls.

He got up and went to the bedroom. All of Callie's clothes were still there. At least she was not leaving him – not yet. He let out a sigh of relief and went to lay on the bed. There was nothing to do until she got home, and now all he could think of was her sleeping with other men. It was not what she wanted to do, and she probably felt as sick to her stomach as he did about the thought of betraying him. He would have to let her know that it was alright and wouldn't change anything between them. Perhaps he could start saving money and open a new shop for her, and if she still had to perform her duties as a succubus, at least she would have the comfort of having her clocks to work on. And if she wanted to live alone, he would also let her. If it was the only way to appease her, then he would do it. He would make any sacrifice for her happiness. The only thing he would not do was give her the watch, for fear that she might use it to go back in time and prevent them from ever meeting.

When he awakened the next morning, Callie was asleep in the bed beside him, in her nightgown. She had pulled the blankets over them. His heart swelled again with the simple joy of seeing her sleeping face and knowing that she had returned home to him. He moved forward and kissed her cheek, but she grunted and rolled over. She still wanted to sleep. So he got up quietly and went into the living room. He had slept in his clothes but did not want to change in the bedroom for fear he might wake her up. He lit a fire in the chimney and put a kettle of water near the flames. There was no kitchen, so they had to eat outside, but they could still make tea in their apartment. Then, he moved back to the sofa, brought the small table they kept against the wall to the middle of the room, and placed the two chairs around it. When the water was boiling, he poured it into the old teapot they had purchased together from an antiques dealer and added some tea leaves. He made sure there was sugar in the matching sugar bowl, and brought out the biscuits Callie loved, and the small bottle of milk they left outside on the windowsill at night, to keep it cold. He heard her stir in the bedroom and sat down at the table, waiting for her with a smile.

She emerged from the bedroom in her white nightgown, wearing only her crimson nightrobe over it, and yawning. She blinked her eyes with surprise when she saw the table set for tea.

"Good morning, my love," he said, smiling. "Milk tea?"

She came and sat at the table and he poured some tea and milk in her cup and added two sugar cubes – just the way she liked it. She smiled faintly.

"You're not asking me who I slept with last night," she then said.

Apparently she had been worried about his reaction, knowing how jealous he was.

"I don't need to know. It's just work," he said, still smiling.

She gazed at him with an expression he could not define, then she poured him a cup of tea and added milk and sugar to it. Payback. She knew he hated milk and sugar in his tea. But he smiled nevertheless, took a sip of it, and tried not to gag when he tasted the milk.

She finally broke into a real smile and her eyes softened.

"You're not going to let us fall apart, are you?" she said.

"No," he replied.

Her eyes moved to her cup of tea and she sighed.

"Of course I didn't want to die, and the cell I was locked up in was disgusting, but... I just wish you had not made a life-changing decision for both of us like that," she said.

She moved her gaze back to him, waiting for his answer.

"I know, Callie, and I'm truly sorry," he said. "But even now, I don't see any other way it could have ended, except with your death, and I didn't want that."

"So, what sort of demon are you?" she asked, sipping on her tea.

"I don't know. I wasn't told," he said.

"Then what is your function?"

"I... I'm not supposed to tell anyone."

"So you're a hitman..." she said, not overly concerned about it. "Well, hopefully, I don't become your target."

"No, darling, you don't need to worry about that. Only major demons should be, not..."

"A lowly succubus?"

"That's not what I meant," he immediately said, apologetic.

She was roasting him now, and he deserved it.

"The good news is you don't have to work at Martha's anymore if you don't want to," he said pleasantly. "I can get money whenever I want. So you can spend your days shopping, or going to suffragette meetings, or even playing tennis."

She laughed softly. It was so good to see her smile again. He truly felt like he had almost lost her the night before, but things were cooling down between them. They would have to figure out their new normal from now on.

"Will you play tennis with me?" she challenged him.

"I can try," he said.

She smiled and poured him another cup of milk tea with sugar, and he swallowed it just to please her.

CHAPTER 10

STANLEY WAITED IN THE darkness for his target. This time he was sent to interrogate and kill a lesser demon simply known as 'Cole'.

After the murder of his lover, Jax was, understandably, upset, and a series of murders had ensued, but nobody knew who he was, nor had they heard his name before. Beelzebub suspected him of having stolen the Time Key, the magical pocket watch, from Belphegor, the Gatekeeper, and now trying to retrieve the item. She quickly found out that the one Stanley had returned to her was a fake, and everyone was looking for this Time Key as though they couldn't just create another one. What did the Gatekeeper use before pocket watches were invented, anyway? But Stanley did not care enough to tell them he had it. He had not become a demon out of loyalty to them, but to save Callie, and now, because of his decision, she resented him. All he wanted was for them to return to what they were before, even with their ups and downs, and though they had settled into a new routine, things just weren't the same anymore. He was angry and frustrated every time she went out to perform her work; he was insanely jealous at the thought of her sleeping with other men, and his only consolation was that she probably didn't enjoy it anymore. As for him, she never touched him anymore, and she had not kissed him since they were reunited. And all of this was his fault, because he decided to go down the wrong way and past the point of no return. If Cat were there, it would probably say: "I told you so."

Yes, he did all of this to himself, and because he had no other outlet to express his anger, he took pleasure in frightening his targets before killing them.

Demons, humans, men, women, he did not care who he killed, and if, at first, he kept track of their numbers, he soon stopped counting. If there even was a chance for him to go back and atone for his sins when he first became a hitman, now there was absolutely none. So he just did what he was good at: terrifying and killing people, and with the money he earned, he spoiled Callie as much as he could. And that night, because Beelzebub had decided it, Cole would die.

The young demon walked past him on the street, and he never saw the invisible fiend lurking in the shadows. Stanley followed him. He did not use his invisibility skills under the rain, because the raindrops would still fall and bounce on him, revealing his presence. But that night, unfortunately for Cole, the sky was perfectly clear.

As he walked, Stanley's thoughts unwillingly reverted back to Callie. She was probably with another prey, or several that night. What did she do with them? Did she prefer doing it with a man who had the right parts down there? She claimed not to have a preference when it came to her sexual partners, but did she see him as a real man or as a woman wearing men's clothes? So many questions he could not ask her for fear of losing her... He tried to quiet his mind. They never asked each other any questions about their professions. She had her body count and he had his; it was just work, nothing more. But her kind of work angered him, and if he became too angry, he would switch into black and red mode - killer mode - and he did not need that now. He needed to remain in invisible mode.

Cole stopped and turned around: he suspected that he was being followed but could not see anyone. Stanley remained perfectly still, facing him. The demon frowned and resumed walking. Another man was walking toward them on the empty street. Cole walked ahead, and as they passed each other, Stanley thought he saw his hand slip something into the hand of the other man. He kept on following Cole, but as the other man approached Stanley, the wind carried his scent to him, and he immediately recognized it. It was a mixture of the scent of woodfire smoke and candy. Jax. The light of the streetlamps was too poor to distinguish his features, but this time, his long hair was blond. He was clad in a long, black cloak, and hid his face under a top hat. He did not wear spectacles. So was this a disguise or was the black-haired Jax his disguise? Who was this man no one seemed to know in the demon world? Stanley would find out soon enough. But before that, he slipped his hand in the man's pocket as he walked by and took whatever item he had just tucked in it. It felt like a small glass vial. He heard the man stop and turn around as though he had felt something, but he did not follow him.

Cole was still walking ahead of him, but looking anxiously to his left, to his right, and sometimes behind him. He then began running, and Stanley had no choice but to chase after him. The demon scrambled down the dark streets, then entered a church - as though God could save him from Stanley. Wrong. Stanley walked right in behind him and the demon ran across the nave and sought refuge near the altar. Stanley closed the heavy wooden doors behind him.

"Who are you and what do you want?" Cole cried, looking in every direction.

Stanley walked down the nave and past him and pressed his fingers on the keys of an old organ behind him, almost scaring the poor man to death.

"Things are not looking good for you tonight... Cole," Stanley said, letting his voice echo all around the apse.

The poor Cole scattered across the nave again, making for the door as Stanley's wicked laughter echoed across the entire church, but before he reached it, it opened and the blond man Stanley had just seen stood before him.

"You?" Cole gasped.

The man pulled out a barley sugar stick from his pocket and bit into it with a crunching sound. He closed the door. Stanley grew quiet and moved closer, but the church was too dark to clearly see his face.

"Someone followed you," the man said calmly.

"Yes... you!" Cole said, backing away. "What's wrong with you? I thought we had a deal! I found out what you wanted!"

The blond man marched forward assuredly, and Cole backed up until he hit the altar again. Stanley didn't like that. Cole was his target, not that other man's. Still, he needed to know who he was and what sort of business he had with Cole.

The blond man raised his hand toward Cole, and the demon's body lifted in the air.

"N-No! Please don't! I beg you!" Cole pleaded, but the blond man only smiled.

"Do you know the best part about killing someone?" he asked, and Stanley was not sure whether he was talking to Cole or to him.

"Please..." Cole said again.

"It's to hear them beg for mercy... and kill them anyway," the blond said.

Cole kicked and struggled, but to no avail. He gasped and tears of blood began to pour out of his eyes as though his head was being crushed from within, then he stopped struggling. He was dead. The blond man finished his barley sugar stick and lowered his hand, and Cole's body fell onto the altar. He sure liked to create a dramatic scene, Stanley thought. But he had sabotaged his mission, so he decided to play with him – just a little. He quietly walked over to the organ and played a few random notes, but the blond was not surprised. He grinned and headed in the direction of the organ, but by the time he had reached it Stanley had already moved to the transept and knocked over some candles.

The blond man's smile widened.

"Someone wants to play..." he said.

He pulled out another barley sugar stick and began to chew on it while walking around the church's nave.

"I know you took something from me. I want it back," he said.

Having no luck making conversation with Stanley, the man sat down on a bench and waited, and Stanley quietly came up behind him.

"I can't see you or hear you move, but I can sense you," the man said, and now Stanley recognized him: he was Belphegor. At least, he looked like him. He clearly remembered Belphegor's woodfire smoke scent. He did not wear any sort of cologne and carried no other scent. This man's scent also carried the sweetness of candy, just like Jax. But if he was actually Jax, he did not seem very distraught over the death of his lover. Unless he was neither of them. Perhaps the one conspiring against Beelzebub was not Berith after all, but someone who wanted her to think he was.

"Who are you?" Stanley said in a cold whisper behind his ear.

The man smiled with satisfaction.

"I'm the candyman," he replied.

So Stanley was right. This candyman had many faces, and he had adopted the features of Belphegor this time. Why? For the Time Key? As Jax, he was already in possession of it and gave it away. What else could he gain from impersonating the Gatekeeper?

"And what's your name?" the man asked him.

"I'm the bogeyman," Stanley whispered, and as he did, the man suddenly turned around and tried to get his hands on him, but Stanley dropped to his knees and rolled, and ran out of the church.

He ran quietly down the empty streets, but the man did not follow him, and after some time, he slowed down his pace and let his heartbeat return to normal. He returned to the hotel room he rented for this mission and turned on the oil lamp, then sat at the small wooden desk and pulled out the glass vial he had stolen from the candyman. It contained a folded piece of paper with the following inscription:

'URCLNCA USUNGAV
Wednesday, Sunday, Friday, Tuesday'

Obviously a coded message, and the code was contained in the weekdays. Stanley frowned and scratched his head. Well, a word game should not be too difficult for his brain. He tried various combinations in his mind, but nothing made sense.

"Let's see," he said to himself. "If Monday was actually Wednesday, and Tuesday Sunday – two days forward, two backward – then Wednesday is Friday, and Thursday is Tuesday."

He applied the same reverse calculation to the letters, two forward, two backward. 'S' was 'U', 'T' was 'R', and so on and then the message read: 'STANLEY SUSPECT'. He got out of his chair, startled. Someone, other than Beelzebub, was looking for him among the demons, and now they had his name – or at least Cole had it, but he never managed to give it to the candyman, a hitman, like him. The question was: who hired him? Surely Beelzebub knew who her enemies were among major demons.

He burned the piece of paper in the flame of the oil lamp and walked over to the mirror on the other side of the room. He did not control mirrors, only his mistress did, and perhaps other major demons too. He had to wait until a gateway was sent to him in order to move across dimensions and space, but she was very good at anticipating how long it would take him to complete an assignment. As he had expected, the surface of the glass was rippled and ready to transport him back to her. He stepped into it and emerged into her bedroom. This time, she was sitting in front of her vanity in her black negligee, and applying her makeup and perfume.

"You wear perfume?" he asked her.

"Every woman wants to smell good," she replied, turning to him.

Should he tell her that it was not very effective with her putrid stench?

"So, what did Cole say?" she asked.

"Nothing. Someone else got to him before me," Stanley said, slipping his hands in the pockets of his trousers.

"Tell me more," she said, intrigued.

He began to pace across the room – partly to get away from her stench.

"Who among the major demons is your enemy?" he asked, frowning.

"All of them. It's a highly competitive function," she said.

He scratched his chin.

"Demons smell like woodfire smoke or other unpleasant things," he said, not wanting to openly offend her. "What creatures of the underworld smell sweet and eat candy?"

She laughed.

"Candy? Not a favorite in the underworld, but vampires are the ones with the sweet scent. Their scent is said to be very floral."

"But vampires and demons do not mingle, correct?"

She lost her smile and now he could see fear in her eyes.

"They do?" he asked.

"They'd better not..." she said in an angry voice.

"Who in the vampire world would be interested in keeping tabs on the demons?" he asked.

"The seraphim," she said.

"Angels?"

"Originally, the title was held by angels, but all of them quit and joined us," she explained. "So other creatures of the underworld now occupy those positions, and many of them are powerful vampires."

He stopped and turned to her.

"There is a mole in the highest spheres of the demon world," he said. "His codename is 'candyman', and he can impersonate anyone. Berith was never involved in a conspiracy against you, but whoever employs the candyman wanted you to believe it."

She got out of her chair, looking furious.

"Those bastards! They have no right to interfere in our business. We had an agreement for thousands of years!"

"Well, apparently not anymore," he said. "Any idea what they want?"

"The Time Key you returned to me was a fake. They must have stolen the real one," she said, now twisting her hands nervously.

They didn't, but he was not ready to share that information with her yet. He needed to find out more.

"I think the theft of the Time Key was a distraction. They know my name and they probably know I am a hitman. I think they want to find out who I work for. Also, I believe that Belphegor is dead," he said.

"Impossible... no one has reported his death," she said, scowling.

"Perhaps because the candyman is impersonating him," he said. "May I go to his office in London and verify this?"

"No. If they are aware of your existence, I need to send someone else," she said.

She turned back to her mirror, and her reflection in it was that of the beast she truly was.

"Seraphim... How dare you?" she said in a dark and hateful whisper.

Stanley returned home, not so much because he wanted to obey his mistress, but because he wanted to see Callie. He had been gone most of the time over the past few weeks and barely got to say good morning to her. She was still up and combing her hair in the bedroom when he walked into their apartment around two that morning.

"Sweetheart, I'm home," he said.

"Still alive, huh?" she replied.

With his new job and its dangers, he might someday not make it home. Both of them were aware of it. At first, she had protested, saying it was too dangerous, but now she had accepted that very real possibility and even joked about it - perhaps as a way to dedramatize their situation.

"Safe and sound, as always," he said, peeking into the bedroom.

"Will you be home tomorrow?" she asked, turning to him.

He removed his hat and jacket.

"Yes, I guess I have a few days off. Why?"

She seemed disappointed.

"I have a two-day assignment," she said, and she returned to the combing of her hair.

"Two days? With no sleep?" he asked, frowning.

"Not two days of sex, silly," she laughed. "I must meet a special client in London. Unlike you, I have to take the train."

Special clients were the overseers and major demons that succubi were obligated to provide sexual favors to when they demanded it. According to her, it was not the most unpleasant of jobs, as demons had more stamina than humans and could keep up with them.

"I'll go with you then - to London, not to meet your client," he said.

He walked over to her and kissed her cheek.

"But Jane and Henrietta were counting on us to attend the next meeting. I was hoping at least you could go there and then tell me about it," she said with a cute child's pout.

She did not want him to go to London with her - probably because she knew how jealous he would be when she went to work. He pursed his lips.

"I had forgotten about it, sorry. Of course I will go to the meeting," he said.

Their relationship had slowly improved over the last few months, and proof of it was that she now wanted them to attend feminist meetings together. She was letting him into her life again, and she never removed the ring on her finger, even if it wasn't truly a wedding ring.

He began to undress and intended to wash in the washbasin before going to bed, but apparently his love had other plans that night. He had not even removed his shirt yet when she got up, grabbed him by the collar, and threw him down on the bed. When sexually frustrated, a succubus could become aggressive, and a man had better not resist her if he wanted to survive the night. Apparently, her last clients had under-performed, and the lustful look in her glowing black eyes let him know that she was absolutely starved. He liked that.

He grinned as she all but tore open his shirt and removed his chest binder. He preferred his chest to remain covered at all times, but as long as she didn't touch it, he did not mind showing it to her. She knew the rules, and she always respected them. With a low and hungry snarl, her tongue came down upon his belly and slowly went up his skin, while her hips rocked against his. He had no idea what she did with other men, but she knew exactly what to do with his body. And his skin, his lips, his loins ached for her now. If he did not have male parts down there, he still felt them, mentally, and he needed to make love to her like a man. For that part, they had toys, but they were not there yet. She still had a lot of teasing and savoring to do.

Her lips found his, and she dove inside them with a kiss like liquid sugar. He closed his eyes in pure ecstasy as she rolled her tongue with his. It had been so long since she kissed him like this. She removed her lips and licked his once more with her hot tongue, and she gazed into his dazzled eyes. When she was in the mood, he was quite happy to become her plaything and let her ravage him with her passion.

With her eager fingers, she then pulled down his trousers and began to tease him there with her tongue. He let out soft cries and arched his back as she played his throbbing member. He did not have a penis, but he preferred to call that part of him so, and Callie did too. She did not waste time in unnecessary questions about her sexual partners; she was a professional of seduction and sex, and her only goal was to pleasure herself and her partner, by whatever means they liked.

Stanley grabbed onto the pillow behind him and bit his lips, then panted, then bit his lips again. The waves of pleasure were making him dizzy and his entire body was twitching, but he knew Callie would want her release soon, so he reached over to their nightstand, pulled the drawer open, and took out her preferred toy. She noticed it and grinned. With a naughty look in her eyes, she crawled over him and unbuttoned the front of her thin nightgown, under which her erect nipples only made Stanley more eager. He reached up and pulled the night-gown down over her shoulders and began to stroke and caress her rounded breasts. He loved women's breasts – he absolutely adored them. He wanted to touch them day and night and fall asleep against them. The only part of women's bodies he liked even more was their precious sanctuary and its juices of love. To be allowed there with his tongue and his lips was like a dream come true, and once again Callie offered him the privilege. She turned around over him so that they could both taste each other at the same time, and he gorged himself on her. He too had been starved.

And when she was ready, they equipped him with the toy and she sat atop him and rocked herself on him, closing her eyes and rolling her head back. This was what she enjoyed the most, he knew it, and he derived great pleasure from pleasuring her. But as he watched her cheeks turn pink and her lips part and moan for him, he began to wonder again how she felt when doing it with other men. As anger and frustration rose again inside him, he began to thrust underneath her with his hips. She liked it a lot, and the more she seemed to enjoy it, the harder he thrust, as to overpower all the men she had ever slept with. She reached her release, and it was apparently so good this time that she began to revert to her true demon form. Her nether parts became hairier, and so did her upper arms and shoulders. Two small black wings similar to a bat's wings came out of her back, and he could feel a long tail whipping his legs. Damn. It must have been really good sex this time.

She let out a deep, languid sigh and returned to her human-like form and collapsed atop him. He wrapped his arms around her and held her. It had been so long since they had been intimate, but now he felt like they truly had reconnected.

"How are you feeling, darling?" he whispered in her ear.

"Tired..." she said, and they laughed together.

And that night again, after a long time, she fell asleep in his arms. Life had returned to normal at last for Stanley... or so he hoped.

That night, in his dreams, he was once again teleported to the tall pine forest somewhere in the mountains. The sky was dark, and the moonlight fell onto the golden thread tied to the ring finger on his right hand, making it shine. Oddly, the ring was still on the ring finger of his left hand. But he knew the golden thread led to his princess. Little by little, he was finding her in the darkness. Callie was like the ocean. Sometimes she came in like a high tide of love, and sometimes she withdrew from him and he had to go and find her. And he smiled when he again found her behind a large rock, in her peasant dress and feathered mask, and she smiled in return.

The moment he took her hand, the pine forest disappeared, and they were at the masquerade ball again, dancing among all the other masked couples. And among all the beautiful young women in the room, Callie was the most beautiful in her lavender pannier gown, her pale, powdered face surrounded by the luscious black curls of her wig. She was shorter and slenderer, and he assumed this was probably what she looked like as a young demon. There was a magical, almost fairy-like charm to her smile, and even the air seemed to sparkle around her. Now he had seen her true form and lived and worked among creatures like her. He understood her world much better. They had been living in entirely different worlds when they met. She was a creature born from magic and sent down to this world among non-magical creatures, who did not think or live like her, and he was one of them. She had undoubtedly had to adapt to his ways and his pace. And now that he could actually be a part of her world, he was discovering her true face. Callie was independent and headstrong. She had her own ideas and hated constraint. She expected the man she loved to be her companion in all her battles, as well as a bed partner, surpassing all others. He could be all that for her. He wanted to be, and he felt like he was slowly getting there.

She lowered her eyes and her cheeks blushed slightly, as though she wanted to be kissed but did not know how to ask, so he leaned forward. At first, his lips went down her neck, breathing in her sweet, lavender-like scent. She sighed softly with surprise and contentment. He then moved up and kissed the back of her ear, making her skin quiver with delight. He was under her spell now, intoxicated by her charms and the magic flowing around her. He moved back to gaze into her eyes and, with a slow gesture, he removed her mask. But the princess he discovered underneath the mask was not Callie. It was Eve. Eve, the kitchen witch, the impassioned public speaker, the dangerous vampire, the one who, like him, was connected to the world of spirits. She observed him with curious eyes, seeming unsure of his intentions. And though she was not Callie, somehow, he did not want to let go of her. He was drawn to her, perhaps even more so than to Callie. Their hearts, it seemed, were beating at the same rhythm that night, and the same magic flowed around their bodies.

This was a dream, after all, wasn't it? And in dreams, everything was permitted. So he leaned closer to her lips, and she did the same, until their lips touched and locked in the most enchanted kiss Stanley had ever experienced. The ballroom around them disappeared, and they were now in the realm of spirits. Not the sort that haunted people, but the ones who lived in the forests, the rivers, the mountains, those who watched over humans and sometimes intervened in their destinies. Eve wrapped her arms around his neck and kissed him passionately, and if one could climax from a kiss, Stanley thought he would right there and then. He tightened his embrace around her as though their hearts could become one. But the clock struck midnight, and their lips parted. They stood once again in the ballroom, except it was dark and empty. Well, not quite empty. Callie stood beside them, gazing at the two of them with cold eyes.

"C–Callie... It's not what you think!" Stanley gasped. "I... I..."

His eyes turned to Eve, who seemed hurt now and wanting him to own up to his actions and choose her. He turned back to Callie, who simply said: "I'm not thinking anything, Stanley, because I don't care what you do."

There was no emotion whatsoever in her voice, and Stanley thought it was because of the pain he had caused her. Her heart was closing its doors to him once again.

"Callie, darling... I swear it was a mistake! I only love you!" he pleaded, and when his eyes moved back to Eve, he saw hers filling with tears. She took a step back, then another, and ran away.

"Wait! Eve!" he cried.

He opened his eyes in his bedroom. Everything was peaceful again, and he could hear little birds chirping outside. Callie was up and dressed already and packing a few things in a carpet bag for her trip.

"You sure slept in late!" she said, her usual smile on her lips.

"What time is it?" he asked, sitting up in the bed.

"Ten o'clock. I must leave soon," she said.

He got out of bed and headed over to the washbasin and washed his face, still feeling guilty about his dream. But it was just that: a dream. It meant absolutely nothing. He then went over to the dresser and looked for his favorite brown suit, but didn't find it.

"Darling, where's my brown suit?" he asked.

"Oh, I threw it away. There were holes in the sleeves. You can wear one of the new suits I got for you," she said casually.

He turned to her and stared at her, astounded.

"It was my favorite suit! We could have had the holes fixed," he said.

"Oh, please Stanley. I can't have you going to meetings in a patched-up suit. Besides, brown doesn't suit you; blue is your color," she replied without even turning to him, and he once again felt like this was some deliberate act on her part.

She finished packing her bag, stepped out of the bedroom, and grabbed her hat in the hallway.

"I'll be home in two days. See you later," she said, and she left the apartment.

'See you later'? Was that all he got after she just told him she had thrown out his favorite suit? Not even a goodbye kiss or an apology?

He slammed the dresser's drawer and picked up the black suit he had left on the chair. He checked the pockets: the watch and the feather were still there. Funny how he had the magical watch all this time, and she never even thought about looking inside his pockets. Well then, since she wanted it that way, he would not go to the feminist meeting; he would travel to London to investigate Belphegor and the candyman. If he hurried, he could still get to Waverley Station and board the same train as Callie unnoticed. So he dressed as quickly as he could, grabbed only his hat and wallet, and rushed out the door.

Waverley Station was just a few blocks away from the building where they lived on Cockburn Street, and he made it there on time and was able to mingle with the crowd and board the Special Scotch Express without being seen. He took a seat at the end of the train, just in case Callie decided to stretch her legs and walk around during the trip. He was angry with her but also with himself for cheating on her in his dream again. Why could he not remain faithful in thought to the only woman he had ever loved? Yes, she could be spiteful sometimes, but she had never cheated on him. He knew of her occupation; she was always upfront with him about it, and he could not honestly accuse her of anything except annoying him with all her feminine games. Now he fully understood the men who said that women were a mystery to them. Whatever he did, however hard he tried, he could never quite figure out what was on Callie's mind, and because she always expected him to guess and he failed to, there would always be tension between them. But he loved her. He gazed at the ring on his finger. No, he would not remove it, no matter what she did. He was the one responsible for their current situation and he still had to make amends for it, and his temperamental nature was not making it easy. His vision was beginning to flicker again; he needed to calm down before he unwillingly killed someone. So he closed his eyes and drew in a deep breath.

Time sometimes flies when one is angry or anxious, and the five-and-a-half-hour trip went by in the blink of an eye. With the one-hour stop it made in York, the train arrived at King's Cross Station in London at approximately five thirty. Stanley lowered his hat, pulled the curtains over the window beside him, and waited until most of the passengers had disembarked before getting off the train. He breathed in deeply when his feet hit the platform. London still stunk. The air was thick and polluted, and he already missed the fresh air of Edinburgh. The demon of jealousy inside him told him to follow Callie, but it would only cause more trouble between them. He knew what she was in town for, and he did not need to know the name of her client. He was just another man, not her lover.

He walked slowly through King's Cross Station, his absent gaze wandering from the long trains and their monster steam engines capable of speeds he would never have thought possible as a child, to the dull-faced people clad in the fashion of the moment. Everyone was in a hurry in London, as always, but the crowd no longer seemed so hostile and annoying to him. He was a part of them now, living like an almost normal man with his wife. A demon hitman and his succubus partner. His life as a broke and solitary paranormal investigator seemed so far away...

He came out on the street and called a cab. For a moment, he thought about returning to his old office and checking on Cornelius and William, but would they even want to see him after he abandoned them? He shook his head sadly and got into the cab.

Stanley knew exactly where to go to pursue his investigation, and that was Belphegor's office. He got off the cab a block away from the office, walked into a dark alleyway, and made himself invisible. It was past six o'clock and the sun was setting. Perfect. He casually walked the rest of the way and stood in front of the small, two-story office building. It was closed, and so were the shutters on the windows. He drew a pocket knife he always carried on him just in case, and tried to force the lock on the door, but it was already broken. Someone else was inside. So, as quietly as he could, he opened the door and walked in.

The door to Belphegor's office was open a crack. He peeked inside and found none other than Callie rummaging through his things. She had lied to him - again - and seemed to know exactly what she was looking for. With the precision of a spy, she reached under the desk and found a small key hidden in a secret compartment. And with it, she opened the desk's top drawer and grabbed the item she had come for: the miniature pocket watch. Her eyes shone with excitement and relief, and she held it against her chest for a few seconds. Then, she turned the crown and nothing happened. Stanley quietly entered the room and stood still behind her in the darkness.

"What? Why isn't it working?" she whispered, trying it again and again.

Stanley let his heartbeat quicken and made himself visible again. She lifted her gaze and saw his reflection in the window, and spun around, startled.

"Callie, what are you doing here?" he asked her, trying to remain calm.

She scowled and lifted her chin defiantly.

"So you followed me?"

"What are you doing here?" he asked again.

"That's none of your business," she said.

"It is my business, since you lied to me," he said. "Why don't you just tell me the truth?"

"The truth?" she said, now in a spiteful voice. "I came here to get my pocket watch back."

"The one you made or the one you stole from Belphegor?" he asked coldly.

"The one I stole," she said.

At least she was talking now, and perhaps he could understand the meaning behind all of this. But her defiant demeanor somehow told him that the truth was much darker and twisted than he had imagined.

"I did steal the Time Key from Belphegor and I was caught. But he offered me a deal," she said. "There was a demon higher in the hierarchy who was looking for someone named 'Sophie Suspect'. They wanted you, but they knew you would be hard to catch, and it would be even harder to convince you to make a pact with them. They knew that if they tried to force you, you might choose death instead, you were capable of it."

Indeed, that sounded like him. If he had found himself trapped with Beelzebub, and if Callie never came into his life, he would have chosen death over becoming her thing.

"My first task was to positively identify you, so I sought out everyone in London with the name 'Suspect'," Callie continued. "It was not easy, since all we had was a photograph of you as a child, and you had changed both your name and appearance, but I eventually located you. I opened a shop and they let me use the Time Key to lure you. You were a paranormal investigator. I knew you could not resist a mystery around time travel, so I made you want to investigate me, and then I made you fall in love with me. Once I successfully delivered you to those who wanted you, the charges against me were formally dropped."

Stanley could feel his blood boiling with anger, and his heartbeat was quickening again. So everything he thought he had – their love, their home – all of it was just a lie... How naïve could he be to never suspect anything? His heart was breaking inside and his world crumbling to pieces, but more than the fact he had been lied to and used, it was the fact that she never loved him at all that crushed him. He had given up everything he had, his life as a human, his freedom, even his closest friends, for a lie.

"But you didn't do it only to be free," he said slowly. "You returned here for the Time Key. Why?"

"To be with Elmer," she said. "I know I can't prevent his death; he died from consumption. But if I could go back in time and just spend a few more years with him, then I would do anything for it!"

"Even destroy another man?" he said.

"Yes, I would do anything to be with the man I love!" she suddenly cried, her eyes filling with tears of anger. "But that's not you, Stanley. It was never you..."

Stanley's vision was beginning to flicker from black to red now, but Callie did not fear him. She tried the pocket watch again, without any results. He pulled the one he was carrying from his pocket.

"Are you looking for this, by any chance?" he asked in a dangerous voice.

"You... You had it all along?" she gasped. "Give it to me!"

She tried to snatch it out of his hand, but he backed away.

"You want it? Come and get it!" he said, and he opened his mouth and swallowed it.

"No!" she cried. "What did you do, you stupid fool?"

Her cries were truly desperate, but her despair was that of a woman who had just lost the only means to be reunited with the man she loved, and that was not Stanley. In a fit of rage, he grabbed her wrists and pushed her against the desk. If she knew so much about him, she knew how dangerous his eyes could be when he was angry, and yet she held his gaze and struggled to free herself.

He was furious, blinded by rage now, and he had only one thought on his mind: to kill the one causing him so much pain. But before he could, Callie's body began to lift in the air and her limbs seemed to twist on their own. She let out a loud cry and struggled, but whatever force was holding her up there was stronger. Stanley turned to his right, and Belphegor stood in the doorway. He looked like Belphegor and wore the same blue suit Stanley had seen him in before, but he carried the scent of candy. The man grinned viciously as he tortured Callie, and hearing her screams only seemed to arouse him more.

"No! Let go of her!" Stanley cried, lunging at him, but the candyman disappeared and reappeared on the other side of the room. Callie then stopped screaming and struggling, and her limp body fell to the ground. Her lifeless eyes were open and staring at Stanley, and tears of blood rolled quietly down her cheeks.

"No! No!" Stanley cried at the top of his lungs.

He dropped to his knees and took her head and cradled it in his arms, calling out her name and crying.

The candyman reached in his pocket, pulled out another piece of barley sugar, and began chewing on it.

"What's the matter? Weren't you just going to kill her yourself?" he asked in a mocking tone.

"How could you?" Stanley cried, turning to him. His vision was so blurred with tears he could barely see him, and he thought he was the one who had just died, so intense was the pain in his chest. The memories of her touch, of their first kiss, the look in her eyes when they made love, and their imperfect home flashed before his eyes, and even if he now knew they were all lies, he wanted all of them back. He would have given anything to have them back. She was the one who had gotten him out of his sordid home in London and shown him magic, the spirits of nature, and everything he could be. Living in Edinburgh with her had been his dream, his fairytale, except it was never meant to end with 'happily ever after'. And though he hated her for lying to him all along, he still loved her with all his heart because she was the one who had made this dream possible. He could not live on without her, not anymore.

"Callie! My love! Please, breathe! Breathe!" he said, choking on his tears, but none of his pleas could bring her back. He could sense that her spirit had already left her body. Demons died differently than humans, and no light came for them. They left their body and simply vanished into the darkness. But even if she was in Hell now, then he wanted to be there with her.

"Kill me! Take my life!" he cried desperately.

"Why be so dramatic? She never even loved you," the candy-man replied casually.

He was a hitman and felt absolutely nothing for those he killed, just like Stanley - most of the time.

Stanley let his head fall on Callie's body and wept loudly. The warm arms that used to hold him were now ice cold, and the chest he used to rest his head on, listening to her fast heartbeat, was quiet. She was no longer inside the body he was cradling in his arms, and never would be. She was gone forever.

"I want to go home! I want to go home!" he cried, and something churned in his stomach.

He had forgotten he had just swallowed the Time Key. If he had not been so stupid, perhaps he could still have used it and turned back time to prevent her death. He would have done anything to turn back time now, to see her alive again, even if she hated him.

His stomach churned again, and he began to feel nauseous. He felt cold at first, then hot, then his body moved on its own like it was being hurled in every direction at the same time from within, and then he crashed into himself again and found himself sitting on the floor, in his childhood home.

CHAPTER 11

STANLEY LOOKED AROUND THE dark room. He was in the dining room of his old house, but not in his upside-down mind this time. The portraits on the walls looked normal, except the one of him and Giselle was missing.

"Callie?" he said, slowly getting up.

His entire body was sore, and he felt sick. The last thing he could remember was begging someone to take him home. He had meant 'I want to go home, before any of this happened', but those were not the words he uttered. So had he actually managed to turn back time, or was he just teleported to a different location?

He slowly walked across the room and the floor creaked under his feet. Immediately, Cornelius came out of the wall to see who the intruder was. He was still the same seven-year-old child, dressed in clothing from the last century.

"Cornelius!" Stanley said, overjoyed, but the child ghost moved back and frowned.

"Who are you?" he said.

"It's me, Stanley!" Stanley said.

And before he could say more, the door pushed open and his child self was standing there, in a long nightgown.

"Who are you?" he also asked.

Stanley stared at his young self in shock, and then he realized that he had actually gone back several years in time. That meant Callie was still alive, somewhere, and if he could find her, perhaps he could change everything and prevent her death. But if he traumatized his child self, he did not know what the consequences might be for his future self in this timeline.

"I'm a friend," he said with a smile. "You need to go back to bed now."

They all heard noise outside, in the backyard, and his child self and Cornelius were scared.

"Stay right here," he told the children, and he stepped out of the room.

He went into the hallway and opened the door to the backyard. It was pitch black and quiet outside, and a light drizzle whipped his face, confirming to him that this was not a dream. He noticed footprints on the ground. They left the small stone path and went into the muddy lawn. As a precaution, he made himself invisible and then followed the footsteps, making sure to step into them and not leave any of his own. With the darkness, even the light rain would not reveal his presence. And there, behind the house, he found his father standing with his back to him. He was wearing a brown suit that night - not his usual colors. He stood before a flower bed as though he was waiting for something to happen, and Stanley thought he heard him whisper: "Giselle!"

The dirt underneath the flower bed began to stir, and a small, blueish hand came out, followed by another. Stanley suddenly recalled his dream: Giselle was about to come out of her grave. So she was buried in their backyard after all, only not where he thought.

His father immediately rushed over to her and dug through the earth with his hands to help her out, and her decayed face then emerged. She wrapped her blue arms around his neck and, in a monstrous voice, said: "Father!"

Stanley's father let out a terrified shriek and immediately disengaged himself from her. Was he only now realizing that no one could bring back the dead – not as they used to be?

"Y-You... what are you?" he said.

"Father..." she said again, but he scrambled back to the house's wall, against which were leaning various gardening tools, including a pitchfork, and grabbed it, shaking.

Giselle crawled out of her grave, her dirt-covered brown hair hiding her face.

"Father...?" she said.

"Don't come near me, you fiend!" their father shouted, but she kept inching closer to him, crawling to him in the dirt.

When she was about to reach him, he moved forward and put the pitchfork through her throat. She did not bleed, since she was already dead, but simply gasped and looked up to him with her yellow eyes. She fell backwards and their father put the pitchfork through her body several more times until she no longer moved. Then he stood there in shock, breathing heavily.

Stanley observed the scene quietly. There would be no point in him intervening. His father had made a mistake, thinking he could bring back the dead, and now he had to face the consequences of it. It seemed like both of them were prone to making stupid and dangerous decisions.

Since there was nothing he could do, he retraced his footsteps and returned to the house, but his foot missed the small step in front of the back door, and he fell forward. He was not sure what happened next, but he remembered thinking: "Forward!" and he opened his eyes, laying on the floor, halfway inside the house and halfway out. He pushed himself up slowly. His chin was sore. He had probably bruised it in his fall. He looked behind him, and the backyard was still and the night sky clear.

"Shit," he said.

He had moved forward in time just by thinking about it, and he had no clue where and when he was now. And then he heard his own voice screaming outside and the sound of a heavy iron carriage door shutting. This was the night his father sent him away.

He jumped to his feet and ran through the hallway and into the dining room. The shutters on the window were closed, and through the cracks he could already see the carriage leaving. But he knew he would be alright: Cornelius would soon appear and rescue him. Perhaps it was even the best thing that had happened to him throughout all his childhood, since after that he was able to live on his own and be free. He would have to face homelessness and become a thief to survive, but eventually, things would get better for him.

He then heard his father's footsteps going up the stairs to the third floor and frowned. He was alone in the house with that bastard now. No child he risked frightening, and he knew what was up in the attic. So he would make his father pay...

Making himself invisible again, he slowly went up the creaking stairs to the second and then the third floor and looked around. All the rooms were empty. That meant his father was in the attic with Beelzebub. He opened the door to the staircase leading up there and made himself visible again. He wanted his father to see him, after all, to see what he had become because of him before he died.

He could still feel the demon's heavy, evil presence everywhere, but he no longer feared it, so he ran up the stairs this time, his vision already flickering in black and red, and kicked the door open. His father was standing in the middle of the room, in the dark, and gazing at the moonlight through the attic's small window. He had covered his shoulders with a long black cape like he was dressing up for Halloween.

"Still playing the wannabe sorcerer? Turn around and face me, you bastard!" Stanley said in a menacing tone.

His father slowly turned around. He was still the old, wrinkled man with thinning brown hair and a light beard Stanley remembered, but now that he had lived in the underworld, he realized that something was different about him. His skin was the color of death itself, and his eyes were no longer hazel, but black. The room was filled with a sweet, almost floral scent. Now Stanley knew exactly what he was, and why he avoided the light.

"A vampire, huh? What a change," he said, smirking.

"Sophie... you too have changed... in the last few minutes," his father said with a certain confusion mixed with anger.

"It's Stanley now, and not only my name has changed," Stanley said, advancing toward him. "I had to become a demon thanks to you and your stupid spells! What the hell were you thinking?" he shouted in his face.

His father had noticed the flickering in his eyes, and his own eyes began to flicker in response, in black and red hues. They walked in circles around each other, their eyes engaged in a silent duel, like beasts preparing to fight.

"I was only correcting a mistake that was made," he said.

"Giselle's death, right? And you thought my life was worth trading for hers?" Stanley said.

"Yes."

His father was a coward, but he had no shame in admitting what he had done to him.

"Why?" Stanley asked.

"Because you are evil – just like me," his father said with a cruel grin.

At least Stanley could not argue that. They were both just as bad.

"I'm not afraid of you," he said.

His father grinned and said: "You should be. Necromancers do not let each other live."

"What the hell is a necromancer?" Stanley said, but his father suddenly vanished.

He looked around the room, certain he was there, and with his enhanced vision in red and black overdrive mode, he could see him moving – or rather flying – quickly around the room. Spirits then emerged from the walls and the floor. Stanley knew some of them already, but others did not belong to this house. But they were not coming forth to his bidding: his father was the one calling them.

"Is that all you can do, 'necromancer'? Call a few ghosts?" Stanley said, laughing.

But the ghosts suddenly converged on him and grabbed his arms and legs, lifting him up in the air, and though he struggled, they were too numerous. He was trapped now, and they were beginning to pull his limbs in every direction. They were going to dismember him.

"You would kill your own child, you bastard?" he shouted.

"Did you not come to kill me?" his father replied in a mocking voice. He was enjoying this, as the new bloodthirsty creature he had become. Stanley was going to die, and in one of the most horrific ways.

His vision flickered faster and faster as he felt that his limbs were about to be torn off, and his heart was beating so fast he thought it might burst out of his chest. He let out a loud shriek, the same he had heard in all his nightmares, and finally freed himself from the spirits. Then, he lunged at his father and caught him mid-flight and pinned him to the floor. They looked into each other's eyes and Stanley could almost see the reflection of his own wrath in his father's twisted, furious face. Both their eyes were flickering now and their hands were on each other's throats, and both said: "DIE!"

Stanley suddenly felt as though all the air had left his lungs, and every limb in his body was paralyzed, and he could see the same happening to his father. They had the same powers and were killing each other. *What a stupid way to die*, he thought. He tried to breathe one last time, and then everything went black.

Darkness had found Stanley again, except it seemed peaceful now after all that had happened to him. He let his heart slow down and his body turn cold, confident now that it was all over. This was finally the end of the road and of all his suffering. He felt his body fall softly to the ground as though it were being carried on a feather bed, and his heart fully stopped. Death was so quiet. There was not a sound around him and all anger, all bitterness flowed out of his body like a disease he had been carrying for too long. He lay there in the silence for what seemed like hours, simply letting the darkness gently lull him to sleep. And then, he felt his soul leaving his body, as light as the air around him, and it flew upward, high above the old house, above humans, and the cities where they suffered. It flew over hills and rivers, and soon met up with the cold northern winds of Scotland, and there it was joined by the sìth and all the spirits of nature. They played together in the clouds with the joy of eternal children, unaffected by the fear and angst of the world beneath them, and then he glided back down to the ground. He was no longer Stanley, but a feather in the sky, ready to let the winds guide him wherever they wanted without offering any resistance.

He slowly opened his eyes again in a forest, laying on a bed of leaves, and all round him small green lights danced like fairies. He remembered his life, from beginning to end, the good times and the bad times. Faces moved before him like the flickering images of a magic lantern. His parents, Giselle, Mary, Annie, Cornelius, William, Marvin, the mysterious author John, Eve, and... Callie. All the pain and suffering she had caused him vanished before her smile, and he let go of the guilt of falling for her. He was not wrong for loving her, and he forgave her for not loving him in return because, somewhere, he knew that she too was lying on the ground, perhaps on a bed of flowers, and she too was letting go of the suffering of her loss. And then he saw Cornelius kneeling beside him, and he was crying like the child he was.

"Don't cry, Cornelius," he whispered.

"S-Stanley... please... don't leave me..." Cornelius sobbed.

"It's too late. I'm already gone," Stanley said.

"No... No..." Cornelius said, crying even harder.

Stanley also felt tears rolling down his cheeks at the thought of being separated from him, and all the time they could still have spent together.

"I'm sorry..." he said softly.

Cornelius disappeared, and in the distance, Stanley could now see Cat approaching. The creature walked slowly over to him and sat beside him on the leaves, crossing its small legs.

"My, what a journey..." it said peacefully.

"You wouldn't believe it," Stanley said. "But it's all over now."

"Is it?" Cat said, grinning.

"Take me home now, where I belong," Stanley said, closing his eyes.

He opened his eyes again to the feeling of a cold, hard surface underneath him. He breathed in deeply and inhaled ashes and began to cough.

"What the hell?" he said, pushing himself up.

He looked around him: he was back in the attic where he had died, and he had been lying on a pile of ashes on the floor. His heart was beating in his chest again, and he realized he was still alive.

"No... No!" he cried in a panic.

He staggered to his feet. The attic was still the same as he had left it, only it looked older and dustier. The window was shattered and birds had made their nest inside, on a beam. He could no longer sense anyone's presence – ghost, demon, or others. Everything was dark and quiet.

Stunned and confused, he crossed the room and walked down to the third floor of the house. It too looked older and dustier, and the top of the walls were stained from apparent roof leaks. Nothing was quite the same anymore – especially not him – but he could not tell what had changed.

He walked into Mary's old bedroom and stepped in front of the wardrobe, which had a tall mirror on it. Yes, he was still Stanley, but his skin was paler now, and every little imperfection on it, every scar and pimple, had been erased. And his eyes, his hazel eyes, were now black with a reddish glow to them. He touched his face, then the mirror, then he opened his mouth and stuck out his tongue. Beelzebub's mark was still on it. But his teeth were different. His canines had grown longer. He frowned and closed his mouth, then smelled his collar. He still smelled somewhat like woodfire smoke, but his scent was also fresh and clean, like that of fresh cut grass in the summer. Now he had no doubt he had become a vampire like his father, but how? He did not remember him biting him before he died. Was there another way one could become a vampire? And what did this new transformation mean?

Still in shock, he left his house. The streets of Kensington were dark and empty and lit only by the few lampposts. Not knowing what to do, he began to walk aimlessly until he came across a solitary cab. He stopped and watched it as it approached him, and the cab also stopped. It looked like an ordinary cab, pulled by a black horse, except the coachman was none other than Cat. It tipped its hat to greet him and said: "Good evening, traveler."

"What happened? Did you do this to me?" Stanley asked him, too confused to feel any anger.

"I did not," Cat said, smiling. "You asked me to take you home. Luckily, I had a nighttime cab in my hat."

"In your hat?" Stanley repeated.

"Will you be riding with me tonight? If so, we should make haste. The sun will rise soon and I believe your kind does not like the sun," Cat said.

Stanley frowned but climbed into the front seat with him. He wanted to talk, but Cat whistled and the black horse's heavy hooves kicked the paved street, and the cab took off into the sky. Stanley looked down, surprised, and held himself to the seat.

"You'd better hang on tight. Seatbelts are optional on this model," Cat said.

"What's a seatbelt?" Stanley asked, but Cat only smiled in response.

The cab flew across the sky and over the city, gliding quietly over the empty streets, the River Thames, the docks and their ships, and everything seemed so small and unimportant that Stanley was almost grateful to be back in his new form, if only to see the world through the eyes of a sith. But reality hit him again when the cab landed in front of his old office, as quietly as it had left the ground.

"It looks like we have arrived," Cat said.

"What day is it?" Stanley asked him.

The sìth pulled out a small notebook and read through the notes it had scribbled inside.

"Let's see... 'Stanley returns to his home on July sixteenth, 1887'."

"1887..." Stanley repeated in shock.

So he had moved forward again, from 1878, the year his father had sent him away, to 1887, and several months after Callie's death. But he did not want to go back in time ever again; there was only sadness there.

"I must leave now. I have a train to catch," Cat said, putting away the notebook. "Unless you would like to return to Edinburgh with me?"

Stanley shook his head. No, he never wanted to return there.

"My home is here, with Cornelius and William," he said.

He got off the cab and turned around.

"Thank you, Cat," he said.

"We will meet again, traveler of the spiritual realm," Cat promised.

It whistled and the black horse's hooves kicked the ground, and this time the cab disappeared underneath the pavement. Stanley stared at it for a moment, then turned around. Nothing surprised him anymore in the sort of world he lived in.

Drawing in a deep breath, he walked up to the door and tried to open it. Of course it was locked, like he had left it. He reached into the pockets of his trousers, not really expecting to find anything there, but he mysteriously found the key. Had Cat slipped it in his pocket when he wasn't looking? He unlocked the door and stepped inside, and his feet immediately hit a pile of mail on the floor. Apparently, William and Cornelius were still angry and had not read his letters.

He walked into his office and lit an oil lamp.

"William! Cornelius! I'm home!" he said aloud, but they did not answer him, so he did what he always did when he got home: he lit a fire in the fireplace, then went over to the windows and made sure the shutters were closed tightly and the curtains pulled. If he truly was a vampire, he did not really want to find out what sunlight could do to him. He would have to do some research on the subject. He then went over to his desk and brushed off the thick layer of dust with his hand. He remembered the last time he did it, for Callie, just before they left London. And now the reality of her death struck him: he was here, in this world, without her. Even traveling through time had not helped save her, and it had only made everything worse for him. His eyes filled with tears again. He needed his friends now, more than ever.

"William! Cornelius! I'm sorry I was gone for so long, I really am..." he said, and Cornelius finally came out of the wall.

"Cornelius!" Stanley said.

He stretched out his arms to him, but Cornelius did not come. Instead, he gazed at him with sad eyes.

"What a welcome!" Stanley said, frowning. "I just died and came back, you know."

Cornelius still did not answer.

"So where's William? Sulking somewhere upstairs?" Stanley asked.

"He's gone," Cornelius said.

"Gone? To another house?" Stanley asked, not understanding.

"No, Stanley. The light came for him. He was scared. I told him everything would be alright, but I don't really know that..."

Stanley stared at him, speechless, and his hands dropped the papers he had been holding as tears slowly rolled down his cold cheeks. William... gone...

"But I had promised him I would be there..." he whispered.

"His time had come. He could not wait for you," Cornelius said, shaking his little head.

Stanley let himself fall to his knees and burst into tears. After all, he had been through, after dying and coming back to life, he would not even have the comfort of seeing his friend again – a friend who had put up with his bad mood for so many years. He let out a cry of pain and wept loudly. Cornelius walked over to him, sat beside him on the floor, and placed his hand on his shoulder.

"I was very sad when you left us, but I always believed you would come back," he said softly. "So when the light came for me next, I hid from it."

Stanley reached for his cold hand and held it, except now his skin was so cold they were the same temperature.

They went to the sofa and sat down together, holding hands.

"I'm so sorry... for everything," Stanley said. "Callie was a fraud... she tricked me from the start, and I fell for it all. I was tricked into becoming a demon, and now it seems like I have graduated from demon to vampire. I just keep getting into more and more trouble. I can't even die peacefully..."

Cornelius let go of his hand and wrapped his little arms around him, and now he was crying, too.

"I don't want you to die and leave me again!" he said.

Stanley embraced him and kissed his hair.

"I'm not going anywhere. Not anymore."

Silence fell upon them and they cried together, letting out all the sadness. They had been apart for so long, and so much had happened, but they were together again, in the place they called home, and Stanley promised himself he would never again leave Cornelius behind, not for anyone in this world.

"On the bright side, now we can be together forever... if you want it," Cornelius said.

"Yes, we'll be together. I will never leave you alone again," Stanley promised.

"So, will you tell me what happened?" Cornelius said.

"It's a long story," Stanley said with a deep sigh.

He told him about Edinburgh and Beelzebub, and how he became a demon for Callie. He then told him about his life as a hitman, how Callie died, and how he returned to his old home and he and his father killed each other. Cornelius quietly listened to him.

"And then I awakened as a vampire and a cat-sìth brought me home in a magical cab," Stanley concluded, wiping away his tears. His eyes were so swollen from crying now he could barely see.

"The cat-sìth brought you *home*..." Cornelius said.

"Yes, to *my* home, with you," Stanley said.

They heard rattling upstairs. Not all spirits had left him - his father's was still there, and he wanted something from him. He looked up at the ceiling.

"You don't have to talk to him if you don't want to," Cornelius said.

"I don't really want to, but I need to..." Stanley said, slowly getting up.

He took the oil lamp, went out into the hallway and up the stairs to his bedroom. There, he placed the lamp on his desk and brought out a chair. He sat on the bed, facing it.

"You can come out now, Father. I'm ready to hear what you have to say," he said in an empty voice.

Cornelius came in through the wall and stood in a corner. He would be there as his emotional support. And then his father appeared, sitting in the chair. He was wearing the same clothing as the night he died and his hands and legs were in chains. His head hung low and he would not look into his son's eyes.

"I killed you, Mother, and Giselle," Stanley said, breaking the silence. "Do you hate me? Is that why you've been haunting me?"

His father shook his head sadly and finally lifted his gaze to meet his. His eyes were hazel again.

"If you hadn't, I probably would have," he said in a defeated voice. "Violence is in our blood."

"Why? Why us?" Stanley asked.

His father shook his head.

"I don't know. Destiny... Or perhaps it is our curse."

Stanley gazed at him with hateful eyes. If anyone was responsible for all of this, it was him. He was the one who gave him this cursed blood.

"I made many mistakes in my life," his father said.

"You did," Stanley said.

"My first mistake was refusing to see that I had a son and not a daughter – that you were Stanley and not Sophie."

"It sure took you a long time to realize that..."

"And I should have seen that you needed my help and not my scorn, that you needed a father."

"Growing up as your child sure was lonely and sad. I don't know what's worse: having parents who ignore you or having no parents at all."

"I was stupid and made a pact with a demon. But as you grew up, I began to change."

"Into a vampire?"

"Yes. It started with a growing desire for violence and the fear of sunlight. And then I began to see your 'imaginary friends', the spirits you were talking to. But I thought we were both insane, so I told you they were not real."

"So you lied to me all those years..." Stanley said.

"What would you do if you knew you were evil, and you had a child just like you?" his father said. "I tried to hide from what I was, to run away by investigating the occult. Having knowledge of the dark world made me feel all-powerful, and I summoned a demon, thinking I could bring back Giselle... But what came out of her grave was not her. And after that, my condition only worsened. I took potions and practiced rituals to rid myself of whatever it was that was devouring me from within, but it only ever got worse. One night I went to bed as a human and awakened as a vampire, thirsting for blood – your blood and Annie's. There were no other vampires around me to tell me what I was, but when I started hunting on the streets to feed my need for human blood, I encountered a few. They told me I was a necromancer, and they feared me. Necromancers are vampires who can summon the dead. Some of them just talk to them, but others can also control them. They are the most dangerous of all vampires. Their desire to collect souls is insatiable, and they may kill ruthlessly until they gather an army of spirits under their control. They are territorial by nature, like spiders, and they do not let each other live. We are both necromancers – soul snatchers. When I realized this, I knew I had to get you away from our house. If I didn't, you would either become like me and I would have to kill you, or the demon I summoned would come for you on your eighteenth birthday. So I sent you away."

Stanley lowered his eyes and wiped away another tear. He could see in his father's eyes that he was finally telling him the truth, all the truth, and there was good and evil inside him. Sending his reclusive child away and possibly having him locked up in an insane asylum was the last thing he could think of to save him – from himself and the forces of darkness.

"I have a question," Stanley said, returning his eyes to him. "Why not just have killed me then and there? Our lives would have been easier, don't you think?"

"Because I love you," his father said. "I hate your bad manners, your temper, and your arrogance, but I am no better than you. I know you were never able to love me, and it's my fault. But I loved you. I will always love you..."

Stanley remained speechless. Neither of his parents had ever told him they loved him.

"I am stuck here until you decide to let me go. I am attached to you until you forgive me," his father then said. "So please, let me move on to the other side. That is all I ask from you."

"I will. But before you go..." Stanley started, but he suddenly burst into tears.

"Yes?" his father said.

"Would you hug me... just once?" Stanley said.

His body was shaking, and he could not lift his gaze. Too much suffering, too many losses at once. He could not endure yet another one. But his father got out of his chair and walked over to him, dragging his chains. He sat on the bed and wrapped his arm around Stanley's shoulder, and Stanley cried even more.

"Even after all that happened, I'm glad you are my son..." he said, finally breaking through the barriers of Stanley's heart. And the moment his anger lifted and he began to forgive his father, a dim light came searching for the sorrowful ghost and he was pulled into it. Stanley held his hand until he disappeared completely, and silence fell upon the room again.

CHAPTER 12

STANLEY FELL ASLEEP BESIDE Cornelius that night, and he slept throughout the next day. And when he opened his eyes, he closed them again. He did not want to be awake, he only wanted to sleep, forever. His soul had aged so much in the last few months of his life that he felt like a hundred-year-old man already. But, with his new body, he still needed to feed, although differently than a human, and hunger eventually awakened him from his slumber. He slowly sat up in the bed, rubbing his eyes.

"I'm starving..." he grunted.

"Do you still eat food?" Cornelius asked.

"I don't think so," Stanley said.

He reached for the oil lamp on the nightstand and lit it and looked around the room. The shutters on the window and the curtains would forever remain closed now. Like it or not, this was his new reality. He might as well get used to it.

"Where is that book?" he asked.

"Which one?" Cornelius said.

"The one by Eve Chauvin. If anyone knows something about vampires, it should be her, since she is one."

"Good idea! Let's read it!" Cornelius immediately said.

He got out of the bed and went through the wall, and soon returned with the book - through the door this time since books could not cross walls. He handed it to Stanley and slipped into the bed with him.

"This is just like the good old times, when I used to read you The Adventures of Tom Sawyer," Stanley said, smiling.

"Oh, I wish you would read me that book again!" Cornelius said.

"We'll find a copy then, and any other books you would like me to read you," Stanley said.

His fingers brushed against the cover of the book as he remembered Eve. Perhaps the only thing he looked forward to in his new life was seeing her again, even if only by attending one of her lectures. She was a vampire and now he was sure that she was, as he had first thought, very old. She had somehow found a way to navigate through her existence in the underworld without being swayed and falling into the wrong hands. He admired her. He was not that smart.

He opened the book to the chapter about vampires and read it again. According to it, vampires fed primarily on human blood, it was their sustenance, and they drank it by biting them. They could bite humans anywhere, but feeding was quicker if they bit the jugular vein. They drank all their victim's blood at once, for if they didn't, the human turned into a hungry ghoul, which was something in between human and vampire. One could not become human again after becoming a ghoul, nor could they become a vampire unless they then drank the vampire's blood, and that was nearly impossible. *'For vampires when they hunt are just like men looking to spend one night with a girl and vanish the next day. Good luck knocking on their door!'* Eve wrote. Stanley smiled as he read her words. He liked her character and spirit.

There were two ways one could become a vampire: one of them was to be bitten by a vampire and then to drink their blood, however this resulted in the human becoming the vampire's eternal servant. And there was another category of vampires: humans who died, usually between their twenties and thirties, and awakened again as undead creatures. If a human destined to become a vampire died of disease or was murdered before their natural transformation, the transformation took place upon their death and they still became a vampire.

Stanley read those lines again. It was what had happened to him and his father. So they would both have become vampires, no matter what...

Eve then went on to explain that vampires did not age and were almost immortal. When injured, the wound healed on its own in a few seconds. But there were ways to eliminate a vampire: a stake through the heart, contact with silver, which burned their skin, injuries causing a sudden and abundant loss of blood such as decapitation, and lastly, boredom. Indeed, Stanley could imagine how after living for thousands of years old vampires might just want to walk into the sunlight and be freed from their curse. According to Eve, starvation could weaken a vampire but not kill them, and neither could drowning. It was an uncomfortable experience, but no vampire ever died from contact with water.

Apart from these few rules to follow and dangers to avoid, she said, vampires could live almost normal lives among humans. They were artists, writers, dressmakers, or even celebrities. They went out and dined in restaurants – red meat dishes were their universal preference – they could enjoy good wine and music, and the best part of it all was that they never aged. After reading this book, Stanley had no doubt that romantic young women might try to meet a handsome vampire and ask him to transform them so they could live a gilded life of eternal youth. But there was something Eve never talked about, something only Stanley knew. It was her he had seen in the pine forest in his dream, he was sure of it, and what she had shared at the meeting he attended led him to believe that she was like him. She was probably born male and identified as a woman. He wondered what the world looked like from the other end of the spectrum. For him, coming out as a man and wearing men's clothes came with privileges he would not have had as 'Sophie'. But Eve would have had all those privileges if she wore the clothing people wanted her to wear. Giving up those privileges to be herself must have been a lot harder than what he gave up, and yet she was fighting for everyone to be equal: men, women, humans, and all the other creatures in this world.

His stomach reminded him of the reason why he was reading the book in the first place: he was hungry. So he closed it, got up and got dressed, and headed out into the streets. He was not the sort of person to question himself endlessly about why he was the way he was. He always knew he was Stanley, not Sophie. When he became a demon, he accepted it, and now that he was a vampire, he also accepted it. He knew he needed to hunt and, with his new instincts and the clarifications provided by Eve's book, he knew how to feed, but he still did not know how to find prey. What human's life was worth taking? He was not quite as sentimental as he had once been, but he did not feel happy about the whole prospect. Still, that made him a hypocrite, because he never even thought about the animal's lives he took when he consumed meat as a human.

His vampire eyes browsed through the faces on the street, and now his sharp senses picked up on their scent as well – much better than before. Some humans smelled very appetizing, others not, and he found that the most attractive to him were young women. He loved women as a human, and now he loved them as his dinner as a vampire. Somehow it made sense to him, though he could not explain why. So he picked an innocent young woman who happened to turn down a dark alley, and he followed her. She soon picked up on her pursuer and turned around. But, perhaps because of his slender figure and perfect, marble-like features, she did not fear him. It was her mistake.

"Who are you?" she asked, but he did not answer.

He walked up to her casually and hooked his eyes on hers, and she seemed paralyzed – not because she was dying, but because she was under his spell. He came closer and looked deeper into her eyes, and in them he saw the reflection of his. They were no longer black but a soft and soothing purple hue. He brushed his fingers against her cheek and tasted her lips in a slow and amorous kiss. She let out soft moans of pleasure under his touch and the gentle strokes of his tongue, fueling his arousal and desire to kill her. He let go of her lips and moved down to her neck and bit it so tenderly she thought he was kissing her again. He did not want to hurt her, he wanted her death to be as peaceful as possible, and only when she felt faint did she try to resist him. He caught her wrists and pinned her to the wall as he finished gorging himself on her blood, and when her heart stopped beating and she fell, he caught her and held her in his arms. Her spirit stood before him in the alley, looking confused, and he felt guilty for taking her life, like the first time he killed as a hitman.

"I'm sorry, my princess..." he whispered.

She shook her head in disbelief and then the light came and took her. Stanley stood beside her lifeless body for a long time, thinking about what he had done and would have to do again. And because he did not want to forget any of the innocents whose lives he would claim, he searched her pockets until he found something he could steal as a token and keep forever. He found a handkerchief and slipped it in his pocket. Then he lay one last kiss on her lips and walked away.

Stanley found that the part he hated the most about being a vampire was having to feed, and even if he tried to make his victims' deaths as gentle as possible, every time he killed, his heart shattered a little more. And to think he was once a cold hitman calling himself the 'bogeyman', who derived pleasure from terrifying his targets before finishing them off. He was that man at a time of his life when he was deeply unhappy without truly understanding why, so he stopped caring about the feelings of others. Now, he was equally unhappy, but at least he knew why, and he felt peaceful about it. He had let it go. And if, now and then, a smile on a stranger's face, a sound, or a scent reminded him of his home in Edinburgh with Callie, he had also let her go. He had removed the ring on his finger and kept it in a box, as a reminder never to fall in love again – not like his heart was capable of it, anyway.

As he slowly settled into this new and dark reality, one in which he was bound to live only at night and fear the sunlight, one without the ghosts of his father and William, one in which he had murdered his relatives and was destined to be evil, he began to wonder why no demon had come after him. Surely the candyman was in Belphegor's office looking for something or someone, and Stanley was not supposed to be there. Was he after the Time Key? If so, couldn't he guess Stanley took it when he suddenly disappeared? But Stanley was tired of fighting, hiding, fearing. So he stayed at home, perhaps waiting for someone to come and quietly end this long, sad dream he was stuck in, but no major demon or their hitmen ever came for him.

Time, he discovered, was different as a vampire. There were vampires like Eve, who went out into the world and socialized with humans and perhaps with their kind, and who seemed to live almost normal lives, and there were others like himself who just let days, nights, and weeks pass without noticing them.

Without any other obligation than having a den to hide in during the daytime – be it a house or a coffin – and having to hunt now and then, life was dull and monotonous. He got up, played cards with Cornelius or read him a book, then went to bed again. Nothing changed around him and he too would never change. He checked his face every evening in the mirror, just in case none of this was true and he was actually still human and would age, but his face was the same every night when he woke up from his daily slumber. Never a pimple or a gray hair or a wrinkle. He was frozen in time and stuck in this body he never wanted, forever.

After some time, because he needed some sort of routine or he thought he would go mad, he began to clean his home. Books scattered around his office and his bedroom returned to their shelves. All surfaces were dusted, and he even picked up the mail on the floor. He brought the stash of letters to the fireplace and proceeded to throw them in the fire, one after the other. Most of them were the letters he had sent Cornelius and William. He had no use for them now that William could no longer read his words. His throat tightened as he watched them burn slowly, like he had burned away his life as a human. Cornelius sat nearby on the sofa and watched him quietly. Apart from those letters were letters from Mister Scarborough, also useless, and when he reached the bottom of the pile was a letter from Eve. He read the name of the sender again, just to make sure he was not mistaken. It was indeed from her. But why would she write him, a stranger, again?

He took the letter and sat on the sofa with Cornelius.

"This one is from Eve... Mademoiselle Chauvin," he said.

"Are you going to read it?" Cornelius asked, who still liked her.

"Why not?" Stanley said after a moment.

He opened the envelope and examined it. It was dated January first, 1887, over eight months ago. Eight months. He had been away from his home, his life, and himself for that long. He began to read it:

'Dear Ernest,

I hope this letter finds you well. Since the tarot reading in your dream intrigued me, I took the liberty of doing another tarot reading for you, and the cards said you were in imminent danger. This danger involves a woman in a position of power (perhaps simply over you), demons or unscrupulous individuals, and the signing of a contract that may lead to your death. If you were considering a business deal with a woman, you should avoid signing the contract. This woman is not telling you the truth. She may have hired or been hired by someone who wants to harm you. I do hope you take my words to heart and don't think I am just a lunatic. And no, I am not the woman trying to swindle you. Please stay safe.

Eve'

"Well, she got it all right, didn't she?" Stanley said.

"She was very worried about you. Are you going to reply to her?" Cornelius asked.

"To tell her what?"

"Everything. She is like you. She will understand."

Stanley sighed and read the letter again. Eve had taken the time to warn him about what awaited him, only her letter came too late. The least he owed her was a thank you note. So he went to his desk, took a piece of paper and a pen, and began to write:

'Dear Eve,

First, let me apologize for the delay in responding to you. By the time your letter reached me, it was too late already, I had met this unscrupulous woman and left London with her. I was in love, but she did not love me. I still wonder how I, a grown-up man, was naïve enough to leave everything for a woman I barely knew. It sounds more like the story of a runaway sixteen-year-old, but I did it. No one forced me...

I'm afraid I already signed the contract that would destroy me, and if I did not die, I came very close to it. During the time I spent away from London, I discovered a whole new world, the existence of which I never suspected. I came in contact with vampires, demons, and the fairy folk. I saw other worlds, other dimensions, I traveled across time and space, I crossed the sky in a magical cab... Entering a world of magic and mystery was as thrilling to me as following this woman was. It was her world, and I wanted to be a part of it, whatever the cost. I gave her all my youth, my heart, and even my soul – quite literally. She took it all and never gave me anything but lies in return. Now she is dead and I am left in this world with nothing but sorrow, still mourning her loss when she would not have mourned mine.

I returned home after the dream ended, only to find I had lost a close friend, and soon after I had to say goodbye to my father. And now I must live with a new condition and adapt to it. To tell the truth, I often wonder why I am still here, what is my purpose in this world. I no longer know. Why do we make stupid decisions when we are in love? The human heart is a fragile thing indeed...

My apologies for this gloomy letter. I trust that you will believe me and not think I made up all of this under the influence of some substance. The next time I make a life-changing decision, I should probably get a tarot reading beforehand.

Your friend, Ernest'

He read out the letter to Cornelius, who frowned slightly.

"You didn't really tell her anything about yourself," he remarked.

"I can't just write to her 'I know you're a vampire and I am too. And by the way, I'm also a crossdresser'," Stanley said.

"Why not?"

"Because she is a stranger and I don't want to intrude on her private life."

"Why?"

"Because it's just rude among adults," Stanley said.

"Oh..." Cornelius said, who was a child and did not understand such restraint.

Stanley had written the letter with a heavy heart, but after writing it he felt better, lighter. He mailed it that evening, not expecting a response, and returned to his daily routine, but a response came less than a week later:

'Dear Ernest,

Thank you so much for your response, and for sharing your story with me. I was so sad to hear about your losses. I'm sure you know, like me, that the souls of those we love never quite leave this world, they are simply pulled away from our sight, beyond a horizon the living cannot cross. Just because they are out of sight does not mean they are forever gone. Still, we mourn their absence because we can no longer resolve anything with them. Disputes, misunderstandings, heartbreaks, everything is left in our hands with seemingly no one to turn to but ourselves. So we turn to a friend, like you did with me, and I truly appreciate you for allowing me, a stranger, to share part of that burden with you.

You were neither naïve nor stupid for falling in love, and the fact that your love was not reciprocated does not make it any less real nor valid. The beauty of love is how it transforms the heart of the person who feels it - much more so than the one who receives it. Each one of us is like a transparent piece of glass, and our life experiences sometimes stain it, sometimes they crack it, and sometimes they even shatter it. And while the stains and cracks can never be removed, we do not remain forever broken. Instead, we become a mosaic of colorful experiences telling a story.

My story may not be one you can relate to, although it does involve magic and mystery, but I too was in love for many years with a man who did not love me, or rather did not love me right. Because I had never experienced love before, I accepted the bits and pieces of love he gave me, along with his criticism and violence, and I thought it was all I deserved. I was not quite like the other women, and therefore I settled for less than they would have. I cannot say I ever found anything more in the hearts of men; perhaps I just keep meeting the wrong ones. But I have found happiness in my friendships with women and fighting for our rights. I have found that love is much more than the embrace and the kiss of a man, it can be found in the smile of a friend, in the gratitude of a stranger, and in the magic of nature all around us. Still, I sometimes cry over the loss of that one man who hurt me so much.

I did another tarot reading for you, and the cards said that your physical ailment is not permanent, or that you will be able to live with it. Make sure to get proper nutrition, perhaps only fluids if you are lacking appetite. I also recommend a rosehip herbal tea daily (unfortunately my shop is out of it, or I would send you some).

Please do take care of yourself, dear friend.

Eve.'

Stanley brushed his fingers over the beautiful letters of her words.

"Are you going to marry her?" Cornelius asked by his side.

"Marry her? We don't even know each other," Stanley said, frowning.

"But I want her to be my mum..." Cornelius said.

"I can't propose to a woman just so she can become the mother of my child ghost friend," Stanley said.

"But you'll write her again, won't you?"

"I don't know..."

Stanley got up from the sofa he was sitting on and placed the letter on his desk. He looked around the room. The light of the dancing flames in the fireplace bathed everything in a warm yellow hue, even the old green wallpaper. As a vampire, his 'day' begun after sunset and ended before dawn. He was a creature of the night now, bound to roam the streets in search of prey. His long 'career' as a killer started with the murders of his relatives, then demons, and now innocent girls on the street who just happened to be his type. He thought about hunting men instead, perhaps even criminals, but he had no appetite for them, so their murders would just be in vain. Whatever he did, it seemed like he could never stray from the path of death, and it broke his heart.

Many nights, after the kill, he walked the streets feeling disgusted with himself, and crying over the loss of another life for his needs. Sometimes, he just wanted to let himself wither away and die, if such a thing was even still possible.

One such night, as he wandered into the darkest streets of Whitechapel, he stumbled upon a peculiar business. The building looked like an old tavern, with most of the windows boarded up. On its side was a small, closed stable, locked with a heavy chain, and behind a barred opening Stanley could distinguish a hearse. A wooden sign near the large doors of the business read: 'Undertakers Inc.'. Hopefully not another demonic shell company. It looked like a legitimate business, though. He wondered whether some of his victims had ended up there.

"Cornelius," he said in a low voice.

The child ghost, who now followed him everywhere, appeared beside him.

"Please unlock the door for me," Stanley said.

"What are you going to do?" Cornelius asked, a little worried about his friend suddenly wanting to trespass into people's homes and businesses.

"I want to feel what my victims feel, laying in a coffin," Stanley said, staring at the door.

"What if you get buried alive?" Cornelius said.

Stanley smirked.

"Well, I already died. I could hardly say I am 'alive'."

Cornelius sighed and passed through the door and un-locked it for him. Stanley quietly opened it and stepped inside. The building was dark and looked empty, but he could smell the scent of several people inside, and at least one of them was a vampire. Whatever.

He walked down the hallway before him and opened the first door to his left. It led to the morgue. Inside it were several closed coffins on biers, an open one with what seemed like ashes at the bottom, and several more of various sizes, leaning against the wall. On a table in a corner was a box filled with wooden and silver stakes. Strange. But this was vampire territory after all. Perhaps they had just killed one in the coffin that night, and that was the scent he caught on when entering the building.

He climbed into the open coffin and lay inside. It was a plain, hard, wooden coffin. Few could afford an expensive burial in this neighborhood.

"Stanley, I don't like this... what if the humans wake up and kill you?" Cornelius said.

"I'll probably kill them first with my eyes," Stanley said. "I'm feeling tired. I think I'll take a nap."

And so he rolled over on his side and closed his eyes. He was awakened some time later by Cornelius' voice.

"Stanley! Stanley!" he said in an anxious whisper by his ear.

Stanley opened his eyes, and the vampire scent he had smelled earlier now filled the room. He turned around, startled, and for a second, he thought Callie was standing beside the coffin. But the woman with the long, black, curly hair and the faded pink dress beside him was not Callie, and not a demon at all. She was a vampire, and he could sense that she was very old and powerful. She was probably the boss in this neighborhood.

"You scared me..." he said, rolling over lazily.

He did not care what happened to him. If she wanted to pick a fight, so be it; he would rather not kill her, but he would if he had to. But she was not in that mood.

"This is a funeral home, not a hotel, young man," she said in a polite but firm voice.

He chuckled.

"'Young man'... yes, I suppose I'm young," he said. "My apologies Madam, I will go home now."

He climbed out of the coffin and walked over to the door, but she called out to him: "Do you need help?"

"No thanks," he said.

Help? Who could ever help someone like him? It wasn't like there was a time and place in the past he could return to and make things right again. He had spent his entire childhood confused and frightened, and his adult years angry or sad. The only time of happiness he had known was a lie. It was not even real. So how could that woman or anyone else help him? As he walked, he gazed at his feet hitting the cold, wet pavement. He was a traveler without a destination, since the place where he wanted to be and the person he wanted there by his side were gone. They had vanished in a haze, like he was slowly disappearing into the thick London fog. His footsteps guided him to a church, and he stood before it, looking up at the belfry, and then he pushed the doors open and entered it.

It was dark and empty, except for a few candles burning on the altar at the end of the nave. It was not a very large church and it had no mosaics or ornaments other than a few statues. Above the altar, hanging from the ceiling with heavy chains, was a statue of Jesus on the cross. He hung there, frozen in marble stillness, his eyes looking into nothingness. From this angle, they oversaw the congregation but never fell upon one person in particular, so all could feel as though Jesus was watching them. Stanley had never been a believer, and all he remembered of the church services he was forced to attend as a child was how boring they were. A priest mumbled something behind his altar, and now and then everyone said 'Amen'. Then they all got up and began singing, and with his reading difficulties, by the time Stanley even found the right hymn in the prayer book, they had all finished singing.

But that night, as he slowly walked down the nave to the altar, he felt like Jesus' eyes were upon him. They were not judging him for all his crimes, just asking him why he chose that path. He did not have an answer for him. He let himself be changed into a demon; Jesus let himself be crucified... Both of them sacrificed themselves, and he did not know what Jesus found on the other side, but he had found nothing down here.

He sat down on a bench and gazed at the small flames of the candles on the altar. He reached in his pocket and pulled out the earring he had stolen from his victim that night, and that he would probably put away in a chest at home with the other tokens from his 'princesses'. He called them so because they were innocent, and he killed them before they could hurt him. He was their prince for a few seconds, and he gave them the illusion of being loved before they died. It was sick and perverted, he knew it.

A crow flew inside the church and perched itself on a bench near him. Stanley smirked. He had not seen that one in a long time.

"What do you want, Calvin?" he asked with a sigh.

"Your mistress has been looking for you," Calvin cawed.

"I'm right here," Stanley said. He turned to him with a forced smile.

"You are under contract with her. You cannot escape," Calvin reminded him.

"If I wanted to escape, wouldn't I be in Spain or Russia now? Why stay here in London?" Stanley said.

"There is a new assignment waiting for you, imbecile," Calvin replied.

"Calvin... come here," Stanley said.

"Why should I come? I don't trust you..." the bird said.

"I have an important message for my mistress," Stanley said. "I won't look at you if you're afraid of my eyes."

The crow made a cawing sound that sounded like a grunt, then flew over and landed on his shoulder. And, his eyes fixed on the statue before him, Stanley suddenly grabbed him and twisted his neck until it broke. He dropped the cursed bird's dead body on the ground and said: "I resign."

"You cannot resign or back out of a contract with a demon," a man said behind him in the dark.

Stanley did not need to turn around to know who he was.

"You should stop eating candy. It's bad for your teeth..." he said.

The man walked down the aisle and sat on the bench beside him. His face had changed again, and he was no longer Belphegor. That night, he was a short and slender man with short brown hair and spectacles. He was wearing a charcoal gray pinstripe suit and hat, with a purple vest and tie.

"Do you even have a name and a face of your own, or are you just always borrowing somebody else's?" Stanley wondered.

The candyman smiled.

"I lost both a long time ago."

"That's too bad," Stanley said.

The candyman was not seeking his compassion and even if he were, he would never get it, not after what he had done to Callie.

"So, are you here to kill me?" Stanley asked.

"No. I'm here to offer you a new job," the candyman replied peacefully.

"As a hitman for whatever other demon you work for?" Stanley said, cynical.

"I don't work for demons these days. I work for the other side," the candyman said.

"What? The seraphim – or whatever they are called?" Stanley said.

"The order of the angels and their overseers, the seraphim, exist to maintain balance between the world of humans and the underworld, whereas demons exist to disrupt this balance," the man explained. "The lowest rank in their hierarchy, the apostles, can be people with any sort of background, but to become an angel or any rank above, candidates must have a pure, untainted heart."

"Well then, that leaves me out," Stanley replied.

"However, there are also special positions for people like you and me, powerful vampires with an innate desire for violence. We are there to do the dirty work the pure-hearted ones could not do."

"Ah, so you're actually a vampire," Stanley said, unimpressed.

"And many other things," the candyman said.

"So they hire ex-demon hitmen?" Stanley said.

"They don't need to know that part of your past," the candyman said, turning to him with an accomplice grin.

"And you, whose side are you on since you work for both?" Stanley asked, turning to him.

The candyman pulled out a piece of barley sugar from his pocket and bit into it.

"Neither. My role is to be invisible and get things done behind the scenes," he said.

"I still don't see why I should work for one side or the other," Stanley said. "I'm tired of everything..."

He rolled his head back and gazed at the tall ceiling of the church.

"That is precisely why they want you. Someone with your talent gone adrift could become quite dangerous for this world," the candyman said.

"And they think they can control me? I'd like to see that."

"Not control you... only channel your powers where they belong," the candyman said. "Think about it: a clean slate, a new life, and a new job doing what you do best. And sometimes you might even protect the innocent."

Stanley did not think he would ever be the hero who saved the innocent, but he needed something to live for, something to occupy his thoughts. He got up and gazed at the man before him. The candyman was right: they were the same: two murderers who trusted no one but themselves, and who could work for whichever side, so long as they could kill. But he would never again work for Beelzebub after the way she and Belphegor and Callie had tricked him. So the other side it would be.

"I'll do it under one condition," he said.

"And what is it?"

"Show me your true face."

The candyman smiled and waved his hand before his face, and in its place was nothing left. Instead of a face, he had a gaping hole filled with smoke. He waved his hand before it again and it returned to what it was a moment before.

"I wasn't lying. I am nobody," he said.

"I hope I don't lose my face. It's not quite the way I want it, but I am attached to it and it to me," Stanley said.

The candyman laughed and extended his hand to him, and Stanley took it.

CHAPTER 13

BIANCA BOWED BEFORE THE crowd and the curtain fell. She could still hear them cheering for her as she left the stage. Other actors awaited her backstage and kissed her cold cheeks.

"Congratulations darling, you were marvelous tonight!" Antonio, the theater's director, said.

"*Grazie, grazie*," she said.

She took the flower bouquets they handed her and blew them kisses, then returned to the dressing room. There, she threw the flowers on a table, kicked off her high-heeled shoes and began to unbutton her costume - a seventeenth century dress all in gold and crimson tones. Only then did she become aware of a presence. She turned around and scrutinized the room with her black eyes.

"Who's there?" she said aloud.

Stanley then appeared behind her, his arms crossed.

"Just a stalker. Get lost!" she said, irritated.

She sat down in front of one of the mirrors and began to remove her thick, curly brown wig. She looked ridiculous, Stanley thought, with her white, powdered face, and the exaggerated rouge on her lips and cheeks.

"Nice way to treat your fans," Stanley said.

"I'm the rising star of Naples. People come from far away to hear me sing," she said with disdain. "And who are you?"

Stanley slowly walked up to her and whispered in her ear: *"L'uomo nero."*

Her eyes suddenly opened wide with fear as she realized he was not there to compliment her on her performance, and she scrambled out of her chair and ran toward the door, but Stanley disappeared and reappeared before her. As a vampire, she was fast, but he had learned to control his time traveling to where he could slow down time for her and casually move where he wanted before she got there.

She stopped in her tracks when she saw him, standing in front of her with his hands in his pockets, when only a second before he had been by the mirror. His lips parted into an evil grin.

"Going somewhere?"

She began to back up and bared her fangs at him.

"Whoever you think you are, I'm more powerful than you!" she hissed in a high-pitched voice.

"I'm nobody," he said. "But you, Madam, are in some serious trouble. You are accused of conspiracy against the Vatican and plotting the murder of the Dark Pope. Your sentence shall be death."

He did not like all these formalities, but his new employers, the seraphim, had their own rules, and one of them was that the criminal needed to be read the charges against them before being eliminated. Stanley did not know why – perhaps because it made them feel good or something. Of course Bianca knew what she did, and she obviously did not care – and neither did he.

"I'd like to see that!" she then said before morphing into a snake.

Oh, great. A shapeshifter. They didn't tell him that about her. She dropped to the floor as a small snake, leaving her clothes behind, and slipped behind a crate.

Stanley sighed. He would have to use a different method to catch her. So he closed his eyes and stretched out his hand, listening to his heartbeat and focusing on it only. He turned his hand around slowly in a clockwise motion and reopened his eyes. The room's walls and floor had now disappeared, and only the furniture remained, and it all flipped upside down and began to fall into emptiness.

"Welcome to my upside-down world," he said, smirking.

With the ease of a cat, he walked into the blackness and caught the snake in his hand while everything else fell. He squeezed the snake's neck in a firm grip and forced Bianca to look into his now flickering eyes. She became paralyzed and stopped struggling, and then her spirit left her body, but it did not cross over. She would not leave him alone and began flying around him in the darkness and hissing.

He dropped her dead snake body into the emptiness beneath him, turned to her, and opened his mouth. With his mind, he ordered her to enter it, and though she tried to resist him, she was eventually pulled inside and he swallowed her whole. The room then returned to normal, and he gagged.

"Disgusting!" he said, placing a hand on his stomach.

He would have to take something later for the indigestion. Swallowing spirits was not something he did very often. For one thing, they tasted like smoke or dust. Secondly, they always gave him an upset stomach. But it was one of the many skills he had mastered in his new form, and it was always a good way to dispose of tenacious spirits who refused to move on.

He checked himself in the mirror: black suit, white shirt, black vest, black tie, and hat. He was back in business as the bogeyman; just another hitman working for another employer. The seraphim of England did not usually send him abroad, but they had partnerships with similar orders in other countries, and the bogeyman was very much in demand these days. Business was good and the pay was fine. The only thing he disliked about this new function was the stupidity of all those goody-goody wannabe angels who were all just creatures of the underworld like himself.

The candyman had first brought him to Westminster Cathedral, which was apparently the headquarters of the seraphim of England, except it was probably not the cathedral humans got to see. It was lit with bright, electric light, even in the dead of night, and white light seemed to pour in through the high windows of the apse. It was not sunlight, for it did not burn his skin or that of any other vampire present. It was only designed to make an impression.

He was presented to two men and a woman, all seated on tall, ornate golden thrones before the altar. Even he could tell they were very powerful, some perhaps more powerful than him. The two men wore all-white suits with what appeared to be medals of honor on the breast pocket, and long, white capes with fur-trimmed shoulder pads. The woman wore a long, white dress that seemed to belong in the Medieval era. The man in the center – their boss – introduced himself as Adeyemi Ojo. In his looks, he was quite a handsome young man, black of skin and hair, with a thin and neatly trimmed beard. Most vampires' eyes were black and turned red when they were hungry or aroused, but his were permanently yellow and he appeared to be blind. He wore on his head a golden crown with more diamonds, sapphires, and rubies than the crowns of kings and queens. The woman to his right simply identified herself as 'Aleksandra'. She was a slender woman who had changed in her late twenties. Her skin was fair and her waist-length hair blond and fine like silk threads. Her eyes were a bright ruby red, and she had typical Slavic features. She smiled with interest when she saw the newcomer. The man to Adeyemi's left introduced himself as Yvan Thompson, he was a middle-aged British vampire as tall as a giant. He was also the most conservative of them, and the first to speak.

"Sophie Suspect... Thank you for accepting our invitation," he said in his deep voice.

"It's Stanley," Stanley grunted.

"What did you say? Speak up," Yvan said.

"My name is Stanley Suspect, and if you want me to work for you, I expect you to use my chosen name and pronouns," Stanley said louder.

"And what are those pronouns?" Aleksandra asked with interest, but Adeyemi gestured to her not to interfere.

Yvan rose from his throne, looking displeased.

"The records show that you were christened 'Sophie'," he said as though it justified his position.

"So if they christened me 'Sausage', would you call me Sausage for the rest of my immortal life?" Stanley responded. "I'm a vampire. What difference does it make what is on the records?"

Aleksandra covered her mouth to hide her laughter and even Adeyemi could hardly suppress a smile, but Yvan looked absolutely appalled.

"You would defy even God and the Church?" he said.

"It's alright," Adeyemi finally said. "You can be Stanley if you want, as long as you do your job."

If he *wanted*? No, Stanley did not *want* to be a man. He *was* a man - just in the wrong body. They were annoying him already. Well, not Aleksandra. She was cute and seemed more open-minded than the others.

"So, what do you want from me?" Stanley asked, slipping his hands in his pockets.

"We know how powerful you are; our spies have seen you at work. You were a hitman targeting demons and you are capable of killing indiscriminately and sadistically... We fear that a vampire as powerful as you could become a threat to our kind. Therefore, our only options are either to hire you, or to eliminate you," Yvan said.

"I didn't know I was such an important person," Stanley said, smirking.

"It's not such a bad proposal," Aleksandra said. "If you could choose between living like a king or being dead, what would you choose?"

"Either way makes no difference to me," Stanley said.

"So you refuse?" Adeyemi said, surprised.

"I didn't say that," Stanley said. "I'll do it, under two conditions: that you call me Stanley and that you don't interfere with my private life."

"We don't care what you do in your private life," Yvan said. "However, you will have to accept our communications whenever they come."

Stanley reached in his vest pocket, pulled out his cigarette case, and lit himself a cigarette - much to Yvan's displeasure.

"And how will you communicate with me?" he asked. "I don't want any creepy creatures flying in through my windows."

"We use the telephone. If you are not equipped with one, we will see to that," Yvan said.

That was not too bad. He hated the idea of having something that could ring in his home any time of day or night, but it was better than mouthy crows.

"I can handle that," he said.

"There is one last verification we need to make," Yvan then said. "We must make sure you do not bear the mark of a demon. We therefore have to examine your body."

"Go right ahead," Stanley shrugged. "Want me to strip here?"

"The examination will be carried out privately by Aleksandra. Please follow her," Adeyemi said.

Aleksandra got up, walked over to him, and invited him to follow her. She took him to a clergy member's office in the church and closed the door.

"Please take off your clothes now," she said with shining eyes.

"Is this an indecent proposal?" he teased her.

"Only if you want it to be," she said with a smile.

He did as he was told and slowly removed all of his clothes, even his binder, and she walked around him, lifted his arms and checked underneath them. She then moved back in front of him.

"Satisfied?" he said.

"There is one last place I ought to check," she said, and, while looking into his eyes, she slipped her fingers in his intimate parts.

He could see what was on her mind, and a year ago he might have been interested, but now even a woman like her left him indifferent.

"I'm not going to do anything with you, if that was your intention," he said calmly.

"Too bad..." she said, before removing her fingers.

"Can I put my clothes back on now?" he asked.

He didn't mind being in the nude before her, he just wanted this interview to be over so he could go home.

"Yes, you may," she said.

He put his clothes back on and she sat on the office's desk, gazing at him with shining eyes.

"So Adeyemi is the big boss, huh? What are his powers?" he asked casually, while buttoning up his shirt.

"The seraphim do not discuss each other's powers," she replied.

"But they sleep together," he remarked.

"What happens behind closed doors is also not discussed," she said.

"Just like the Church then," he said. "Alright, sweetheart, what's the next step? Do I sign a contract?"

She giggled as he called her 'sweetheart'.

"Indeed."

A thick bundle of documents appeared in her hands and she placed it on the desk.

"Seriously, I have to read through all of this?" he asked, picking it up.

"The majority of it is just our rules," she said. "You can skip to the last page and sign."

He went straight to the last page and signed his name.

"Done."

"Excellent."

She slipped the papers in a folder and handed them to him.

"Congratulations, Stanley Suspect. You are now a special agent of the seraphim," she then said, smiling.

As they had promised, he was only visited once by one of the cherubim, a vampire lower than them in the hierarchy, who installed a telephone in his home, and then he was left alone. He received few calls from them, and only during the night, when he was awake. The assignments he was given were easy, and the vampires he eliminated were actual criminals. He chose the time, place, and means of the kill. The only two requirements were that he read them the charges before proceeding, and that he refrained from biting them and drinking their blood, which apparently was the vampire form of mating with each other. He did not know that. The other long list of rules they were supposed to agree to but that no one seemed to actually follow included abstaining from sex or sexual thoughts, not killing humans except to feed, not carrying out personal vengeance, and not mingling with the vampire court of England and its dark lord, who was the equivalent of their king. The seraphim ruled over dark lords and ladies, and he was told he may have to eliminate one or two, eventually. Not like he cared.

He settled again in the same sort of routine he had with Callie, being away for days at a time, except now he only returned home to Cornelius, whom he did not want following him on assignments and seeing what he did. He brought him back toys and books, and they read them together before going to bed. Stanley never did get his parents to read him a bedtime story, but now he could read them to Cornelius, not like a parent, but like his eternal big brother. He was contented with his life, but nothing ever quite lifted the sadness in his heart, not even the letters he received regularly from Eve. Seasons passed and the world carried on without him. Like the candyman, he had become invisible, and that was what he wanted.

April 4th, 1889. Stanley returned home with his hands full of books and picked up the mail on the floor in the hallway.

"Cornelius! I have a surprise for you!" he said cheerfully.

He was going to walk into the office, but Cornelius came flying through the wall and wrapped his arms around his legs, almost making him fall.

"More books?" he said, excited.

"Lots of books," Stanley said. "I got to Marvin's before closing time tonight."

"Do they have pictures?" Cornelius asked. Those were his favorites.

"Lots of pictures," Stanley said.

With great difficulty, he made his way into the office, dragging Cornelius along, and set the books on the table.

"Can I look at one now? Please? Please?" Cornelius said.

At least the misunderstanding between them was over now, and because Stanley was no longer moody, Cornelius was also happier.

"Here you go. I want to read my mail before we read a book," Stanley said, handing him a book of fairy tales.

Cornelius cried with joy, took it, and went to sit on the sofa. Stanley removed his coat and hat and sat on the sofa beside him with the letter he had received. It was from Eve. Their correspondence was always polite and cautious, and neither of them talked about their past very much. Since he had expressed his interest in the suffragette cause, she sent him the latest news from Paris, as well as the results of her occasional tarot readings. He enjoyed receiving her letters; they were the only thing that still brightened his days – or rather his nights since he slept all day. He had told her he was a paranormal investigator – which was technically not a lie since he had not quit his profession, he just stopped advertising his services since it would most likely involve meeting clients in the daytime and he couldn't – and he had told her about life with Cornelius. He smiled, opened the letter, and began to read it quietly:

Dear Ernest,

I hope your health is improving and that little Cornelius is also doing well. I had an intuition, and as a Moon in Gemini native I always try to explain my intuitions, so I did another tarot reading for you. You will soon receive a message inviting you to a duel or a challenge. You must not accept it. This duel is a trap and great harm could come to you if you partake in it. I know you are a cautious man and not the sort to throw yourself into a duel, but I just thought I had better advise you. Sagittarius natives can sometimes make decisions they will later regret when provoked.

Life in Paris is the same as always: busy. I will not be attending any feminist lectures this month as I need to take care of my shop. Do

*you suffer from hair loss? I am launching a new line of hair growth
products and would be happy to send you a sample.'*

Stanley laughed.

"Hair loss? How old does she think I am?"

But he liked the way her mind jumped from one topic to
another. Or perhaps she had so few friends because of her busy
life that she just wrote to him everything that came to her mind
at the same time. He continued reading:

*'I think of little Cornelius often and wonder how he keeps himself
busy. Being a ghost child must get boring after a while. You did not
tell me whether he was the sort of ghost who could touch and move
objects, but I included some printed paper to make origami. It is a
game played by children in Japan. I have enclosed instructions for
him.*

I look forward to your next letter.

Your friend, Eve.'

Stanley looked inside the envelope again and found a set of
small paper squares and instructions to make animal shapes by
folding them.

"Oh, look Cornelius, Eve sent you some paper to make
'origami' – whatever that is," he said.

"Really? For me?" Cornelius said, putting down his book.

Stanley gave him the paper squares, and they tried to make
a crane together. Cornelius loved the new game, but Stanley
gave up after a few unsuccessful attempts. He was not good at
anything requiring manual dexterity or patience.

"I think you should marry Eve," Cornelius then remarked as
he played with the paper crane.

"Cornelius..." Stanley said with a sigh. "For the hundredth
time, Eve is just a friend, and I will never marry anyone. I don't
even think vampires marry each other."

Cornelius looked disappointed, but did not insist.

"So what else did she say in her letter?" he asked.

"Someone is going to challenge me to a duel apparently, but all I have to do is refuse," Stanley said, and no sooner had he said it than the telephone rang. He got up and picked up the receiver, wondering where they were sending him next.

"Yes?" he said.

"We have a new assignment for you, Sophie," Yvan said on the other end.

"It's Stanley," Stanley said.

He hated the old vampire who couldn't stray one step away from his religious upbringing in the Middle Ages despite no longer being a creature of God. And, as always, Yvan ignored him.

"Your target's name is Joseph Stein," he said.

Stanley grabbed a piece of paper and wrote down the name.

"Vampire?" he said.

"Necromancer, like you," Yvan said.

Great, another one like Stanley and his father. That meant he was probably very powerful and dangerous.

"Interesting. What did he do?" he asked.

"He has recently become an Apostle for the Dark Lord of England, but we are suspicious of his motives," Yvan explained. "We want you to investigate him and find out if he also works for someone else. Do not kill him now."

"So he hasn't committed any crime yet... isn't everyone innocent until proven guilty?" Stanley asked, frowning.

"That is our call. Your job is to obey our orders."

"So you just want me to investigate him and report to you?"

"Exactly."

"Alright, I need his address and the names of places where he usually goes."

"We only have his home address. He does not appear to have much of a social life," Yvan said.

"What's his address?" Stanley asked, and he wrote down the address Yvan gave him, then hung up the phone.

"Where are you going this time?" Cornelius asked.

He understood his brother's new role, but he worried about him. He was facing powerful vampires and could potentially lose his life – his undead life this time.

"Just an investigation," Stanley said. "But the target is another necromancer, so he can likely see you. I'm afraid you'll have to stay home again."

"Is this the duel Eve was talking about?" Cornelius asked, anxious.

"No, I was not asked to fight him or kill him," Stanley said.

He looked at the name and address on the paper again and frowned. What if this was in fact what she had seen in her tarot reading? He remembered his father's words: necromancers did not let each other live. What if the man challenged him to a duel? He would have to make sure not to be seen or heard during his investigation. He checked the clock: seven twenty-five. Most vampires, if they had to run errands, would run them early in the evening before shops closed. Those who frequented salons or the theater could be out all night.

"Alright, I'd better get to work," he said, getting up.

He put on his coat and hat and headed out.

As it turned out, his necromancer target did not live very far from him at all, only a few blocks away, and the fact they never came across each other while hunting was probably a miracle. He rented a small room in an old building, and the other tenants all seemed to be bachelors or theatricals. He liked a quiet dwelling, but to be surrounded by eccentrics and people who did not live like everyone else. Stanley took mental notes.

Using his invisible mode, he watched the building for some time, looking for a vampire among the faces that came in and out, until he thought he spotted one - and immediately recognized him. He was the romance author Stanley had once met as a human, John Silverstake, and now that he saw him again, he was clearly a vampire. That probably explained why he refused to meet him again in the daylight, and also why he could see Cornelius. A good thing Stanley did not bring him along.

The man still looked as young as he did back then, short, with overgrown, curly black hair and an air of melancholy on his face, only now as a vampire Stanley could tell he was very old - much older than any other he had met so far. He was dressed in a black suit that night, with a matching hat and a cream-colored scarf, and was obviously going out. Stanley followed him at a distance.

Spring had come, but the air was still cold at night, and he regretted not wearing warmer clothes. But the man was not going very far: he joined a group of other vampires, all young men like him, and they chatted for a moment in front of a restaurant. With them, he seemed much livelier and more enthusiastic. He was telling a young man a story, probably from his next novel, and mimicking the characters with gestures, and the young man laughed. Stanley could not get close enough to hear all of their conversation. The wind was against him, but it seemed innocent enough and his target looked... happy. He clearly had a few friends of his kind, something Stanley did not have, but he did not even know if he would be accepted in their world any more than he had been in the world of humans. There was just no place for him.

The group of young men then entered the restaurant, and Joseph parted with them. He headed on to a flower shop where he purchased a bouquet of white roses and walked to a nearby cemetery where he deposited them on a grave. He kneeled beside the grave for some time, just gazing at it quietly, then he got up and left. When he was far enough, Stanley walked over to the grave: it was that of a woman named Alice Broomfield, who died in her old age – nothing supernatural about her or her grave. He then noticed a small note Joseph had slipped inside the bouquet. He took it and read it:

'Dear Alice,

So many years have passed since you left me, and yet there is not a single day I don't think about you. You were the one who told me to come to London, and for you I came. You showed me who I could be. Now you are gone and somehow I cannot bring myself to leave the city where my dreams flourished, though I should. Time passes, but not for me. My dreams live in the past, and I see no future, not without you. So many times I have thought about ending it all and joining you, but even if I died, I am not sure I would go to the beautiful realm where you probably live. You were a rose, destined to Heaven, and I am but a black-feathered poet, writing words of love to you who will never read them. Please, give me the strength to live on, for I cannot find it on my own...

Your devoted Joseph'

The man was obviously depressed over the loss of a lover or a woman he admired, and he was a bit melodramatic about it, but Stanley understood his conflicting desires to leave this place behind and live again or remain here in the dream he lost and think about her all the time. Either way, this posed no threat to the seraphim, so he carefully replaced the note in the bouquet as it was intended, and left the cemetery.

He had lost track of his target, but he had an easily recogniz-able rose-like scent. He followed it back to the building where he lived, and once there, he waited in the shadows. Hours passed, and his hands and feet were stiff, but the man did not come out again, not that night nor any of the next few nights Stanley stalked him. So on the fourth night, he decided he would have to get into his room somehow, to gather evidence.

That night, he entered the building, invisible as always, and followed Joseph's scent until he found his room, the number thirteen. He had made sure to wash before leaving his home, then stand near the fireplace, so that his scent would only be that of woodfire smoke and not that of a necromancer vampire. After checking the empty hallway once more, he knocked loudly on the door and waited. The man took a long time to open the door, as though he hoped whoever knocked would already be gone, but he finally opened it a crack, then shut it when he saw no one. Damn it, he sure was antisocial. So Stanley walked up to the door and knocked on it again, then retreated. The man opened it again, and this time came out into the poorly lit hallway and looked around him. That night he looked rather sloppy in his wrinkled shirt that had probably once been white but was now more of a cream color and his black trousers held up with brown suspenders. He still smelled like roses, but also strongly of gin. He had been drinking. He walked over to the room closest to his and knocked on the door.

"James, did you need something?" he asked aloud.

A human – likely James – opened the door.

"Oh, hey Joe. No, I didn't need anything. Why?"

"Someone knocked on my door. I thought it might be you," Joseph said, his cheeks growing red. He was also shy.

Stanley moved quickly, while he was busy talking, and slipped into his room. There, he slowed down time and quickly went through the papers on the man's desk. Nothing interesting there, only novel chapters and poetry. He looked around for other places where he might hide evidence of criminal activity, but the whole room was a mess: there were clothing scattered all over the bed and the floor, more papers with poetry, books, playing cards, ashtrays filled with cigarette butts, and empty bottles of liquor. This man was really just a depressed, introverted writer, and probably an alcoholic. He was friendly to his neighbors and strangers, and even the random ghosts he met, and earned a living writing about love. He seemed very likeable. Perhaps even someone Stanley might have wanted to become friends with, not the sort of dangerous criminals he usually hunted down.

"Not me. Miss Meyers, perhaps? Are you late on rent again?" he heard James saying in the hallway.

"I don't think so. Well, good night," Joseph said.

James closed the door and Joseph returned to his room before Stanley could get out and closed the door. He was trapped now, just like Eve had foreseen - this time in another necromancer's den. If the vampire could not see him, he could probably sense his presence, and he was blocking the door. Stanley remained perfectly still. As he had expected, the moment Joseph entered the room, he stopped and looked around it.

"Who is there?" he asked.

Stanley did not make a sound.

"If you are a spirit, you can come out. You have nothing to fear," Joseph said, looking at the walls.

He did not seem very dangerous at all, but his demeanor quickly changed.

"But if you're not a spirit, then you'd better come out before I find you," he warned, and his voice had the same sadistic tone Stanley used to frighten his targets. But there could only be one bogeyman...

"You want to play that game? Fine. I have the means to find you," Joseph said, and he stood still and closed his eyes.

Stanley had not thought about the possibility that other vampires than himself or the candyman could make themselves invisible or see those who could. A terrible miscalculation on his part. A black halo now surrounded the other necromancer's body, and his power level increased dramatically. He was already more powerful than all the seraphim, and his power was still going up, as though there was no limit to it. Stanley had never seen anything like it. He couldn't remain there and wait to see what sort of magic he was about to use, so he slowed down time again and rushed over to the door, pushing the vampire out of the way, swung the door open and ran out. Joseph fell to the ground, wondering what had just happened, then he sat up and touched his chest, trying to recall his perceptions.

"A short person, small hands, slender fingers," he said to himself, frowning. "Perhaps a ghost who was looking for someone else and got scared when I closed the door?"

He let his power level return to normal, shrugged and returned to his desk and the novel he was writing. He looked at the page before him, crossed out what he had just written, and wrote instead: *'Eleanor's burning skin quivered under the cold whisper of Patrick, the ghost of her teenage lover...'*

He read it again and smiled, satisfied.

Stanley burst into his office out of breath and removed his coat and hat. Cornelius, who was waiting for him on the sofa, immediately got up and said: "What happened?"

"Nothing - luckily," Stanley said.

He dropped into a chair and loosened his tie.

"Then why did you run back home?" Cornelius asked.

"Do you remember the other clairvoyant we once met at the bookstore, the one who could see you?" Stanley said. "Well, he's my new target. He's a necromancer like me."

"Is he a criminal?" Cornelius asked with a frown.

"I didn't find any evidence, but I suppose they have something against him," Stanley said.

Cornelius stood still before him, looking serious.

"What?" Stanley said.

"Stanley, you need to stop risking your life. I don't want to lose you again," the child ghost said.

"Hey, I was not in any danger. I'm alright," Stanley replied with a smile.

But he could have been. In fact, he could have been shredded to pieces by that old vampire.

"You didn't have to accept this new job for the seraphim. Why do you always go looking for danger?" Cornelius said, stomping off.

Because he was a ghost, he walked right through the wall and disappeared.

"Cornelius... are you going to throw a tantrum?" Stanley said. "Come back here, please."

Cornelius's head only came out of the wall.

"You just take orders from the seraphim and never question them," he pointed out.

"Yes, that's my job. I'm a hitman, not the police. I do the dirty work they can't do."

"What if they asked you to kill an innocent?"

"They won't, because I have to read out all the charges to my target before making the kill."

"Then what are the charges against him?" Cornelius asked.

"None. I don't know," Stanley said. "Listen, this is just an investigation. If I don't find anything, then there won't be any charges, and the man will live. If I do find something, that will mean he is a criminal, and I eliminate criminals."

"I'll warn him!" Cornelius threatened.

"No, you won't, because he knows you and that would blow my cover," Stanley said firmly. "I know you want me to be safe and you like this man, but the truth is neither of us knows him."

"But you don't know this Yvan Thompson either," Cornelius said.

Stanley sighed and ran his fingers through his messy hair, then let his head fall in his hands.

"Stanley?" Cornelius said in a small voice.

He flew over to him.

"I just need something..." Stanley said in a choked voice. "I need to do something. I can't live for all eternity, never aging, and just thinking about what I lost..."

Cornelius placed his little hand on his shoulder and rubbed it softly.

"You're not happy..." he said.

"I'm happy with you, but... every time I go out and see couples and families, I think about her," Stanley said softly. "I'll never be alright, Cornelius. I can never erase what she did to me. She gave me a dream and then snatched it from me!"

"But you can have other dreams," Cornelius told him. "You can make new friends, people you can trust, like Eve. What if there are other people like you who have suffered and would like to be your friends?"

"Friends with a murderer? Are you insane?" Stanley said in a cynical voice.

"Well, the seraphim are not your friends. They don't care whether you are happy; they won't even call you by your name," Cornelius said.

Stanley rubbed the tears away from his face and looked once again at the letter on his desk. Eve did not know what sort of job he truly did, but she sensed a trap. Why would the seraphim want to trap him? Was this Joseph another one of their hitmen they wanted to get rid of? And if they could decide to get rid of him, they could also decide to get rid of Stanley. If that was the case, he didn't have time to write Eve and ask her for another tarot reading. His options were limited. But there was someone he could ask about Yvan Thompson and Joseph Stein, someone not involved with the demons or the vampires, and who had helped him in the past.

He reached into his breast pocket and pulled out Cat's feather. He always carried it on him as a good luck charm.

"Cat!" he said. "Cat-sìth!"

He did not have to wait too long until Cat appeared, but not where he expected it. The sìth fell down the chimney in which, luckily, the fire had died out. Cat got up, rubbing its bottom, and Stanley jumped out of his chair, startled.

"These chimneys are so bumpy!" Cat said.

"Uh... sorry," Stanley said.

The creature always appeared in such odd places... It dusted its suit to remove all the ashes.

"How can I help you, lost traveler?" it then said with a feline grin and sparkling eyes.

"I'm lost, and you've always helped me find my way," Stanley said, lowering his eyes.

"That is what cat guides do best," Cat said proudly.

"I don't know who to trust anymore," Stanley said.

"Ah. That is always a complex question," Cat said.

"Do you know anything about Yvan Thompson and Joseph Stein?" Stanley asked.

"I can check. One moment," Cat said.

It pulled out a small notebook and wrote down both names, one after another, and underneath each of them, information appeared on the paper.

"What would you like to know?" it asked.

"Is Joseph Stein a criminal?"

"What is a criminal in your world? Please be more precise."

"Murderers, hitmen, conspirators..."

Cat wrote down notes.

"And does feeding count as murder in the vampire world?" it asked.

"No, that is allowed, as well as formal duels," Stanley said. "A murderer in the vampire world would be someone who kills ruthlessly, out of revenge, or to hide a crime."

Cat seemed to add up numbers, then turned back to him with a smile.

"Yes, he has committed fifty-two murders."

"Alright, we have our answer," Stanley told Cornelius, but Cornelius said: "Wait, how many murders has Yvan Thompson committed?"

Cat looked at the notebook again.

"Do witch hunts also count as murder?" it asked.

"I suppose, if they were carried out by a vampire for no other reason than sheer cruelty," Stanley said, frowning.

Cat nodded and jotted down notes.

"What about people dying after being tortured?"

"Also... wait, what did this man do?" Stanley asked.

Cat once again added up the numbers.

"Yvan Thompson has committed or ordered one thousand three-hundred and forty-eight murders," it said.

"One thousand..." Stanley repeated, astounded.

"Any other questions?" Cat asked.

"Are the seraphim trying to get rid of me?" Stanley asked.

Cat scratched the back of its head, pondering the question, then said: "Unfortunately, only the predictable sequence of the immediate future is written in my notebook."

"Then there's no way to find out..." Stanley said, disappointed.

"Who ever said that?" Cat said. "For unanswered questions, we can always use a crystal ball."

And with this, it waved its hand over Stanley's desk and a crystal ball appeared. Then, it sat in the chair and looked into it. Stanley and Cornelius gathered around it. They also looked into the ball, but they could see nothing.

"Oh... interesting," Cat said, leaning forward. "The answer is..."

Stanley waited, but Cat only said: "...Up to you."

"Cat! You're not being helpful!" Stanley said, irritated.

Cat turned back to him and smiled.

"Oh, you wanted all the details? My apologies," it said. "Joseph Stein met Yvan Thompson several hundred years ago and brought him another vampire who became an archangel, but Yvan didn't trust Joseph because of his dark nature as a necromancer - which is really the pot calling the kettle black since Yvan ordered the burning of hundreds of supposed witches during the Inquisition - and as a result Joseph also didn't trust him. Then the archangel, who was more loyal to Joseph than Yvan, decided to take a vacation from her duties, and Yvan was not happy about it because he was counting on her to spy on Joseph for him, but then she and Joseph had a fallout, then they became friends again, then the archangel requested Yvan's help to harbor fugitives... Anyway, all of them are involved with each other and their loyalties seem to go back and forth, they have all committed murders, but also done good deeds. So it is up to you to decide who to trust."

"That still doesn't help me much." Stanley sighed. "If only I had intuitions like Eve..."

"If I remember correctly, the last time I visited your mind, it was full of intuitions. You just always followed the least intuitive path," Cat remarked.

It was right. Before Stanley made that pact with Beelzebub, didn't all the arrows along the path he followed tell him exactly where he was going? And he went ahead and chose the wrong way rather than the way out. He always did things backwards. But now he had another guide, one whose intuitions were a lot better and more precise than his. He looked once more at Eve's letter on the desk.

"So, what path will you follow this time?" Cat asked.

"The one that I want to follow," Stanley said with a smile.

CHAPTER 14

CORNELIUS QUIETLY WALKED UP to the room with the number thirteen on the door. He listened for a moment, but heard no noise inside, so he crossed through the wall. The room he entered was small and cluttered, with clothing all over the bed and papers on the desk. This was definitely the place Stanley had described to him. The necromancer was gone, so the child ghost walked over to the desk and sat down in the chair. He picked up the fountain pen laying on the desk. It was a brand-new invention, and he had only ever written using quills, but he knew that these new pens did not need to be dipped in ink. He tried it out on a clean sheet of paper and it traced a smooth ink line just like magic. He giggled with excitement, then proceeded to draw a house, a tree, and a cloud above them. Then he remembered why he was there and began to write the message Stanley had him memorize: *'Leave London now. Danger.'*

It was not the entire message. Stanley wanted him to write something about the seraphim, but he did not know how to spell that word, so he drew a small pair of wings at the end of it.

He left the message on the desk, then took his drawing and hung it on a nail on the wall for the kind vampire who could see him. Stanley hadn't asked him to do that, but he wouldn't know, would he? Then, he quietly left the room, and when the tenant returned and sat at his desk, he saw the message and read it.

"Leave London?" he whispered, frowning.

He then looked up to the wall and saw the child's drawing and smiled.

"Thank you, little one," he said.

'April 12th, 1890,

Dearest Eve,

I apologize for the long silence; I was called abroad for work. I hope you received my postcards from Siberia (a dreadfully cold place). Thank you again for your advice about the duel. I am proud to say this time I followed it. I'm not sure what the outcome might have been if I hadn't, but I am now safe and sound. I decided to follow my own intuition (is that a Sagittarius trait?) and listen to yours. I may also have sought guidance from the fairy folk and Cornelius. Cornelius thinks I need more friends I can trust. He says I am not letting new people into my life I could become friends with. Perhaps he is right. But here I am writing you. I think that's a good starting point.

I am not in need of any hair growth lotion, however if you have a potion to make me wiser, please do send it! I could sure use a little wisdom now and then.

The weather in London is nice. By this, I mean cloudy. I do not like the sunshine and much prefer walking outside at night, in the moonlight. The moon in the sky watches over the gentle spirits of the earth, only we are too noisy and busy here in London to see them. I have briefly lived in Edinburgh, and I fondly remember the magic that permeated the land and the city. Edinburgh was the place where my dreams began and ended. I have too many bittersweet memories to ever return there. Is this what happens to every youth as they grow older? Do they go out into the world, their hearts filled with magic and dreams, only to get hurt and lose everything, and return home as adults? But I am letting my mind wander again...

I hope to read your words again soon, and I am sure you can explain my melancholy through the stars and their signs.

Your friend (hopefully),

Ernest'

'April 20th, 1890,

Dearest Ernest,

It is always with great pleasure I read your letters, please do not hesitate to share your thoughts with me. The weather in Paris is very pleasant, and perhaps a little sunnier than where you are. I would not know because I too am a solitary person who likes to walk by the moonlight. I often stroll through Montmartre, watching the people come and go in the cabarets and the café-concert venues. I sometimes wish I was younger so I could go to all the salons the artists frequent. A secret dream of mine is to become an artist's muse and model. I do sometimes buy a painting from an unknown artist on the banks of the Seine River, but that is the full extent of my interactions with that world.

I do not need the stars to explain to you your melancholy, for I feel the same. After some time, all our youthful dreams filled with magic and possibilities do seem to fade away, and we are left facing a reality that can be dull. Perhaps we do become adults when we give up on magic. My own bittersweet memories are in the south of France, where I grew up. I come from the mountains there. I still sometimes dream of the forests with the tall pine trees, their secret trails and mysteries. Now you know my secret: I am a peasant girl. Please don't share it with the press if I ever become famous!

How old are you, dear Ernest? I look twenty, but I feel like I am over a hundred years old sometimes!

Reading your letters always brings me joy, so please do write me again.

Your friend,

Eve'

'*April 27th, 1890,*

Dearest Eve,

Your last letter troubled me, and I feel like I ought to share with you the reason. When I lived in Edinburgh, a few years ago, I had a recurring dream. In this dream, I awakened in a pine forest somewhere in the mountains. A golden thread was tied to my finger. I followed the thread and found a young girl dressed in peasants' clothes. The other end of the golden thread was tied to her finger. I did not see her face, for she was wearing a mask. As the dream progressed, I saw myself dancing with her at a masquerade ball in the last century. Perhaps this is all the product of my imagination, but after reading your letter I cannot help but wonder if you traveled through my dreams and met me in the pine forest?

I apologize if I sound like a lunatic or yet another bad man trying to seduce you. That is not my intention and I would never dare mislead a woman. I just wanted to share my dream with you.

By the way, I am twenty-six, but I also feel like an old man! Life has really made me age quickly, but reading your letters makes me feel young again.

Your friend,

Ernest'

'*May 6th, 1890,*

Dearest Ernest,

Your letter did not upset me in any way. On the contrary, it made me very happy. I must confess that I have had the same dream, only in it the man I met was wearing a mask. I do believe we traveled in each other's dreams, or our spirits met in the realm of magic somehow. A legend says that two souls destined to meet are tied together by an invisible thread. Perhaps we were destined to meet in this life, and since it did not happen in the real world, our souls sought each other out in their dreams.

In my dream, you were tall (taller than me, that is), and had brown hair. Is this true? I dare not send you a photograph of me, but I am short and have black hair. The place you saw in your dream are the mountains of Gevaudan, where I come from. I grew up on a small farm, listening to the local folktales and legends and the spirits of the mountain. Everything in nature, from the soil to the trees, is inhabited by spirits, and those humans who listen carefully can still hear their voices. Of course, in Paris, one can hardly hear them, but I am sure someone like you would see many ghosts walking down the old, paved streets. Have you ever heard of the Catacombs underneath the city, where the bones of thousands of people are said to be kept? I bet you it is one of our most haunted places. If you ever come to visit me, I would love to go into them with you, and perhaps you could tell me what the dead whisper to you.

Do write me again and tell me more about you.

Your friend,

Eve'

'May 12th, 1890,

Dearest Eve,

I read about your home region in France. What a fascinating place to grow up in, surrounded by all this magic and mystery! And I would love to visit Paris and its Catacombs with you, if you are not afraid (but I do not think you fear the unknown, rather you embrace it as part of this world). I'm afraid I grew up in an average middle-class home in Kensington. My family was wealthy enough to have a maid and a governess and mingle with society, but they held no title and they were not great land owners. Because of a slight speech impediment, I was kept at home, where I spent most of my time playing with Cornelius. There were many spirits in my home, and some of them were frightening. Unlike you, I did not embrace the unknown, and yet I could never escape it. Perhaps that is why I chose to become a paranormal investigator. Like you, I cannot hear the spirits of the earth in London, but I did hear and see them in Scotland. Have you heard of the legend of the cat-sìth? I believe I may have met it, in a train. I still cannot tell whether I was dreaming or awake, but I saw many spirits sitting in the train that night, among the passengers. They all looked somewhat like children, and some even had furry ears! They wore colorful clothing and trinkets, and all had a sort of green aura about them.

You do not need to send me your photograph. I was able to attend one of your lectures once, although you would never have noticed someone like me. You were very beautiful, much more so than all the other women present. I dare to say you have something more than they do. I should not send you a photograph of me, for I fear you may be terribly disappointed. I am not your average man. I was born in a female body, but always thought of myself as a boy, and later a man as I grew up. But my physique is what it is: I am not very tall, rather skinny, and I do have brown hair. Very few people know what I am, but I wanted to share it with you because I trust you and I know you will understand...

Hoping to hear from you again soon,
Your admirer,
Ernest'

'May 21st, 1890,
Dearest Ernest,
Thank you for sharing with me the magic you witnessed in Scotland. My heart swells with joy every time I read your letters and

find out how similar we are. I have never felt close to any man in my life, not even the one I loved for so many years. I am grateful that the golden thread of fate led me to you and you to me. I do not live in your world, but through your letters I feel like I am already a part of it. You do not need to worry about your appearance or how manly you are. Since you have shared your secret with me, I will also share mine with you: I was born in a male body but, like you, I always identified as the opposite. You and I are the same, Ernest, I understand everything you have been through growing up and probably still go through every day. I always felt a special connection between us, from the moment I received your first letter and traveled in your dreams, and now I can understand why. Oh, Ernest, can we meet in person? I am very busy, but if you ever come to one of my lectures again, please do not hide in the crowd. Come and talk to me. I have so much affection for you already, if only I could put a face on your name...

Write me again, traveler of my heart,

Your admirer,

Eve'

'June 7ᵗʰ, 1890,

Dearest Eve,

I read your letter over and over and held it to my heart. Yes, you and I are the same, and the golden thread of fate led us to each other. I had never met someone who understands me and the world I live in like you do, a woman not afraid to hear my stories of hauntings or visit the Catacombs of Paris with me, a woman who would guide me through the pine forests of Gevaudan and tell me what the spirits there whisper, a woman who can see the essence of my soul, and never judges me, but embraces what is unique about me. All the kindness and magic of the spirits seem to flow through your golden heart, and I am in awe before you. You are so much more than all the other women I have met... I have framed a photograph of you I found in *the newspaper and placed it beside my bed, so that I may always see you when I wake up and imagine that you are there with me. Your presence in my life brings me comfort and joy, and I would love to meet you if my work did not keep me away from home so often...*

Do write me again, sweet angel,

Your Ernest'

'June 15th, 1890,

Dearest Ernest,

If only you knew how your words touch my heart every time I read them, how they echo with mine! I still don't have a photograph of you (will you ever send me one?) You are the one I secretly think of while at work, while I walk down the banks of the Seine River at night, the one who appears in my dreams and dances with me in the masquerade ball of Time. Should I say more? Will you hate me if I do? I do not want these feelings to remain locked up in my heart... Every time one of your letters comes in the mail, my heart races with the excitement of a young girl in love. You too are much more than all the other men. Not only do you understand me perfectly, but you are not afraid of the world I live in, nor are you afraid of me like so many others. I have waited so long to find a man with enough courage to accept me as I am, but I have found you at last. But we cannot meet in person yet, so I shall have to be brave and write you the words in my heart. I think I am falling in love with you, Ernest, and it is the most beautiful feeling I have ever experienced. I tremble with fear as I write these words, hoping you will accept them like you have already accepted me... I am so scared of being betrayed and abused again, but with you I feel safe, safe enough to open my heart to you. There is still so much I need to tell you, and I do hope to tell you about myself face to face soon.

Your Eve'

'*June 22nd, 1890,*

Dearest Eve, my sweet angel,

I am not sure how to respond to your letter. I read it a thousand times, wondering what I should say, how to express my feelings with words... In the end, I found myself holding it to my heart and wishing it was you my arms were holding. My hands trembled as I held your letter and read it, wondering if it could be true, if you felt for me the way I feel for you. I had promised myself I would never fall in love again, but my heart has fallen for you, and yet in this free fall it is the high skies I reach with you! I repeat your name endlessly, and caress your portrait, and hold it when I sleep. I wish you were the one in my arms, so my fingers could caress your skin instead, and adorn it with kisses. I would fall to my knees for you and worship you, I would steal the moon from the sky of London and send it to you in Paris! Oh Eve, how could I have lived my life until now without knowing you? If love is madness, then I think I have become mad for you, but it is such a sweet and beautiful feeling! My heart is at peace now, knowing it belongs to you and no other, and I want it to be always yours...

Your lovestruck Ernest'

'*July 23rd, 1890,*

My dearest Eve,

Over a month and you never replied to me... I am terribly sorry if I got carried away. It was inappropriate of me to say such things, and I do hope I did not frighten you. I am just a stranger, a pen friend. You do not need to reply to me when I am getting too bold and assertive, I completely understand. Please do not make anything of my words and let us be friends again.

Ernest'

'*August 8th 1890,*

Dear Eve,

Why this silence? I thought we were close friends, who trusted each other. If I have done something wrong, please tell me honestly so I may correct myself. I do not want to lose our friendship over some words I should not have said...

Ernest'

'*August 19th, 1890,*

Dear Eve,

This will be the last letter I send you. I still don't know what happened and I ask myself every day what I did wrong, but you will not tell me. I have cried myself to sleep over the loss of what we had. Please Eve, if you care about me at all, send me just one word, let me know why you suddenly hate me. I never wanted to lose you, but it seems like I have after all...

Farewell,

Ernest'

Stanley put his pen down and let his tears fall on the page. Once again, a woman left him, and this time without a word of explanation. Was he a fool for believing there was something between them, just because they shared the same dream and exchanged a few letters? Did he frighten her when he got carried away and talked about worshipping her? Had he gone too far, too fast?

Cornelius came to him and slipped his little arm around his shoulders.

"I'm sure there is an explanation," he said. "Maybe something happened."

"Nothing happened to her. I read in the newspaper that she gave a lecture in Liverpool last week," Stanley said. "She's just ignoring me, and I'm not sure why. She's the one who first talked about love..."

"I'm sorry, Stanley," Cornelius said.

"I guess I was just wrong again. I trusted the wrong person," Stanley said.

He pulled out a handkerchief from his pocket and wiped his moist eyes.

After he warned the necromancer, he had left London, and the seraphim had lost track of him in France. They contacted the French equivalent to their order, the Freemasons, but they refused to cooperate due to old rivalries between the two countries. France did not have a vampire dark lord, they had beheaded him during the Revolution. Their underworld had its own system of governance which was not so involved with the Church. But none of it mattered to Stanley anymore. He had completed his assignment and reported that he found no evidence against Joseph Stein, then accepted another assignment and another. He was often away from home for several days at a time, sometimes weeks or months, but he always made sure to write Eve when he returned, and at first she had replied. The timing of her letters showed that she usually replied to him within less than two days, and he thought it meant something. And when she told him she had been having the same dreams as him, something in his heart opened up again. He who had promised himself he would never love again had begun to feel something for her. It began with trust. Even though he still could not bring himself to be honest with her about being a vampire and a demon and a hitman, he told her about Cornelius, and she already accepted him as her own ghost. Though she had not yet told him what he already knew, that she was a vampire, she had begun giving him hints that she may be older than he thought and that she lived at night. And when she told him she felt something for him, too, he was over-joyed. He remembered reading her letter over and over and holding it to his heart as though it were her. She seemed ready to move on from her past heartbreaks, perhaps with him, so he felt confident enough to respond with the same. But perhaps the expression of his feelings was too intense for her. Now that he thought about it, what woman would want her pen friend to obsess over her day and night and hold her portrait when he slept? He probably sounded like a crazy stalker or some other kind of deranged individual. Perhaps he was. His only other experience of love was with Callie, and when she tricked him he fell face forward into her lies, ready to believe anything she told him just to get the bits and pieces of love she threw out there for him like a master would throw food to their dog.

He shook his head. There was no point in losing himself in endless questioning. Women were obscure, manipulative creatures, and the less he trusted them, the better. He mailed the letter to Eve without any hopes, then went hunting. He was not so gentle with his prey that night and did not give her the 'prince's kiss' nor take a token from her after she was gone, nor did he apologize to her spirit when it left her body. She had suffered and died, just like he did, only his suffering had been longer and the curse upon him was eternal. He then returned home with a heavy heart, took Eve's letters, her framed picture, and walked over to the fireplace.

"Are you really going to burn them?" Cornelius asked him in a small voice.

He was lying on the sofa, holding a cushion. He too felt sad because he was the one who had always encouraged Stanley and Eve's relationship, and in the end, it had only hurt him.

Stanley gazed at the dancing flames for a long time, still wondering how he could have let himself develop feelings for yet another cunning and manipulative woman.

"She obviously didn't mean any of the things she wrote me. She was just playing with me, like Callie," he said, and he threw the whole stash of letters and the portrait into the fire and watched them burn. The glass on the frame cracked and burst, and the picture also went up in flames. Then, not willing to talk anymore, he went to bed. Cornelius followed him and tucked him under the blankets.

Stanley was getting used to heartbreaks now, and when he awakened the next evening, though a great and terrible sadness still gripped his heart, he knew he would get over it, eventually. All he had to do was focus on other things for some time, like his work. Killing people, wasn't it the best way to get over a heartache? If it wasn't, at least it would give him an outlet for his anger. But he did not have any assignments at the moment.

He got out of bed, feeling heavier than ever before, and got dressed. Then he mechanically went downstairs to the kitchen and fixed himself some strong black tea - something he could still enjoy as a vampire - and brought it up to the office, where Cornelius awaited him.

"Looks like a quiet night. I might go to the bookstore," he said, trying to sound cheerful, but he could not fool his best friend.

"Stanley, you don't have to pretend for me," Cornelius reminded him.

"I'm not pretending. I'm perfectly fine," Stanley said.

He took the newspaper and began to read it. Or pretend to read it. Just the headlines. He could not focus on anything, really. He needed some distraction, and right now. And, as though his silent plea had been heard, someone knocked on the front door. He got up and headed into the hallway, and quickly checked himself in the small oval mirror hanging on the wall. At least now as a vampire he always looked good, even after a heartbreak. Whoever was at the door – a salesperson, a vengeful demon sent by Beelzebub – he could deal with them. But it was neither. Aleksandra was the one who had knocked on the door. In her elegant royal blue ball gown with purple lace, her shoulders covered with a long black and purple silk cape, and her hair up in a loose bun and decorated with black feathers, she looked more like a demon than an angel, and like she had come to the wrong neighborhood.

"Good evening," she said with a smile.

"Aleksandra? How did you even make it here? It's a wonder no one attacked you in this neighborhood dressed like this," Stanley said, surprised.

"I am a vampire. If a man attacks me, he is likely to become my dinner," she reminded him.

"True. So what brings you here?" he asked, trying to sound casual.

He did not dislike her; she seemed to be the funniest among the seraphim, and at least she called him by the right name.

"You haven't had any assignments in a while. I was afraid you might be bored. So I thought perhaps I could take you to a party," she said.

"You know I, of all people, am not allowed to show my face at social events with members of the Order," he said.

"But this will be a masked banquet," she said, handing him a small black mask. The mischievous sparkle in her eyes meant that tonight she wanted to shed her seraph robe and just have fun – preferably with him.

"A masked vampire banquet? Never heard of that," he said.

"Sometimes we too want to enjoy the good things in life," she said. "So, are you coming or shall I have to ask the candyman?"

He smirked.

"I'm afraid you're not muscular enough to be his type," he said. "Fine, I'll be your date. Give me just a moment."

He was habitually well dressed now, always in his black suit and tie, so he did not need to change, just to let Cornelius know he was going out. So he grabbed his hat and peeked into the office.

"I'm going to a party. You stay here," he told him.

"What kind of party? Why can't I go?" Cornelius asked.

"It's an adult party with vampires. You might see things you don't want to see," Stanley said. He did not know what a vampire banquet entailed, but there was likely going to be a lot of blood spilled - not a suitable sight for a seven-year-old.

He went outside, closed the door, offered Aleksandra his arm, and they began walking.

"So where are we going?"

"Not too far from here, just a few streets up. A cherub has a mansion there - he is the one who throws the wildest parties," she said with a wink.

"I hope old Yvan is not invited then. He's likely to bring a Bible and start preaching," he joked and she laughed.

"Yvan is never invited," she said with an accomplice grin.

He also smiled. Perhaps he would be able to think about something else than his heartbreak that night after all.

The banquet was to take place in an old and fairly large Tudor mansion on a gated property. They put on their masks before they arrived, and they were greeted at the door by a masked human who either did not know or did not care what the guests were going to eat that night. Stanley and Aleksandra mingled with the guests on the first floor in the large ballroom, then went up to the second floor, where they sat down on sofas. Stanley looked around the room. If the outside of the mansion looked old and the garden in need of some work, the inside was quite luxurious, with typical white walls and ceiling and the thick brown beams supporting it. The polished wooden floors sparkled under the candlelight, and a warm fire burned in the large stone chimney. The furniture was mostly from the time period, with the addition of modern chairs and sofas, but the banquet table was missing. Three human musicians in a corner played a slow and relaxing song for the guests. Most people knew who was coming or not, but everyone was there anonymously, to get up to all the mischief their order did not permit.

"How do you like it?" Aleksandra asked, leaning over to her companion.

"Where's the table?" Stanley asked.

"Oh, it's takeout tonight. I hope you like fresh young men," she said.

"Unfortunately I prefer young women," he said. Men tasted to him like milk tea and sugar: bad.

"Well, there might be other things on the menu," she said with a grin.

"Tell me more," he said, leaning over to her.

"Later," she said.

He did not know what he was doing that night, nor did he care. He was not the only one breaking the rules of the Order. Apparently everyone did, and they were all there as strangers that night, they owed no explanations to anyone.

After wine and appetizers were served, the unsuspecting humans were also served - even the musicians. There were far more humans present than vampires, so the vampires could gorge themselves without restraint, ignoring the most basic rule of the vampire society: to feed only when necessary. Guests took the prey they wanted outside or to a separate room, and the poor humans never knew that they had not walked into an orgy but into a banquet in which they were the main course. Aleksandra took three young men with her and soon returned and slouched on the sofa beside Stanley, who had not fed yet.

"Oh, I'm so full!" she complained.

He smirked.

"Don't give yourself indigestion."

The vampires with musical skills picked up the discarded violins and began to play them, and the lights were dimmed. Guests were returning from the garden and the back rooms smelling like fresh blood and lust. People having affairs sat on each other's lap and began getting comfortable and petting.

"Oh, dear friend, aren't you going to eat something?" Aleksandra told Stanley in a sweet voice.

"You?" he said, turning to her with a grin.

"You can touch, but you can't bite, naughty boy!" she said.

"That still leaves me a lot of other options," he said.

"Come," she said, getting up and inviting him to follow her.

She took him through the lazy crowd of sleepy or aroused guests, some laying on each other on the sofas, others on cushions on the floor. The whole thing had gone from banquet to orgy very quickly. Stanley knew the Order was probably not as pure as what they preached, but he never imagined to what extent.

"Is it always like this?" he whispered to Aleksandra, casually taking her hand.

She giggled and turned to him.

"It's not nearly as wild as when we bring in the clergy!"

"That must be interesting!" he laughed with her.

Because she knew he would not feel comfortable taking off his clothes in front of other people, she took him to a small closet that had been a servant's room and contained a bed. They had brought with them only one candle. She set in on a small shelf on the wall and locked the door. He sat on the bed, removed his tie, and unbuttoned the top of his shirt, still not knowing how far she wanted to go, but she was apparently very much in the mood. and immediately sat on his lap and began kissing him.

"You taste sweet," she whispered when their lips parted.

"Not as sweet as you," he said, and he kissed her again.

Now he was getting in the mood too. In normal times, he was not very attracted to blondes and preferred brunettes, but that night he was sad and he wanted to forget everything and be comforted, even by a stranger.

With eager hands, he tore open the front of her dress and the laces of her corset, and she giggled with delight. Then, he lay her on the bed and tore open the rest of her dress to get to his banquet, and she let out soft cries and moans as he tasted her in slow but hungry strokes. The small closet was getting hot, despite their vampire bodies being only lukewarm at their highest levels of arousal, and the naughty seraph grabbed Stanley's hair as he devoured her, always pressing him for more, then they switched places and he fully unbuttoned his shirt while she rid him of his trousers. She then tried to remove his binder, but he gently pushed her away – she was not allowed to be that intimate with him. She smiled and tasted him next, looking up to him with languid eyes under her mask, just like Callie used to do. It made him suddenly uncomfortable and brought back memories he wanted to forget, so he grabbed her hair and pushed her head down. She liked that too. He let her do her business and lay back, thinking of nothing, and then she sat on his lap and rubbed herself against him, and he pleasured her with his fingers while drowning his somber thoughts in the softness of her breasts.

The little vixen had enormous appetites, but nothing he couldn't handle after being with a succubus, and when they were all spent, they lay together in the near darkness and she sighed with contentment. But he was in a bad mood. Images of him and Callie danced through his mind now, along with Eve's words and the pain he had felt, when she suddenly stopped answering him. He had loved Callie with all his young heart, but things were different with Eve. The connection between him and Callie was largely physical – because she was a succubus, and back then he loved with his body as much as he loved with his heart – but the connection he thought he had with Eve was intellectual and emotional. She lived in the same sort of world as him and seemed to understand him so perfectly... or not, since she abandoned him. He closed his eyes in pain and frustration.

"Oh, what's the matter?" Aleksandra asked like she would ask a child who was pouting.

"Nothing," he said.

Aleksandra then laughed to herself and said: "If only Yvan knew what we all do behind closed doors..."

"Don't tell him, he might faint," Stanley joked, and she laughed again. "What's his problem, anyway? I'm pretty sure undead creatures don't go to Heaven, so why is he so bent on calling me the wrong name and imposing chastity on us – down to our thoughts?" he asked.

"Yvan was a devout Christian lord in the Medieval Ages. Some say he participated in the Crusades," she explained. "He was certain a place in Heaven awaited him when he died, but he found out instead that his place would be down on Earth, as a vampire. After he became a seraph, he worked in close connection with the human clergy to make sure all creatures of the underworld submitted to the authority of God. I'm not sure what he is hoping for, honestly."

"One of those men, huh?" he said. "What about you, honey?"

"Me? I was once a great queen of Kievan Rus..." she said with some regret. "My armies conquered, burned, and looted villages of pagan idol-worshippers. All knew my name and I was feared."

"I thought you couldn't be part of the Order if you had committed senseless murder," he said. Yvan had too, and now he was sure Adeyemi's hands were not any cleaner. But she laughed.

"Christians see the murder of non-Christians as heroic. I was called a saint..."

"Are you even Christian?" he asked.

"Not one bit," she laughed. "Are you?"

"I only believe in myself," he said, smirking.

He'd had enough cuddling with her, so he stretched out and lit himself a cigarette. She took one from him and also lit it, and they sat facing each other on the small bed, their legs intertwined.

"Dear Stanley, I wonder what kind of woman you would ever let into your heart," she said, smiling.

The lying, deceitful ones apparently.

"Is it necessary to let anyone in?" he asked in response. "So, do I get promoted now that I officially slept with my boss?" he joked, and she laughed even harder.

"You need to do a lot more than that!"

"Oh yeah?" he said.

And he crawled over to her and kissed her once more. He still needed to release some tension, and she was ready for a rematch.

They left the banquet in the early hours of morning and parted ways on the corner of a street. A thick fog had settled over the city – nothing unusual for London – but Stanley sensed something else in the fog, something dark and oppressive. He stopped and turned to look around him. It could be a demon or another enemy. He made himself invisible as a precaution and resumed walking. Then, seemingly out of nowhere, a small, red toy ball came rolling past his feet. He stopped and remained quiet, and the ball stopped for a few seconds, then continued rolling. This time he followed it at a distance. It rolled slowly down the street, then turned the corner and eventually caught up with Aleksandra, who was walking alone, and hit the heel of her boot. Stanley quietly moved into the shadows and observed her. She turned around, picked up the ball, and looked around her, frowning. Like Stanley, she sensed the presence of something, but neither of them knew who or what was there. Stanley thought about making himself visible and joining her, but after all, she was just a stranger to him and he was not even supposed to be there. She did not expect his protection, neither did he owe it to her.

Seconds passed and nothing happened, but just as Aleksandra was about to toss the ball, it began to shake in her hand and a large jack-in-the-box head suddenly burst out of it. Surprised but wary of such tricks, Aleksandra quietly dropped the ball and began to run, and it followed her, nipping at her ankles, until she tripped over an invisible string and fell. Stanley followed them, still hidden in the shadows. So far, nothing much was happening. Someone was obviously trying to frighten Aleksandra, and the level of danger she was in would depend on how powerful that creature was. As a seraph, Aleksandra had the means to defend herself, and her body began to liquefy like water. She was a shapeshifter. But a small hand suddenly appeared out of the fog and traced a symbol in the air. A childlike voice then said: "Ice!"

The bizarre spell immediately turned her liquid form into ice and frost formed on the ground around her. Stanley took a step back, surprised, and his foot hit a small stone, signaling his presence. The jack-in-the-box immediately started rolling in his direction, and a yo-yo came out of the fog from his side. Stanley dodged both and rolled on the ground, but another yo-yo attacked him, this time from the other side. Either the creature in the mist had doppelgangers, or it could teleport parts of its body through the mist. That had to be it. So where was the one controlling and coordinating the attacks? Stanley slowed down time and quickly looked around him until he noticed a small figure hidden under a dark blue cloak in the shadows of an alleyway. He rushed over to it and as he came closer, he caught a glimpse of the mysterious one: she was a young girl of about twelve, with cropped blond hair mostly hidden under the hood of her cloak, and her face was painted like a clown's - a sad clown. Of course, professional assassins, whatever their age, would not want to be easily identifiable, and this one certainly wasn't. He sensed something supernatural about her, but she was neither a vampire nor a demon. Either way, she had attacked him, so she had to be eliminated.

He quickly moved behind her and grabbed her with one arm and placed the blade of his pocketknife against her throat. Time returned to normal, and she seemed startled.

"Don't move," he whispered, but she began to laugh.

Immediately, her body dissolved into thousands of droplets of water, leaving only the cloak in his hands, and she reappeared near the frozen body of Aleksandra. Now he could see her full body shape and it was indeed that of a child, but her moves were like that of an automaton. She wore nothing but a light, short-sleeved white dress, and the joints of her elbows, her wrists, her knees and ankles looked like those of a puppet.

She turned her expressionless face in his direction again and suddenly smiled and crushed Aleksandra's head with her foot. The vampire's body dissolved into ashes.

"I don't know who you are, but this is none of your business," she said, looking in Stanley's direction.

He did not move or answer. After all, she could be working for another jealous and vindicative seraph. No one could be trusted in the underworld.

She then turned around and stretched out her hand, and the jack-in-the-box came rolling back to her. She picked it up and softly petted its head, and it returned to the ball.

"Let's play again next time," she then said, this time in a friendly voice, before disappearing into the fog.

CHAPTER 15

STANLEY RETURNED HOME BEFORE dawn, and not feeling one bit better than he had before.

"You were out all night..." Cornelius said, who had been waiting for him in his bedroom, reading a book on the bed.

"Sorry," Stanley said.

He removed his jacket and set it on the back of the chair, then he proceeded to remove his tie.

"Who did you get in trouble with this time?" Cornelius asked in a reproachful voice.

"Nobody,' Stanley lied.

Cornelius returned to his book while he changed into his nightshirt.

"Then who was the woman who knocked on the door?" he asked.

"Just a coworker."

Cornelius lifted his gazed and gave him that look again.

"What? I don't know her, she doesn't know me, we just went to a party together," Stanley said.

"But every time you go out without me, you seem to get yourself into more trouble," Cornelius said.

"I'm already in trouble with a major demon and possibly a seraph and all those who work for them. How much worse does it get?" Stanley said, cynical.

He got under the blankets and rolled over.

"Stanley..."

"What?"

"You're not happy," Cornelius said.

"Is anyone happy in this world?" Stanley said bitterly. "Now go to bed, or at least let me sleep. I'm tired."

But that night, as though fate was mocking him, he dreamed of the pine forest again. The sky was dark, the air bitterly cold, and he was standing in knee-high snow. He looked at the golden thread on his finger and it was hanging in the snow, and when he tugged at it the end appeared. It was broken, because Eve had broken off whatever they had. But he still remembered the path to find her in this forest, so he followed it, his heartbeat quickening. Anger was growing in his heart again at the thought she had abandoned him.

He eventually found the large rock behind which she was usually hiding, and when he went around it he found her. She was sitting near the stone hearth of an ancient kitchen, in her peasant dress, like Cinderella. She wore no mask that night and her face was sad. Her empty eyes gazed at the letter she was holding in her hands. One of his letters? All around them, Stanley could hear the echoes of women's voices:

"Et alors, Eve? Ton Anglais?"

"Un Anglais? Et ton Allemand?"

"Shh... les filles! Au travail!" That was Eve's voice.

"Quelle chance quand-même, avec tous tes hommes!"

Stanley barely spoke a word of French, but in his dream, he could understand it perfectly. Eve's name sounded so beautiful in her native language... But the other women were talking about 'her Englishman and her German', and how many men she had. Stanley's heart was crushed. So she stopped writing him because she had someone else - possibly several men. But the young girl sitting in the hearth was crying, and her hands shaking as she read the letter. She covered her mouth as though she could not believe what she was reading, then dropped the letter and covered her face with her hands and wept loudly. Stanley frowned and picked up the letter and read it. It was his letter, his handwriting, his style, but it appeared to have been edited:

'Dearest Eve,

I am not sure how to respond to your letter. I read it a thousand times, wondering what I should say, how to express my feelings with words. I think of you as a dear friend, and I never imagined anything more. I only shared my secret with you because I thought you would understand. I have recently met someone and we are now living together. I was going to announce it to you in this letter and I hoped you would be happy for us, but now I realize I may have only hurt your feelings. I am so sorry for any misunderstanding I may have created.

Ernest'

"Eve! This is... this is not my letter!" he said, turning to her.

But she could not hear or see him. Instead, Cat walked out of the shadows, carrying a large pair of scissors.

"You? Did you do this? Did you cut the golden thread between us?" Stanley shouted, furious.

"Me? No, I did not," Cat replied, looking confused.

"Then why are you carrying scissors?" Stanley said.

"To cut a rose," Cat said, showing him a red rose pinned to its breast pocket.

"In the middle of winter?" Stanley said.

Cat looked at him, then at the poor girl crying in the hearth, then said: "Did I miss something?"

Stanley handed over the letter and Cat read it.

"Ouch, that was cold..." it then said.

"Those were not my words!" Stanley said. "In my letter, I told her how much I loved her!"

"How strange... I wonder if someone edited your letter," Cat said.

"Someone certainly did! And if not you, then who?" Stanley said, still agitated.

Cat reached in one of its pockets, then in the other, then pulled out a large magnifying glass and read the letter again, using it.

"Oh... what clever magic! I almost didn't see it," it said.

"Magic? Did a demon do this?" Stanley said.

"Someone with magical abilities for sure," Cat said, handing the letter back to him. "Is it a demon? Someone else? I do not know."

"Then why don't you just look into your crystal ball to find out?" Stanley said.

"Why don't you just turn back time and deliver your letter in person? This would prevent any misunderstanding from happening," Cat said in response.

"I can't..." Stanley said, lowering his head in defeat. "Eve can't know what I am."

"Why not?"

"Because I'm a hitman, a murderer. She will hate me if she finds out."

"Are you sure about it?"

"Yes... Besides, it sounds like she has someone else."

Stanley crumpled the letter in his hands. If he had not been honest with her, then neither had she. He felt terrible about the fact that she received that fake letter and it made her cry, but wouldn't he have cried anyway when he found out she was only playing games with him?

"I guess I should just give up. This dream meant nothing in the end," he said softly.

"I do not think so. I would always rather trust a dream than what I am told," Cat said.

"Why? There is only one truth, and now I know it," Stanley said, shaking his head.

"But you will not know that truth until you ask her," Cat said. "Apparently, she too trusted the words on a letter over her dream."

"I don't understand what you're trying to tell me..."

"As I told you before, there is no such thing as absolute happiness or absolute sadness in this world," Cat said with a grin. "Likewise, many things happen in people's lives that affect the decisions they make. At some point, this young woman read the words on the letter she received and made a decision based on them. Now you are making a decision based on words you heard, and yet neither of you has exchanged a word in real life yet."

"So you're saying I should go meet her and talk to her face to face?" Stanley said.

"I think that if you do, you may find out more about her and she about you – the good and the bad. The result of your meeting will depend on what is truly in your hearts, and only you and her know the answer."

The young girl wiped away her tears and got up. She took a broomstick and began to sweep the hearth. A shadow moved among the trees, like a creature lurking, but she did not notice it. Stanley immediately stepped in front of Eve, between her and whatever was stalking her, and the creature retreated, leaving behind the scent of woodfire smoke. A demon.

"Is that you Beelzebub? What do you want?" he said in a low and angry snarl.

"It looks like Cinderella has not yet found her prince. I do hope the wolf does not find her first," Cat said, turning to him.

"Who was it and what do they want?" Stanley asked anxiously.

"I do not know. Do you have enemies?" Cat said.

"Dozens for sure," Stanley said. "Is it after me?"

"Who knows... However, it seems like it does not want you and Eve to find each other," Cat said.

Stanley turned back to Eve and gazed at her sad face and her swollen, puffy eyes. Was she in danger? But if so, what could he do for her now? She no longer trusted him, and he did not know whether he should trust her.

"It looks like your fairy tale is only just beginning, Stanley," Cat then said, its grin widening.

"But I'm not the prince she is waiting for," Stanley said. "More like an evil wizard..."

"But isn't she a witch?"

Stanley smirked. Indeed, perhaps they were not a prince and a princess, but a wizard and a witch. In a way, they were a good match.

Cat stepped forward and handed him the rose from its breast pocket.

"Here is another magical token for your journey. You seem to need them a lot," it said.

The rose floated over to his chest and disappeared inside him.

"Will it be difficult? What am I up against?" he asked.

"I sense that your journey will be difficult, but, like any hero, you will find help along the way."

"But who should I trust?" Stanley asked.

"You have learned to follow your intuitions now. I think you will be fine," Cat said, smiling.

Stanley turned back to the dark pine forest surrounding them and began to power up.

"Alright, demon, are you ready for the bogeyman?" he said, before rushing into the darkness.

Cat smiled and said: "I love fairy tales..."

Stanley awakened to the sound of the telephone ringing. He did not know what time it was: he had disposed of all timepieces he owned after all that happened with Callie and the Time Key.

"Leave me alone!" he grunted.

He rolled over in his bed and pulled the pillow over his head. Now he no longer had William or his father to awaken him, but he had the seraphim instead. After a few minutes, the telephone stopped ringing. He sat up in his bed, disheveled. What was that dream all about? Did Beelzebub find out he had stolen the Time Key, and this was her revenge? Probably not, or a swarm of demons and vengeful spirits would already be surrounding his home. Unless she was dead... He tried to replay in his mind all that had happened in the last year – everything unusual, that is. First, he received that warning from Eve about a duel, and he was sent to investigate another necromancer, which could have resulted in a duel and his death if not for the fact this Joseph Stein was such a kind man. Then, after he advised him to leave London, someone messed with his correspondence with Eve, and the moment he gave up on her Aleksandra appeared out of nowhere to seduce him, but she got murdered. The three events could be unrelated, or they could all have been planned by someone who wanted to show him just how much control they had over his life. That someone wanted him to know they could send him to his death with another necromancer, kill anyone who came too close to him, and even destroy his relationship with a stranger in another country. One name immediately came to his mind: Yvan Thompson. But what could his motive be? Certainly not his religious bigotry. It had to be something more. Power... Of course. Stanley, Eve, Joseph, and Aleksandra were all very powerful vampires, and Yvan saw at least one of them as a threat, even if he had done nothing wrong. What if he was secretly coveting Adeyemi's throne and getting rid of all potential rivals, or keeping them from forming alliances? And what was the candyman's involvement in all of this, since he worked both for demons and angels? Yvan could have made an alliance with a major demon, he wouldn't put it past him... Stanley rubbed his face and growled in frustration. This was all too confusing, even for him. He really could use a vacation.

"Stanley! What happened?" Cornelius asked, who had been sleeping in the wall.

He came out and climbed onto his friend's bed.

"I had a dream..." Stanley said. "Eve received a letter that appeared to be from me but was not. That's why she stopped writing me. Someone doesn't want us to develop any kind of relationship."

"The seraphim?" Cornelius asked.

"I don't know. There is a demon lurking around her – in her dreams at least," Stanley said. "There is something else I didn't tell you. Last night I encountered another assassin, a little girl who killed Aleksandra. There was nothing I could do."

Cornelius shook his head disapprovingly.

"It's getting too dangerous, Stanley. You need to back out of all of it."

Stanley ignored him. He quickly got out of bed and got dressed, then grabbed a carpet bag and threw a few clothes in it.

"Are you going somewhere?" Cornelius asked, getting off the bed.

"We are," Stanley said. "To France."

"France? Are we going to meet Eve?" Cornelius said, suddenly excited.

"That's right," Stanley said with a smile. "There are a lot of things going on between the angels and the demons here, and I'm pretty sure I can handle them. But if someone is going to harm Eve, then they will have to face me first. Nobody touches my girl."

Cornelius smiled with sheer joy, but the telephone started ringing again. Really? This was not a good time. Stanley rushed down the stairs with his bag and into his office and picked up the phone.

"Who the hell is it?" he shouted into the receiver.

"Yvan," Yvan's deep voice said on the other side.

Of course. Who else would it be?

"I'm a little busy right now," Stanley said.

"Then you'll make time for me," Yvan said in a menacing tone.

"Who says?"

"I say. You work for us."

Stanley grunted and sat down on the chair.

"Alright, go ahead. What do you want?"

He had expected Yvan to question him about Aleksandra's death, but he didn't, which confirmed to him that he was connected to it.

"I'm still waiting on your report about Joseph Stein," Yvan said.

"Didn't I already submit it? The man is innocent. He's not involved with demons or plotting anything against you," Stanley said with growing impatience.

"You only followed him for a few days, then he mysteriously vanished and you handed us an empty report," Yvan said.

"The report was empty because I didn't find anything," Stanley said. "He met up with friends and talked about a new book he was writing, visited a grave, then spent the rest of his time drowning his sorrow in alcohol."

"I find it rather surprising that you even got close to him and he did not kill you. Necromancers do not let each other live..." Yvan said.

"Perhaps he had other things on his mind than killing me," Stanley replied.

"And obviously so did you..."

"I did not know my orders were to kill him."

"They were not," Yvan agreed. "Nevertheless, after he disappeared, he published a book exposing the vampire society and the existence of the Dark Lord of England and his apostles,"

"Vampires exposing themselves to humans is a class D crime, according to your own book of rules. It falls under the jurisdiction of the apostles, not the seraphim," Stanley reminded him.

In the vampire society, like in human society, crimes were handled in accordance with their severity and how dangerous the criminal was. Class D crimes were petty crimes and were handled by the apostles. The angels, cherubim, and seraphim dealt with high-profile criminals, such as spies or people in positions of power.

"A bounty has been issued on him," Yvan said.

Stanley didn't like that. But Joseph certainly knew the rules of the vampire society, he knew what he was getting himself into.

"Still not my problem," he said.

"Joseph is too powerful. No ordinary vampire will be able to capture or defeat him," Yvan said. "We were thinking about offering him a position instead."

"As a hitman?" Stanley asked, surprised.

"No, a position of power, when one comes up."

"And how is any of this related to my job?"

"Let's just say it would be simpler for everyone if he was eliminated now," Yvan said.

"Is this an assignment from the seraphim... or from you?" Stanley asked.

"From me," Yvan said. "We know that he fled to France, then boarded a ship for the Americas several months ago, then we lost track of him. Find him and kill him."

Stanley chuckled. Yvan didn't like that.

"You must obey our orders," he said.

"You would send your best hitman all the way across the world to eliminate a man who has committed only a petty crime, just because you're terrified of him being in a position of power someday?" Stanley said.

"Who ever said you were the best?" Yvan retorted.

Stanley held his breath for a moment, then said: "No."

"You cannot refuse. You are under contract with us," Yvan reminded him.

"Yvan Thompson," he said coldly. "I have another theory. It was never about Joseph Stein, it was about eliminating those who are a threat to you, and that means both I and Joseph, and probably others too. You sent me to him hoping that, because our powers are similar, we would kill each other. Joseph is a sweet man, but I did get a glimpse of his dark side. I can see yours too. In fact, I investigated you a little and found out that you have a tendency to work behind the scenes to eliminate those who might threaten your power. You were involved in the witch hunts, and I'm sure many of your personal enemies got tortured and burned at the stake. What an easy way to get rid of vampires while keeping your little seraph hands clean!"

Silence on the other end. It meant Stanley was right. His heart was racing now, with excitement and some fear. He could just have remained quiet and accepted the assignment and run away, but now that they were trying to hurt Eve, his anger had no limits, and he was ready to challenge the entire Order for her.

"You're playing with fire, Sophie Suspect," Yvan warned him.

"Listen up, you nincompoop," Stanley suddenly shouted. "My name is Stanley and you're the one playing with fire... I told you not to interfere in my personal life, but you did anyway. I swear if you ever try to hurt someone dear to me, you're going to see what the real Stanley is capable of, and it's going to be a lot scarier than what Joseph Stein can do!"

"If you actually read your contract, and I doubt you have, you would know that the penalty for disobeying our orders is death," Yvan said.

"I'm right here at home. Come and get me!" Stanley said, before slamming the receiver on the phone. He then unplugged the damned device and threw it across the room.

"There! We're done! No more hypocrites, no more dead-naming, no more lies!" he shouted. "Cornelius! Come! We're leaving!"

Cornelius showed up at the front door, ready and waiting. Stanley smiled, picked up his bag, and they headed out.

"Do you speak any French?" Stanley asked as they walked down the dark street.

"No, do you?" Cornelius said.

"No. I guess we'll just have to figure our way around Paris," Stanley said. "Alright, let's go to the docks and find out what boats are departing for France."

But before they could even turn the street corner, five men came out of the shadows and surrounded them. They were all humans, dressed in long black cloaks and top hats, and all wore around their neck a silver medal. Vampire hunters. Stanley saw them now and then when he was hunting. They posed no threat whatsoever to someone like him with their silver jewelry to ward off creatures of the night, and the pistols with blessed silver bullets he knew they carried underneath their cloaks would only work if they could actually see him.

"Is that all you've got, Yvan? I'm disappointed," he said.

But, just as he was about to make himself invisible and flip them upside down in his distorted reality, another one dropped from the roof right behind him and covered his eyes. A hand-kerchief with chloroform then covered his mouth and the last thing he heard before passing out was Cornelius crying out his name.

CHAPTER 16

"AND THAT'S HOW I woke up in a chair in a straitjacket, with those three humans trying to confirm whether I was a vampire or a demon so they could eliminate me accordingly," Stanley said. "Obviously, this was just a teaser. I'm sure Yvan knew I could get out of his trap easily and he will be sending me some terrifying clown puppet who can freeze me or breathe fire on me in my sleep, or whatever."

Belial, who had listened to the whole story attentively, leaned back and applauded again.

"Stanley Suspect, or should I say 'bogeyman'? You are absolutely fantastic!" he said. "But I am curious about something: as a vampire, how can you walk out in the daylight and not catch fire when you touch silver?"

Stanley grinned.

"Simple, I project myself backward and forward in time by only a fraction of a second, therefore I am not actually 'there' long enough to get hurt. I don't like using the Time Key though. It gives me an upset stomach, and I've found that the results of time travel can be unpredictable."

"I would assume so," Belial said. "But now I wonder why you would share all this information with me, a major demon, when both demons and angels have played some nasty tricks on you."

Stanley shrugged.

"You call me by my name and you're not gross like some others," he said, lighting himself another cigar.

"Indeed, I look a lot better than Beelzebub," Belial said. "We had a fling back in the day, but it didn't last."

"Let me guess: bad breath?" Stanley said. "Speaking of her, I'm surprised she hasn't sent another hitman after me yet. They must know who stole the Time Key."

"At this point, the Evil Trinity does not know who is in possession of the Time Key - except for me, of course," Belial said. "Which brings me to the whole point of our interview."

"Go ahead," Stanley said.

"How would you feel about working on a team where you can be yourself and even make friends?" Belial said.

"Oh, please no. I hate teamwork," Stanley said, rolling his eyes.

"Well, they are not aware that they are on my team. I just keep them close to me," Belial said. He leaned forward and his expression turned serious. "Beelzebub was murdered some time ago, after you stole the Time Key," he said.

"Wasn't me. I was busy killing my father and becoming a vampire," Stanley said.

"I know it wasn't you. It could only be one of two people: the head of the seraphim or my associate, Astaroth."

"It could be a lot more people, believe me," Stanley said, smirking. "I'm not the only hitman powerful enough to kill a major demon."

"Hitmen always work for somebody," Belial said.

"So, why does her murder matter? I thought you didn't like her."

"Beelzebub was part of the Evil Trinity, along with myself and Astaroth," the demon said, "If one of us disappears, someone else has to take over their powers to maintain the balance of this world."

"I thought the angels maintained the balance and the demons disrupted it," Stanley said.

He didn't really care either way. Belial grinned.

"I suppose the seraphim told you that, but that is not true. All of us major demons were originally angels. I used to be a secretary for the God of the North," Belial said.

"Wait, there are other gods?" Stanley said.

"Of course. The world is not just limited to Europe," Belial said. "My former employer loves humans, but you could call it 'tough love'. He makes rules they cannot possibly follow and that are the condition to entering his realm. And if they fail to follow them - like over ninety-nine percent of them - he terrifies them by threatening to send them to Hell - which is a place of repentance, but for real criminals. Most humans don't actually qualify and end up in Purgatory instead, which is neither good nor bad, except it is getting very crowded. We had to build extensions."

Stanley put down his glass and listened. Now the demon was getting interesting.

"So you used to work for the old man? That must have been awful," Stanley said.

"The workload was a nightmare. I suffered from anxiety and lack of sleep. I eventually had to quit - the whole department did," Belial said, frowning as he remembered the unpleasant experience.

"So now you're the big boss of Hell?" Stanley said, leaning forward.

"As the most powerful demon alive, yes. I am the lord of all demons," Belial said with some pride. "But in everyday life, I am just an attorney with a side job as administrative director of Hell."

"And so you think Astaroth murdered Beelzebub? What is his motive?" Stanley asked.

"I cannot prove that he did it and he has no apparent motive," Belial said. "However, several major demons have recently been murdered, including the Gatekeeper of time, Belphegor. Astaroth would not gain anything from eliminating Belphegor since he was already his overseer. He now has to appoint someone else and have a new Time Key manufactured, which is more trouble than it's worth. The seraphim were always the ones trying to get their hands on the Time Key so they can change history to their advantage."

"Oh, I sense a plot involving people on both sides..." Stanley said with a grin. "And I suppose you want to know what I know."

"I know that hitmen work under codenames, so any names you might provide me would not help," Belial said.

"So why do you specifically need me?" Stanley asked.

"Because only you can infiltrate Astaroth's private circle," Belial said. "Recently, he has begun gathering around him transgender creatures of the underworld, people like you. Major demons often have a 'harem' - a group of people we form pacts with for pleasure. Every demon has their own preference, and I thought he simply had a new fascination for transgender people, but I discovered that the people he collects also all happen to be spiritual vampires."

"Transgender? Spiritual vampires?" Stanley said, puzzled.

"Transgender is a new word used by medical science to describe people like you, who do not identify as the gender assigned to them based on their reproductive organs," Belial explained. "Spirituals are vampires with the ability to leave their body or project their spirit. Not all spirituals are transgender and not all transgender vampires are spirituals, but there just happen to be many among your group."

"I can understand why. I would do anything to get out of this body," Stanley said.

"I want you to find out what Astaroth is up to. And who knows? You might even make some friends," Belial said with his charming smile.

"And in exchange, I have to make another pact with you," Stanley said.

"You will, but this pact only entails your loyalty to me, nothing more," Belial said. "You will be free to do whatever you want once your mission is complete and you will never be forced to do anything you don't want to do."

"What if I decide I don't want to carry out this mission after making a pact with you?"

Belial's grin widened.

"I think you will want to do it," he said. "This young woman you are acquainted with, Eve, she is a spiritual and therefore a potential target for Astaroth. He could be the demon you saw lurking around her in a dream."

"What?" Stanley suddenly said, grabbing the arms of his chair.

His eyes began to flicker with anger. Belial gestured to him to calm down.

"There is no need to get angry, Stanley, and I would advise you against it," he said. "Though I want to be your friend, I do have the means to restrain you if necessary."

Stanley breathed in deeply and let his heartbeat slow down.

"Why don't you just recruit Eve then?" he asked.

"She is – how should I put it? – difficult to approach," Belial said with an accomplice smile.

"You just don't know how to rub women the right way," Stanley replied with a grin.

"Do you want to bet on that?"

"Sure thing."

Belial rose and began to walk around the room, his hands casually slipped in his pockets.

"So do you agree to work with me, Stanley?" he asked. "It sounds like you are in trouble with a lot of people, and I can both protect you from them and set you free."

Stanley turned his gaze to Cornelius, who had been listening to them from a corner of the room, but Belial also turned to him and said: "Don't worry, your friend will be safe with me."

"You can see him?" Stanley said, surprised.

"No, not in this realm, but I can feel his presence," Belial said.

"Well, why not? Let's make a new pact," Stanley said. "How do we do it?"

"I'm afraid my mark will have to cover Beelzebub's. I am a little territorial," Belial said.

Stanley rolled his eyes again and said: "Alright, come."

The demon grinned and walked over to him. Then, leaning over him, he cupped his face and opened his mouth with his thumb and slowly kissed him – not like Beelzebub's foul, deepthroat kiss – this one was both gentle and sensual, and it awakened new desires in Stanley's loins. When he was done languidly rolling his tongue inside his mouth, the demon let go of him, leaving Stanley's tongue tingling and his cheeks blushing.

"Hopefully it was not too horrible," Belial said. He sounded quite sure of his kissing skills.

Stanley shrugged.

"It was not so bad. So is the pact concluded, then?"

"It is," Belial said.

He began to pace across the room, then looked like he had forgotten something and came back.

"Just one last thing, Stanley."

"Yes?" Stanley said, still blushing.

Belial extended his hand to him and said: "My wallet, please."

Stanley grinned and returned his wallet to him.

About the Author

JC COMPTON IS A non-binary author with an international background, being born in France and now living in the USA. They have a degree in East Asian Studies and are particularly passionate about Japan and China. Their multicultural experiences and friendships are reflected in the diversity of their characters and the worlds they create.

"If you want to reach the sky, aim even higher" could be their life motto.

JC writes diverse LGBTQIA+ fantasy, sci-fi, and paranormal romance stories, and is the author of the self-published series Undertakers Inc. They hope to bring readers exciting, empowering, fun, and creative stories where the LGBTQIA characters are the lead and their friends of all backgrounds and orientations are also represented.

Excellent LGBTQ+ fiction by unique, wonderful authors.
Thrillers
Mystery
Romance
Young Adult
& More

Join our mailing list here for news, offers and free books!

Visit our website for more Spectrum Books
www.spectrum-books.com

Or find us on Instagram
@spectrumbookpublisher

www.ingramcontent.com/pod-product-compliance
Lightning Source LLC
La Vergne TN
LVHW011320080426
835513LV00006B/138